Social Theory and Postcommunism

Social Theory and Postcommunism

William Outhwaite and Larry Ray

Blackwell
Publishing

BLACKWELL PUBLISHING
350 Main Street, Malden, MA 02148-5020, USA
108 Cowley Road, Oxford OX4 1JF, UK
550 Swanston Street, Carlton, Victoria 3053, Australia

First published 2005 by Blackwell Publishing Ltd

Library of Congress Cataloging-in-Publication Data

Outhwaite, William.
    Social theory and postcommunism / William Outhwaite and Larry Ray.
       p. cm.
    Includes bibliographical references and index.
    ISBN 0-631-21111-X (hardback : alk. paper) – ISBN 0-631-21112-8
(pbk. : alk. paper)
1. Postmodernism – Social aspects. 2. Post-communism.
I. Ray, Larry J. II. Title.

HM449.O9 2005
301'.01–dc22

                                            2004011682

A catalogue record for this title is available from the British Library.

Set in 10.5pt/13pt Sabon
by Kolam Information Services Pvt. Ltd., Pondicherry, India
Printed and bound in the United Kingdom
by MPG Books Ltd, Bodmin, Cornwall

The publisher's policy is to use permanent paper from mills that operate a sustainable forestry policy, and which has been manufactured from pulp processed using acid-free and elementary chlorine-free practices. Furthermore, the publisher ensures that the text paper and cover board used have met acceptable environmental accreditation standards.

For further information on
Blackwell Publishing, visit our website:
www.blackwellpublishing.com

Contents

Preface

The rise and fall of communism represented one of the most dramatic and world-historical forces of the twentieth century and shapes the context in which events unfold in the early decades of the twenty-first. This phenomenon has, of course, been subjected to enormous scholarly and political, journalistic, and cultural commentary; the division of the world into competing ideological and military systems was the fundamental point of reference for politics for much of the last century. Yet the departure from the world stage not only of the Soviet system but also, at least as it seems at present, of the idea of socialism, occurred with a whimper rather than a bang. Rapidly and, with a few tragic exceptions, largely peacefully the Soviet systems fell within the space of a few years between 1989 and 1991, to be replaced, by what? This is where the course of world development becomes less clear and where there are competing futures and realities emerging within the former countries of the Soviet Union and Eastern Europe. Indeed the emergence of a postcommunist condition opens up a new stage in global history the contours of which are still taking shape. This book develops an analysis of these events using a range of sociological approaches and theories, while asking throughout how these monumental events might affect the process of sociological theorizing itself. We bear in mind that most of the latter has been undertaken with the Western world in the forefront of our perceptions, as to a large extent it is still.

This is, then, a contribution to social theorizing about social change and development with a view to considering how existing debates can be reinvigorated and developed by seriously embracing issues raised by the postcommunist condition. It raises questions about the consequences of living in a world without (systemic) alternatives in which issues of social justice and inequality remain as pertinent and demanding of solutions as ever. The arguments are grounded in classical social theory but also move beyond these, recognizing the important gulf that separates us from the world of the classical theorists. In the wake of the rapid and profound social changes of the later twentieth century, it is important to question whether our theoretical frames of reference are appropriate for these novel configurations of culture, economy, and society. Sociologists further need to ask whether recent theoretical preoccupations – for example with the "cultural turn," postmodernism, deconstruction, globalization, and identity adequately grasp social processes in the new millennium. Sociology is still reluctant to forget its classical founders, and the relevance of this tradition is both powerful and problematic. It is powerful because the classics constitute a rich source of insights, concepts, and analyses that can be deployed and reinterpreted to grasp current problems. But it is problematic because the social world of the classics is largely that of industrial, imperial, and high-bourgeois European societies prior to World War I. How do we begin to relate the concepts formed in this milieu to the concerns of the globalized social world that is postcolonial, postindustrial, and has seen the rise and collapse of Soviet socialism? In addressing these questions we intend to provide a book that will be relevant to students and will contribute to wider thinking about the discipline.

Acknowledgments

Thanks are due to many friends and colleagues who have contributed in various ways to the development of this book. William Outhwaite would like to acknowledge in particular helpful comments by Justin Rosenberg and other participants at a Social and Political Thought seminar at Sussex on a paper related to this project, and by participants at a conference at Schloss Elmau, Upper Bavaria, organized by Gerard Delanty. Seminars by colleagues at, and visitors to, the Sussex European Institute also provided valuable background. Larry Ray would like to thank Georgi Dimitrov (Sofia University), Benjamin Forest (Dartmouth College, US), Sławomir Kapralski (Center for Social Studies, Warsaw), Barbara Misztal (Leicester University), and Richard Sakwa (University of Kent) for assistance, helpful comments and discussions of the issues addressed here.

We are also grateful to Pearson Education for permission to reproduce Figure 3.1 (on p. 51).

W.O.
L.R.

Introduction:
Being Taken by Surprise

For much of the twentieth century, around half the world's population lived under regimes, the official ideology of which was "communist." The world was divided into hostile camps of "capitalism" and "communism" until the end of the Cold War in the late 1980s, which was followed by the dramatic collapse of European and Soviet variants of communism. The prime focus of this book is to argue that these events have serious consequences for the project of social theorizing – many of which are even now widely unacknowledged. We review a number of central theoretical issues, asking how the communist and postcommunist experience has changed our thinking about social theory. In summary, these are social class, social solidarity, social change and convergence, modernity, globalization, civil society and the state, and memory and identity. In each case we set out the current state of the debates, identify some key issues and then attempt to show how the postcommunist transformation might cast new light on these. More broadly, we ask how the postcommunist condition poses new challenges to sociological analysis. The world of the Cold War was a world of borders *par excellence* – both physical borders epitomized by the Berlin Wall, and symbolic borders of "us" and "them" in which crossing a land frontier involved the frisson of transgression. In the postcommunist world borders are more porous, yet subject to repeated panics over migration and "asylum." The phenomenon of global migration has been given huge impetus by the end of European and western Asian communism and has become embroiled in postcommunist fears around security and identity.

Most mainstream social theory was rooted in the economic, political, and cultural experiences of the "Western world," that is, the world of "advanced capitalism" in Western Europe, North America, and Australasia. Where the rest of the world appeared it did so within particular specialisms such as the "sociology of development," "world systems," and "sociology of Eastern Europe/communism." The former were for brief periods of central concern in sociology, and are now largely replaced by globalization theories. However, mainstream sociology generally approached communism through theories of industrial society and convergence. This limited focus was rather odd, in view of the crucial significance of the "East–West" divide for the fate of contemporary societies and, indeed, the world itself. The nuclear stand-off between the US and USSR did after all threaten to destroy most of the world on a number of occasions and the superpowers' involvement was evident in many local conflicts in the latter half of the century. However, while one might expect social theorists to take an interest in these issues because of their intrinsic importance, there are other reasons why the communist experience is crucial to our evaluation of social theory.

These reasons are as follows. Firstly, the project of social reconstruction in line with the putative "laws" of social evolution, which is what the communist parties claimed to be doing, was linked to and had much in common with the central project of sociology. An early sociological ambition that one finds in theories as politically diverse as positivism and Marxism was to identify "laws" of social development.[1] The belief that history followed a determinate and therefore predictable course was an illusion, but one that has proved remarkably tenacious, as we will show a little later.

Secondly, the origin and fate of capitalism is one of the central concerns of social theory. There is now a chance to observe the construction of capitalism under novel circumstances and this has implications for how the core concepts in the discipline might be considered. The social sciences often bewail the impossibility of experimentation in more than the most banal social situations. The communist experiment itself, its collapse, and the process of postcommunist development are surely among the most valuable resources available to social science and not to be confined to the backwaters of area studies or "transitology."

Thirdly, there is the question of the legacy of Europe after communism, which involves an examination of the limits of globalization and postcommunist integration (including EU enlargement), as well as current issues of asylum and post-Cold War migration. Fourthly, the sociological enterprise has, in different ways, often claimed to be critical of prevailing social conditions. However, critique is dependent on the existence of a potential or imaginable alternative to existing social forms. The end of communism thus has two different possible implications. One is that there is now no "really existing" alternative to capitalism, and possibly therefore never will be. Another is that now communism has finally shuffled off the historical stage, it is perhaps possible to imagine non-authoritarian and genuine alternatives to capitalism, although we need also to acknowledge that the fate of the Soviet system has seriously damaged, for the present at least, the idea of systemic alternatives. In this sense we may have to wait a while for the rehabilitation of socialism that Weber predicted following the Russian Revolution.[2]

What implications, then, does the fall of communism have for sociological theory? We have chosen to discuss these issues in relation to recognizable concerns of classical social theory, not because we believe that nothing much has happened in social theory since the time of the classical writers but because they drew up a number of fundamental lines of approach, paradigms in the strict sense, which remain relevant. The next chapter discusses issues of markets and class relations in terms which are still recognizably influenced by Marx and Weber. Chapter 2 follows a Durkheimian agenda, though not Durkheim's substantive claims, in its analysis of solidarity and the nature of society and social determination. Chapter 3 takes as its initial frame of reference a later body of theory: the models of the convergence of industrial societies common in the 1950s and 1960s. We argue that although the idea of a gradual convergence of capitalist and state socialist systems was clearly dealt a death blow in the autumn of 1989, with China alone following a path of convergence towards capitalism of the kind sometimes predicted for the Soviet Union, the idea of a spontaneously developing or externally encouraged convergence to similar patterns of political, economic, and more broadly social organization has a good deal of mileage in it.

The subsequent chapters draw substantially on more recent theories of modernity (and to some extent postmodernity) and globalization, though these themselves revisit more long-standing themes in Marx and the late nineteenth- and early twentieth-century classics, and the thematic of civil society recalls Tocqueville's analysis of democracy as well as the revival of the concept in the dissident movements of the 1980s.

We begin the book with the theme of "being taken by surprise" by the fall of communism, and the concluding chapter reviews this and the other surprises of the postcommunist transition. First, we refer to the relatively peaceful nature of 1989 and the post-1989 scene in Europe, with, of course, the tragic exception of Yugoslavia and the partial exception of Russia, noting that an alternative and far bloodier bloc-wide scenario was just as possible. Secondly, we suggest that the outcome of 1989 lends support to Theda Skocpol's model of revolution, with its stress on regime collapse, and more generally to those who emphasize the importance of relatively intangible ideological and legimatory resources, rather than military hardware.

Another surprise which we register in the course of the book is that, with so much apparently up for grabs at the end of 1989 and in the early months of 1990, so much fell into rather conventional "Western" European patterns. In many cases things just happened faster in the East than in the West: the rise and fall of civil society movements, the destruction (called *Abwicklung* in Germany) of "old" industrial resources, the drastic reshaping of social welfare provision. Part of the explanation for the rapid adoption of fairly "standard" political and other social forms throughout the former bloc was no doubt the widespread sense that the whole telos of postcommunist transition was indeed to return to "Europe" and to "normality." East European citizens had been through a social and political experiment and did not want more. The gradual (except in Germany) arrival on the agenda of the prospect of EU accession merely reinforced an existing trend.

All this, however, raises broader questions about not so much the predictability, but the determination of social processes. How could futures which seemed so radically open, for better or worse, fall so quickly into familiar patterns? Were the apparent freedoms illusory, or just not exploited? Were the models adopted because they had proved themselves to be evolutionarily or at least practically optimal, or just because they were familiar from the West and open to imitation? Theorists as different as Luhmann and Giddens have stressed the way in which human beings manage complexity through, for example, routines, while middle-range theories of path-dependence, drawing on Jon Elster's earlier work on counterfactual conditionals and branching points in history (Elster 1978), achieved a deserved prominence in charting particular developments.

A related set of questions concerns the weights to be attached to the political, the economic, the social, and the cultural in the analysis of social formations. Very crudely, one can see the collapse of communism as further evidence, if this were needed, against Marxist emphases on the primacy of the economic – which is not to deny that the slow-down and general malaise of the state socialist economies in the 1980s was a crucial element in their loss of legitimacy and their ultimate collapse.

One could make a strong case for the primacy of the political, since many of the movement activists were motivated more by the pursuit of freedom and democracy than by economic considerations, and it was a specifically political collapse, precipitated by the withdrawal of the Soviet guarantee, that occurred in 1989. If Gorbachev had lost power or backtracked on his policies in the late 1980s, then "1989" might have happened many years later; conversely, Gorbachevian policies in the 1970s might have produced a similar outcome a decade sooner. The cultural erosion of the regimes may also deserve more attention than it has often received. Cultural forms from poetry to rock music were increasingly recalcitrant to central management, and pop culture in particular made the regimes seem like something from the past.

The 1990s saw the triumph of economically and politically deterministic models at the expense of more socially and culturally oriented ones. Ralf Dahrendorf (1990: 85) drew the classic distinction between the "hour of the (constitutional) lawyers," its immediate successor or accompaniment, "the hour of the politicians," and the much later "hour of the citizen" (Dahrendorf 1990: 92–3). Dahrendorf's prediction of sixty years for the completion of civil society is of course a high estimate, but the general analysis now seems prophetic. What happened in postcommunist Europe is, broadly speaking, the adoption of political and economic fixes which were at least meant to be quick, with the social left to fend for itself insofar as it was not understood as merely the object of administrative "social" policy. EU accession negotiations, in the second half of the 1990s, reinforced this legalistic emphasis; analyses that differentiated between formal and substantive democracy, such as Kaldor and Vejvoda (1999 [2002]), were the exception.

This "forgetting of society," to borrow the title of a book by the Swiss Canadian sociologist Michel Freitag (2002), is of course paralleled by the marginalization of the concept of society in social theory. Yet the postcommunist experience, though beset by contingencies of all kinds, also demonstrates the importance of notions such as society or civil society and social structure. Economic systems can be rapidly transformed by changes in resources (for example oil) or markets; political systems can be changed in their formal constitution (in both senses of the word), but societies, still largely shaped according to the frontiers of the territorial national state, retain a substantial quality, a "stickiness," which defies attempts at short-term transformation.

Communitarians turn considerations of this kind into a political philosophy. While we have little sympathy for such substantialist approaches, we share their sense that intangible but deeply entrenched "habits of the heart," as Tocqueville called them, are an important element in any adequate account of contemporary societies, no less than those of the past. This version of modernity may be "lighter," in Bauman's sense – more informal and fluid – but it is still a variant of the same underlying form of societal modernity. These issues lead us finally to some consideration of aspects of the EU's Eastern Enlargement in 2004. The apparent banality or normality of the postcommunist transition, in Germany and in much of the former bloc, and now to be reinforced by a "second transition" in the Enlargement process, conceals more fundamental changes which deserve more attention than they have so far attracted from European social scientists.

Having sketched out a rather ambitious agenda for this book, we should say a word about what we do not aim to cover. While we have tried to avoid the almost exclusive emphasis in much of the literature on postcommunism, including some of the best studies, on the holy trinity of Poland, Hungary, and Czechoslovakia/Czech Republic, we have focused largely on Europe, including Russia, and within Europe mainly on countries in the forefront of postcommunist transition. We say very little about China, despite its enormous and growing importance on the world scene, because its postcommunist economic development has not so far been accompanied by fundamental political change. (In many ways the Chinese path of economic liberalization combined with continuing political control illustrates a path predicted for, but not taken by, the Soviet Union and the bloc as a whole.) Elsewhere in Asia, both in the Southeast and in the former Soviet Southwest, both political and economic changes in residually communist or postcommunist societies have been too uneven to yield clear theoretical implications.

Secondly, while we register the end of the bipolar world and the emergence of new cleavages and conflicts, we do not make this a principal focus of the book. We resist the temptation to opt for the irenic vision of Fukuyama or for Huntington's equally overstated apocalyptic model, and politely decline the challenge to offer our own vision of the world's geopolitical future. In particular, we are skeptical about the rather overblown reaction to the current wave of world terrorism. This, as Bergesen (2003) has interestingly pointed out, in its development from the 1970s to the present in some ways replicates a century later the terrorist wave of the late nineteenth and early twentieth centuries which ended with the outbreak of World War I and the Russian Revolution (and, one might add, the state terror of the Soviet and fascist regimes). These are all important issues, but we could not have addressed them adequately without exceeding both our own expertise and the reasonable limits of a book with a more precise theoretical purpose.

1

Theory after the Fall

Since the postcommunist transition meant pulling up an established social system by its roots, we propose to go back to first principles in asking what social theoretical resources might be most relevant in understanding these societies. A possible starting point is Marxism. A humorous guide to the Soviet Union is subtitled "From an original idea by Karl Marx" (Polonsky and Taylor 1986), and most studies of the USSR and the rest of the bloc began with some reference to Marxist theory and the aims of the Bolshevik leadership and their successors. There was never, of course, a single Marxist account of the nature of the Russian Revolution or the Soviet state; theories varied from the official state doctrine of scientific communism, still taught in the 1980s in Soviet and East German universities as part of the core curriculum, to a variety of anarchist, Maoist, and Trotskyist critiques. The Mensheviks were in many ways better Marxists than the Bolsheviks when they argued that conditions in Russia were not ripe for a communist revolution; the Revolution could be seen either as a vindication of Lenin's break with orthodoxy or as a "revolution against Marxism" which called into question its deterministic emphasis.

Similarly, the suggestion that the end of communism demonstrates the theoretical as well as the practical failure of Marxism is only one of many possible conclusions. Gandhi, when asked what he thought of Western civilization, replied that it sounded like a good idea, and it remains possible to make the same reply on behalf of communism, that it was never tried properly, under properly favorable conditions. And even if the Marxist prognosis of capitalism was wrong, and the cure, as standardly applied, worse than the disease, the diagnosis might still be valid. On the other hand, even if Marxism can offer a good theory of capitalism, it seems less confident in explaining the original communist revolutions or takeovers, the operation of communist systems, or their overthrow and the process of postcommunist transition. Economic reductionism seems unhelpful in explaining what look more like essentially political and military processes at the beginning and end of the communist era, and in systems in which, to use Giddens's terminology, authoritative resources seem more important than allocative ones (Giddens 1985).

If Marxism is poorly equipped to address the details of these processes, it can offer an admittedly crude, but by no means ridiculous, account in which the (low) level of development of the productive forces, if it did not explain the original communist revolution in Russia and its military/geopolitical extension to Eastern Europe and elsewhere, can reasonably explain the failure of communism, its eventual collapse, and the somewhat bleak prospects of postcommunist states in the 1990s and beyond. Such an account of postcommunism will tend to play down any institutional or political differences from other variants of capitalism, stressing instead the peripheral or handicapped position of the postcommunist countries or regions in modern global capitalism. Seen in this way, Marxism can turn its political defeat into a theoretical advantage, as it reverts to the terrain on which it is most comfortable, the analysis of capitalism.

But if we are going to give Marxism, at least provisionally, so much of the benefit of the doubt, we should be at least as generous toward other traditions of social theory. The axis between Marxism and critics such as Max Weber, who attack its determinism and economic reductionism, is perhaps the most obvious one, but we should bear in mind also a rather different axis between Hobbes and Tocqueville. It is, of course, no accident that Hobbes, writing in the revolutionary turmoil of the mid-seventeenth century, looked to the establishment of a strong sovereign power, and many postcommunist thinkers, particularly in Russia, have been similarly attracted by a Hobbesian alternative to a situation of radical economic and political disorder. Even those, the majority, who would not feel comfortable arguing for a(nother) dictatorship, can hardly deny that almost a defining feature of postcommunist states is their pathological weakness (cf. Staniszkis 1999: ch. 4). Theories of postcommunism *before* 1989 tended to stress Latin American models as pointing to a possible future for the USSR and the rest of the bloc, and although, of course, the original prognosis of a gradual "Mexicanization"[1] of the ruling parties and their regimes was abruptly refuted in 1989, something of the underlying analysis remains useful.

At the other extreme from this approach is one which stresses the need for democratization and the development of intermediate institutions, built on the ruins of the all-powerful Stalinist and neo-Stalinist state and nurturing the civil society which that state had so badly fragmented and distorted. Tocqueville's model of civic activity in American democracy has been a significant reference point here (Wellmer 1993). More broadly, there have been a number of studies concerned to trace and evaluate the democratization process in cross-cultural contexts, encouraged by the substantial short-term evidence for a global democratizing shift in the last two decades of the twentieth century (see, for example, Wolton 1993; Pridham et al. 1994; Held 1995; Fischer 1996; Nagle and Mahr 1999; also the earlier and somewhat prophetic texts in Lefort 1981). Finally, as we will see in more detail in the chapters on convergence and civil society, the EU's insistence on democratization as a precondition for membership has exercised an important effect in East Central Europe, both as an overall parameter and in the details of the expansion and democratization of civil society in individual postcommunist countries.

A third axis might be that between Spencer and Durkheim or, in their more modern form, the neoliberal economic and political theorist Friedrich von Hayek and the communitarians. Communist societies had, because of their ruling charters, to interpret themselves, officially, in primarily Marxist terms, but in practice their official self-image was much more a Durkheimian one: a harmoniously integrated national community, motivated by shared beliefs and values and in which the division of labor had lost its antagonistic, anomic, or forced character. The US sociologist Alvin Gouldner (1971) rightly pointed to the parallels between American functionalism, which took up much of this underlying model while on the whole avoiding the dangerously leftist term "solidarity," and Soviet Marxism-Leninism and scientific communism. One can, of course, debate what solidarity meant in practice in state socialist societies, but a first approximation might be to say that the official rhetoric of solidarity coincided both with a substantial degree of mutual indifference, encouraged by the feeling that any systematic social disadvantage was the responsibility of the state, but also with the cultivation of self-help networks in the face of general material shortages.[2]

The indifference seems to have survived postcommunist transition better than the informal practices of mutual assistance, and the collapse of the latter has been a well-documented source of anxiety throughout the region. The perceived responsibility of the state has in many ways simply been transferred to a reified and personified market, seen as giving everyone their just deserts. More worrying still, much of the basis of social solidarity has been eroded by the collapse of many institutions and the criminalization of much of ordinary life. Durkheim's concern for social solidarity in the previous *fin de siècle*, and his sense that market relations alone were unable to sustain it, is reiterated, with good reason, in the late twentieth and early twenty-first centuries. (The attention paid in East Central Europe to Putnam's analyses of Italy and the US is a striking example of this concern.)

Max Weber's critique of Marxism's one-dimensional reductionism and his early responses to the Russian Revolution and the beginnings of bureaucratic socialism now seem quite prophetic. His stress on autonomous, i.e. not class-determined, power, including the military power of the nation state, also acts as a corrective to Marxism. More broadly, Weber's sensitive analysis of modernity and patterns of individual motivation in his sociology of religion and elsewhere has been an important source of analyses of communism and postcommunism, which make modernity rather than industrialism or capitalism their primary organizing category (Arnason 1993). Here, Weber rides together with Simmel and Elias's later work in the same vein. Simmel is also relevant as a precursor of what we have come to call a postmodernist stress on the fragmentation of the contemporary world. Whatever the weaknesses of postmodernism as a theoretical model or a historical thesis, we should not be surprised that it has found considerable resonance in a region where it often seems that almost everything has become shifting and uncertain and where oppositions such as legitimate/illegitimate, profitable/unprofitable, or economic/political often seem inapplicable.

Postmodern theory, as originally developed by Jean-François Lyotard (1979) defined the postmodern as "incredulity" towards "metanarratives" (tr.: xxiv) or "grands récits." "I will use the term 'modern' to designate any science that legitimates itself with reference to a metadiscourse . . . making an explicit appeal to some grand narrative, such as the dialectics of the Spirit, the hermeneutics of meaning, the emancipation of the rational or working subject, or the creation of wealth" (tr.: xxiii). In this long list a special place is occupied, at least in Lyotard's own biography, by the Marxist narrative of the emancipation of the working subject, since he was for a long time a rather unorthodox Marxist involved in the production of the journal *Socialisme ou Barbarie,* which was particularly concerned with the critical analysis of state socialism. From Lyotard's later post-Marxist position, as developed by subsequent postmodernists, both capitalism and, even more so, state socialism can be seen as modernist as well as, rather more plausibly, Fordist. The ruling communist parties were certainly also modernist in terms of Zygmunt Bauman's influential distinction between conceptions of intellectuals as legislators and interpreters (Bauman 1987). They laid down the law on the basis of their self-certified insight into the logic of historical development – something foreshadowed in Engels's conception of "the development of socialism from utopia to science." Although one can question this conception of modernism, Bauman's distinction is all too relevant to state socialism (see also the influential analysis by Konrád and Szelényi 1979).

We shall return to these issues in chapter 5, but two points may usefully be made here. First, "critical theory" in the narrow, Frankfurt School sense of the term offered elements of a powerful account of Stalinism, displaying a greater sensitivity to its authoritarian power dynamics than more orthodox Marxist analyses focusing on the productive systems (see, for example, Marcuse 1958). Although Habermas and Wellmer, the leading theorists of second-generation critical theory, did not address these issues directly until the fall of communism (Habermas 1990; Wellmer 1993), their approach inspired a good deal of work in West Germany and elsewhere (see, for example, Arato 1982; Guldimann 1984; Meuschel 1992). These thinkers mostly worked in the 1970s and 1980s in quite close contact with opposition social theorists in East Central Europe itself, many of whom should be included in a somewhat broader definition of critical theory. Konrád and

Szelényi (1979) and Fehér et al. (1983) in Hungary, Staniszkis (1985, 1992) in Poland, and the "Praxis group" in Yugoslavia are particularly worthy of note. Regular meetings at the Inter-University Center in Dubrovnik and the Yugoslav journal *Praxis* (after 1981, *Praxis International*) formed a focus for much of this collaborative work. More recently, Claus Offe and Ulrich Preuss have concentrated their work on the critical analysis of postcommunism (see, in particular, Offe 1994, 2000, Elster et al. 1998).

Secondly, it is worth noting the contribution of three French thinkers who have not worked substantially on communist or postcommunist societies, and in one case did not have the opportunity to comment on postcommunism, but whose work is highly pertinent: the French theorists Michel Foucault, Alain Touraine, and Pierre Bourdieu. Foucault (1975) introduced to social theory the theme of panoptical surveillance; this was, of course, all too relevant to the study of heavily policed communist societies, as was, more broadly, the notion that welfare policy regimes, of the kind most fully developed in state socialism, should also be seen in these terms. Foucault dramatically extended reflection on power from what he rightly saw as an unduly limited concern with state power and sovereignty; the notion of power being located in an intricate web of explicitly political and other social institutions was again of exceptional relevance in a communist context. When French thinkers in the late 1970s and 1980s addressed the issue of communist totalitarianism, their thinking was shaped by Foucault's contribution. Elsewhere, thinkers such as Anthony Giddens (1985) made surveillance central to their analyses of the state, and Giddens (1990) went so far as to describe it as one of the core elements of modernity, along with industrialism, capitalism, and military power. The discovery after 1989 that the surveillance apparatuses of the communist states had been even more pervasive than previously believed, especially in Germany and Romania, lent a new twist to this line of analysis.

Touraine conducted one of his major interactive social movement studies with Solidarność (Touraine 1982), and his more recent work on social solidarity and his critiques of neoliberalism (Touraine 1997, 1999) are highly relevant to the postcommunist world. In a more general way, Bourdieu's model of social stratification, which lays especial importance on "cultural" or "symbolic" capital, can be shown to illuminate the postcommunist world, in which foreign contacts, languages, and so on may be more important for individual life-chances than economic resources or formal qualifications derived from the communist period. A concern with the intersection of culture and social stratification is also central to feminist analyses of postcommunism. Western critical theory of the late twentieth century developed in close connection with feminism, though in an often tense relationship (Hartmann 1981). The encounter between Western feminism and Eastern European reality was similarly tense and problematic, though the best of this work takes one to the heart of social dilemmas in postcommunist societies (see, for example, *Feminist Review* 1991; Einhorn 1993; Einhorn et al. 1996).

So far we have been concentrating on theoretical models mostly developed or cultivated in Western Europe, and this is not just for accidental reasons of geography and linguistic competence. One of the disappointments of the 1990s was the realization that the removal of restrictions on publishing, and the social transformations themselves, in Central and Eastern Europe had not led to an explosion of new home-grown analyses of communist and postcommunist reality. Systematic retrospective or prospective analyses such as that by Jadwiga Staniszkis (1999) were the exception rather than the rule. Yet Western social and political theorists, as opposed to economic technicians, had learned two crucially important lessons from the process. Firstly, as is noted below, the permanent possibility of being taken by surprise. Secondly, that legal, constitutional, and more broadly institutional processes are not part of an epiphenomenal superstructure and are too important to be left to the attention of specialists. Offe has rightly stressed the centrality of "institutional design," not as a substitute, but as a complement, to other processes of social transformation.

This forms part of a broader process in Western social and political theory, which had seen from the late 1970s a new emphasis on the importance of state power – what Theda Skocpol, a leading exponent of this approach, called "bringing the state back in." Skocpol and others argued that both Marxist and pluralist sociologists and political scientists had tended to see the state as a mere epiphenomenon of class forces or other social pressures. Looking back to Max Weber and to the German historian Otto Hintze, Skocpol argued that social scientists should pay more attention to the internal dynamics and organization of the state – whether in the initiation of policy or in increasing the susceptibility of societies to revolutionary challenge. Although there was little systematic work on the state in state socialism to match the vast outpouring of work on "the" capitalist state, it was clear that states were even more central to Soviet-type societies than to those of the West; Giddens, whose work had always had a strongly comparative emphasis, and others reflected this. However simplistic the contrast between "state-centered" and "society-centered" approaches, it helped to sharpen up thinking in this area.

At the normative pole of social and political thinking, too, issues of state power, human rights, and the rule of law had taken on a new importance. Thinkers on the political left who tended to marginalize the legal-political "superstructure" and to treat human rights discourse as a liberal indulgence were pushed into a response to the much greater prominence of human rights-based activity in the wake of the Helsinki European Conference on Security and Cooperation (ECSC) of 1972–5 and the citizens' assemblies to which it gave rise. Western peace movements, too, began to cultivate contact with dissident groups in the East as well as with the official peace committees largely animated by the security services. In the UK, where constitutionalism was, and remains, bizarrely underdeveloped in both theory and practice, the Thatcher government's attacks on established rights and practices led to the creation of a pressure group, Charter 88, borrowing its name from the Czechoslovak Charter 77. In the realm of theory, Habermas in the late 1980s brought his theoretical model of communicative action to bear on the interrelations between law, morality, and the democratic state, culminating in his major treatise of 1992.

The Communist System

Before proceeding with discussion of theoretical approaches to postcommunism we should briefly characterize what we understand by communism. This view will be elaborated later, especially in chapter 5 on modernity and modernization. There are many detailed sociological discussions of communism, which this section will not repeat (e.g. Ray 1996; Lane 1985; Staniszkis 1992). However, there were relatively few attempts to theorize the system in a creative way. Among these were Fehér et al. (1983) who drew on Weber's concept of goal-directed action to define the system in terms of the goal function of *Zweck der Produktion*, production as an end in itself. Abolition of the market, they argued, left no room for contingencies and the articulation of needs, no objective basis for calculation of human cost, no welfare system, and no concept of rights-based individualism.[3] Rather, there was a "dictatorship over needs" in which people were bound to the state as atomized subjects of a sovereign power through complex systems of dependency. The only constraints on production were those of extent and technological capacity that were mobilized without reference to articulated needs, producing a system of unparalleled waste and scarcity (1983: 236). Dictatorship over needs is a historical "dead end," and once the system begins to reform, they suggested, it would abolish itself. The following depiction draws loosely on their analysis (and on Ray 1996).

The Soviet system was a project of *dirigiste*, state-directed modernization on a "heroic" scale attempting to fashion a Promethean modernity based on rapidly increasing productivity through forces of industrialization and collectivization of agriculture. Throughout the life of the Soviet Union, and despite efforts to correct this imbalance, the production of consumption goods was subordinated to the heavy industrial and military sectors. Published economic growth rates (always highly unreliable) indicated high increases in the mid-twentieth century, declining rapidly thereafter.[4] This developmental model was driven by an extensive bureaucratic state for which Marxism-Leninism was a scientific and technological vision of progress towards a communist society that represented the future for humanity as a whole. Following Lenin's concept of a professional, theoretically guided, revolutionary elite, the Communist Party claimed to be the vanguard of the proletariat in whose name it ruled and whose true consciousness it embodied. Soviet Marxism further promoted a particular form of hegemonic masculinity that idealized the roles of warrior/revolutionary and proletarian Promethean strength. At the same time a particular cult of femininity was developed in which women often featured in propaganda alongside men (or alone) enacting "masculine" roles – such as manual workers or soldiers – encapsulating an ideal of equality through common participation in the revolutionary struggle. Although women were more highly represented in public life in state socialist than in most Western countries (though rarely in leading political positions) they were also subject to the "double burden" of paid employment and domestic work (e.g. Corin 1992). This was especially the case following World War II, when women faced the conflicting responsibilities of rebuilding the economy and repopulating the Soviet Union, and the press bombarded them with images of women who successfully fulfilled all the demands placed upon them (Bucher 2000).

Having superseded the market as a means of resource allocation (although some limited market exchanges would continue during the transition to communism), allocation was managed by a massive system of state planning, usually based on five-year targets. Planners attempted to replace the impersonal, indeterminate outcomes of markets by administratively set production quotas and prices. However, the unpredictability of demand and needs in what were becoming increasingly complex industrial societies meant that it was impossible for central authorities to flexibly control millions of prices and production decisions (Nove 1991: 80ff). Despite periodic campaigns against "bureaucratism," this system required multiple bureaucracies that exercised mutual surveillance on one another. In particular, there were dual lines of authority via the state enterprises on the one hand and the Party on the other, both of which came under the constant vigilance of security services. This is not to say that power rested with the bureaucracy, since during the 1930s each functional layer, including that of state security (NKVD), itself was subject to purges. The bureaucratic mode of execution of power was a consequence of a mode of political domination exercised by the Party (Fehér et al. 1983: 175). Within the bureaucracy career paths and admission to the new ruling stratum, the *nomenklatura*, were based on high degrees of clientelism, patronage, and personal loyalties – a system that Stalin attempted to break through periodic purges. In the Great Purge of 1937–8 virtually the entire top stratum of managers and government personnel (the old Bolshevik "Red Directors") was removed in favor of the *vydvizhentsy*, new technical graduates who were too young to have developed loyalties in the immediate post-Revolutionary period, whose loyalty to Stalin could be forged. Terror created a collective and visceral fear of the constant possibility of denunciation and arrest as a "saboteur," "Trotskyite," or other form of anti-Soviet deviant.

During the Stalinist period (1928–53) forced industrialization and collectivization were pursued at the cost of a death toll of genocidal proportions.

Supposedly justified by the necessity to increase agricultural productivity to meet the needs of a growing industrial and urban population, collectivization was also waged as "class war" against the *kulaks* ("better-off peasants," literally "fist"). In the process some 3 million died in the famine in the Ukraine and the mass deportations that accompanied collectivization. At the same time the population of the gulag system of labor camps during the 1930s, crucial sources of labor for industrialization, amounted to somewhere around 15 million by 1938. The total numbers of deaths that resulted from the camp system, purges, executions, and famine are matters of dispute but many estimates put them at 15–20 million during the Stalin period (Hosking 1992: 203). Although terror and mass death diminished after Stalin's death, partly because of a mutual security pact entered into by the surviving political elite, the memory of terror remained within the system, was never really expiated (despite de-Stalinization under Khrushchev), and always threatened to undermine the tenuous legitimacy of the ruling party. This was especially the case among the Soviet "satellite" states of Eastern Europe that were brought into the socialist bloc at the end of World War II, where communism was often regarded as a foreign system. Furthermore, as the complexity and extent of the system increased, its underlying systemic limitations became increasingly apparent.

Officially, communism as a state of substantive equality and rational resource allocation based on need represented the developmental goal of the system, to which the Soviet Union was in the process of transition. In this it took a leading role over the East European People's Democracies, which (with the exception of Yugoslavia) were integrated into a military alliance (the Warsaw Pact) and economic association (Council for Mutual Economic Assistance, CMEA). The Soviet Union was dominant in both, and attempts to break free from this comradely alliance of socialist peoples, such as Hungary's in 1956, would be met with military suppression. Even so, by the 1950s the political thresholds of terror had become apparent in that mass arrests and deportations were failing to address underlying systemic crisis tendencies and were actually reducing the Party's capacity to address them. Several of these arose from problems inherent in the planning process. First, the absence of constraints on deployment of resources created chronic over-investment and imbalances – overproduction in some areas (especially capital goods), combined with shortages in others (especially consumption goods). This in turn resulted in periodic manifestations of unrest associated with rising prices and shortages (notably in Poland in 1956, 1971, and 1980–1). Secondly, the exhaustion of the Stalinist growth model and the emergence of informal decentralization, such as local deals and exchanges between enterprises, meant that the "plan" became increasingly fictional and unrelated to actual social and economic life. The planning system was in practice replaced by negotiation between enterprises and planners in which the former would understate their productive potential to obtain manageable targets. At the same time planners knew that enterprises hoarded labor and materials and allowed for this in plan targets. In turn, managers would further underreport inventories in order to anticipate planners' adjustments, all of which encouraged falsification of data and concealment of worsening conditions. This, thirdly, created conditions for cynicism and withdrawal from the system in the forms of apathy, illness, ritualism, and a drain of labor from the state sector that in turn reduced productivity. Fourthly, the more these problems were articulated (at least within higher echelons of the Party) the less even the Party intelligentsia were committed to the symbolism and political culture associated with the vanguard role. They began to seek models elsewhere, including Western liberalism and social democracy (examples of this are given in Ray 1996: 4–6).

Nonetheless, there were serious attempts in the post-Stalin period to shift from the extensive growth model towards more intensive growth, based on increasing labor productivity. These required the reduction of supply shortages; improvements in quality of capital and consumer goods; less variability in production; and the availability of consumption goods as a reward for labor. But the central planning mechanism found it impossible to deliver this and alternative models were experimented with in the Soviet Union (e.g. the Lieberman Reforms, 1965–8) and across the socialist bloc, giving rise to a wide range of variation within the system. This included, in particular, varieties of "market socialism" in which the scope for market-based systems of allocation was increased (these harked back to Lenin's New Economic Policy in the 1920s) (see Nove 1991). One example of this was the Yugoslavian model of self-management and state coordination with extensive market and competition. Another was the Hungarian New Economic Mechanism in the 1970s in which the plan was limited to capital goods and energy production, and an extensive legal "second economy" (along with a less legal informal economy) emerged. In the Gorbachev period, after 1985, such models were actively promoted in the Soviet Union too, although it was still publicly acknowledged that inherent problems in the system (of efficiency and innovation) were not being tackled (e.g. Aganbegyan 1988). By the late 1980s reform communism in the Soviet Union and elsewhere (e.g. Hungary) expanded democracy, civic freedoms, and markets while trying to retain the "socialist" character of the system. Questions of "what if" are inherently speculative but there does remain, we feel, such a question over the eventual fate of the system and whether its demise was inevitable (thus confirming Fehér et al.'s thesis) or whether an alternative route might have been possible.

Challenges of Postcommunism

What then is postcommunism? Leslie Holmes (1997: 16–21) outlines a model of the key issues within postcommunism that provides a starting point for our discussion (though not in the order he presents them). The fall of communism was a comprehensive revolution entailing the unprecedented simultaneous transition from a centralized state economy and polity to a privatized economy and at the same time political democratization. This not surprisingly created widespread insecurity, especially following the reduction of welfare systems and an end to full employment. Political instability, legitimation problems, frequent elections and changes of government, and in some cases civil war followed, although in many parts of central and eastern Europe this was relatively short-lived. There was general rejection of "grand theories" of social reconstruction, and an insistence on "return to normality" rather than more social experiments (although given the uniqueness of the transformation it is difficult to see how it could be other than another experiment). The collapse of Soviet ideology created an ideological vacuum into which nationalism and religious ideas entered, often accompanied by unrealistic expectations about the amount of national independence that was possible within a complex global system. There was an absence of a culture of compromise in a situation in which democratic culture and civil society were undeveloped, combined with high expectations placed on "charismatic" leaders. At the same time there was cynicism towards political institutions often linked to a legacy of corruption and a moral vacuum in which social solidarity was weak and crime rates were soaring. Yet postcommunism is a temporally specific phenomenon (all transitions must end) and dynamic – it passes through a trajectory of changes.

To what extent does living in the postcommunist condition affect our core concepts and theories of the social? These questions will be examined with reference to some central themes in current sociology, including postindustrialism, modernization, globalization, postmodernism, social differentiation, and the problem of agency in social change. This will involve considering both the relevance of dominant Western concerns for understanding the crisis and transition of state socialism and the actual and potential impact of the transformation on sociology. We argue that, whatever one regards as the underlying tendencies of contemporary social organization, the continuing diversity of possible institutional responses to the global environment should be acknowledged.

The first challenge posed by the anticommunist revolutions is that they took us by surprise. This widely held view has a degree of validity. Dahrendorf (1990) commented that while (Western) sociologists were eager to "explain things that had not taken place," such as the imminent downfall of capitalism, they were struck speechless by the revolutions of 1989. Offe (1991) lamented the "a-theoretical character" of the changes, which followed no historical model and were not informed by a revolutionary theory.[5] Again, the *American Journal of Sociology* (AJS) Symposium (Hechter 1995) debated the reproach that sociologists failed to predict the revolutions.[6] Here, Randall Collins, who *did* predict the fall of the USSR (Collins

1986), claims to offer a geopolitical theory of the disintegration of large empires. However, others (e.g. Charles Tilly) argue that revolutions are non-linear events and cannot ever be predicted, even if they have recurrent causes. There has been an extensive and at times acrimonious debate among former Soviet area specialists as to whether the end was foretold, and if not, why not? (e.g. King 2000; Lipset and Bence 1994).

Actually, although no sociologists predicted specifically when communism would disintegrate (would one expect them to?), there were numerous general predictions of its imminent demise (e.g. Fehér et al. 1983: 21–2; Bugajski and Pollack 1989: 1). Many Eastern European scholars juggled the views that, on the one hand, Soviet systems were incapable of reform (so would last indefinitely) and on the other, that reform such as *glasnost* would serve only to render their latent irrationality manifest. This paradox was epitomized by Fehér et al. (1983) who argued that the communist systems were dominated by a "will to production" – a new form of domination that established an irrational dictatorship over genuine needs. Reforms that attempted to reduce the irrationality and oppressive nature of the system would signal its imminent demise since this form of domination was incompatible with the rational and democratic articulation of needs. To some extent, it seems, both views were right – the systems were unreformable and the reforms made manifest their unviability. One should not overlook, though, the extent to which institutional and cultural aspects of the former systems survived the transformation and continue to shape present-day social practices.

However, the charge of failing to predict the anticommunist revolutions is surprising, because the problem of prediction has latterly received little attention in sociological theory (see Kemp and Holmwood 2003). Most sociologists appeared convinced by arguments from diverse positions – systems theorists, Popperians, realists – that it was not the task of sociologists to predict the future. We may attempt to identify trends – in demography, consumption patterns, technological development, and so forth – on the basis of which we project what life may be like in the next half century or so. But we do so in the knowledge that present-day trends can be misleading in many ways and that, like weather fronts, they can change direction and take us by surprise. The idea, central to the sociology of August Comte in the nineteenth century, that sociologists can make scientific predictions on the basis of law-like propositions about the course of social development, has proved to be mistaken. Complex dynamic systems defy the prediction of specific outcomes and the problem arises only for those who believe in the scientific, predictive power of social science (Sójka 1994). All in all, prediction is probably better left to sorcerers and astrologers who, while they may not be much good at it, do it with flair.

The real challenges for us are to explain what happened and how the postcommunist transformations affect our understanding of the social. This book focuses on the latter. But why might we expect the fall of communism to have *any* particular implications for social theory? It is possible, after all, that the whole experience can be incorporated comfortably into existing modes of analysis. We argue against this view, not least because the configuration of the post-Cold War world as a world in which all alternatives to capitalism have been exhausted, poses questions that could not have been addressed in mid-twentieth-century social theory. These include the possibility of the most remote corners of the world being incorporated in an all-encompassing process of globalization; the way homogeneity and particularity will play themselves out in a world of increasing integration *and* diversity; the implications of postcommunism for debates about modernity and postmodernity; and the ability of or necessity for social theorists to engage in critical analysis at all.

The end of the Cold War brought new optimism, risk, and uncertainties. The various "Civic Forum" movements, which had begun in Leipzig (and Czechoslovakia) and spread rapidly throughout the communist states, suggested new models of politics and citizenship that would surpass the old representational politics of the Western democracies. Some like Habermas argued, albeit briefly, that 1989 offered Europe a "second chance" to realize the idea of a communicative civil society in both East and West, but this time free from "Eurocentric narcissistic self-absorption" (1994: 72). Optimism about a world in which major conflicts had been resolved and as Anthony Giddens claimed, "no one has any enemies" was widespread (this is discussed further in chapter 6). Writing after September 11, Stephen Holmes (2001) talks about the end of "the long postcommunist 'decade' " which had been the "heyday of happy globalization." The long postcommunist decade ran from the fall of the Berlin Wall in 1989 to the fall of the Twin Towers in 2001, during which time there was widespread optimism that as capitalism gained access to the whole planet it opened a decade of "frictionless competition" bringing prosperity to the poor, peaceful dialogue and progress toward democracy and the rule of law. After September 11 globalization took on more sinister and threatening connotations. But the two events were connected in that the collapse of the Soviet bloc left in its wake significant areas of the world free from governmental control or where the government humored autonomous armed groups like al-Qaeda. In the process, the lines between military and civilian, state and society, civil and political became unstable (see Kaldor 1998).

However, the region of the world now described as postcommunist has not generally been at the forefront of Western sociological concerns. The anxieties that have arisen in the postcommunist world have less to do with poor prediction, and more with the unease that momentous social changes arose from a part of the world that had received little direct attention from mainstream sociology. Sociological theory, as we noted earlier, has been largely grounded in the experience of modernity in North America and

Western Europe and its frames of analysis have tended to reflect this. It has, moreover, tended to assume that the West represents the normal developmental model, prefiguring the future of other societies.[7] While social differentiation has been an important theme in recent sociological theory, this has tended to refer to differentiation of function (polity, economy, civil society, family, etc.) which is compatible with the view that the structural and cultural patterns of modern societies are becoming homogeneous. It will be suggested here that this idea has several manifestations in contemporary sociology, in addition to its classical formulation in Parsonian theories. For the latter, homogeneity arises from the evolution of optimal systems of co-ordination combined with cultural diffusion. Richard Münch (1990: 463), for example, argues that "social differentiation is the only possible answer to the problem of social order under modern conditions" (see also Schwinn 2001). The view that societies are increasingly conforming to core organizational forms has been reinforced by the collapse of communism, previously the only "actually existing" competitor to capitalism. Recently, theories of modernization have been dusted down in response to problems of socio-economic adjustment in Eastern Europe (e.g. Alexander 1995; Inkeles 1991; Lipset and Bence 1994; Tiryakian 1991, 2001). One of the best-known exponents of this view is Fukuyama, who claims that "modernization theory looks much more persuasive . . . than it did 15–20 years earlier. . . . There are few versions of modernity other than the capitalist liberal-democratic one that look like they are going concerns" (1992: 133). Modernization and neomodernization theories have entered many debates about postcommunism, such as:

- investigating the importance of the urban–rural balance in successful democratization (Kurtz and Barnes 2002);
- the emergence of cultural difference as opposed to increasing homogenization and conformity (Blaney and Inayatullah 2002; Hörschelmann 2002);
- the development of ecological policies in postcommunist countries (Andersen 2002);
- Europeanization vs. Latinization as models for understanding the emergence of postcommunist political forms (Goetz 2001);
- developing models of the postsocialist urban area (Ott 2001).

As well as these classical and neoclassical formulations, there are more recent theories of convergence between Eastern and Western social systems. The classical versions envisaged a convergence around principles of social welfare and state-managed industrialism, which Wagner (1994) calls "organized modernity." Recent theories, if they do not speak explicitly about "convergence," nevertheless imply that there is a tendency for all developed societies to share features of post-(or "late") modernity. These diverse trends are often associated with globalization, postmodernization, and reflexive modernization. Crook et al. (1994) see a common tendency within contemporary societies towards:

- cultural fragmentation, semiotic promiscuity, and pastiche;
- decentralization of the state and decoupling from economics – the "remoralization of politics";
- post-welfare societies in which the politics of redistribution has less importance than that of identity, lifestyle, and consumption;
- the erosion of the public/private boundary and transformation of class and gender relations;
- the emergence of ephemeral and informal social movements;
- flexible specialization in work organization;
- the erosion of scientific authority.

In this vein, Soviet societies are viewed as having been a variant of industrial or modern society, now undergoing a similar process of crisis and restructuring as Western capitalism. Such arguments refer to things like the "crisis of corporatism," state decentralization, new social movements, economic privatization and a "shrinking state," deregulation, and globalization (e.g. Crook et al. 1994: 42n; Wagner 1994: 100–1).

However, it may be premature to expect former communist societies to converge around (what some perceive to be) the main features of privatized, post-welfare neoliberalism. It can be argued (as did Latour 1991: 8ff) that the "year of miracles, 1989" exposed modernity's failure, permitting a "return of the repressed" – of passions previously excluded by the modernist paradigm. History, he claims, has run in reverse. The Bolsheviks announced the end of exploitation; but now, with popular approval, the repressed returns as "voracious elites take up the old work of exploitation in banks, businesses, and factories." Kumar (1995) makes a similar point, arguing that the resurgence of revolution, nationalism, and religion as bases of social mobilization indicate the need for a reassessment of the modernist project. Not so much a convergence, then, as a rethinking of the core assumptions of contemporary social organization.

We will suggest that the changes pose several challenges to sociological theory. Communism, as Steve Smith (1994) has said, now has a narrative structure, a "beginning, middle, and end." This enables us to review, in the light of hindsight, questions about the underlying tendencies of industrial systems that have exercised sociologists for decades, appearing in "convergence theories," but in many other forms too. Then there are the questions of social organization thrown up by the anticommunist revolutions themselves, which have put ideas of civil society, democracy, the foundations and regulation of market relations back into the foreground of sociological debates.

There are also important implications for theories of globalization. The events of 1989–91 were "global" in several respects:

- the fall of communism signaled the end of a world-historical idea;
- the successive collapses of the regimes were world media spectacles;
- the rapidity of televisual transmission partly accounted for the speed with which the regimes fell;
- the availability of alternative social models to state socialism had been demonstrated by satellite TV;
- their impact was global, in that the postcommunist world confronts new questions of security, volatility, migration, and so forth.

Yet globalization in turn bears on the questions posed above. To speak about social differentiation, diffusion, transition, and so on, we need to specify where these occur. However, contemporary theories of fragmentation, globalization, and new virtual forms of sociality call into question precisely the traditional object of sociological theory: a "society" situated within the borders of the nation state. This in turn relates to current debates about the nature of modernity, "neo" and "post," as Alexander puts it. The transformations of postcommunist societies in the context of an increasingly globalized but unstable world are crucial for our understanding of these very processes. Clearly, postcommunist societies are undergoing a process of transformation, but from and towards what? Here there is less agreement. Are the problems of the transformation largely peculiar to the postcommunist societies, or do they address more general concerns about the values, action, choices, and indeed, the "fate" of modernity itself?

Beyond Postcommunism?

Before proceeding further, though, a few words of justification of the very idea of postcommunism are needed. Although the term has entered into widespread use since 1989 (e.g. Sakwa 1999), the diversity of postcommunist societies leads some to argue like King (2000) that "the idea of 'post-communism' is genuinely useless." "The label," he says, "ten years into the transition, now seems bizarre as a moniker for governments, societies and economies as vastly different as those of Poland and Tajikistan." Have we already arrived in the period beyond postcommunism? In some ways, perhaps. It is true that there is considerable social, cultural, political, and economic diversity among the countries that were once communist. But when we speak of "postcommunism" we use the term (as does Sakwa 1999) to denote not only the geographic European and Asian region of former communist states, but also the wider postcommunist global condition. By the latter we mean the complex political, social, and intellectual transformation brought about by the collapse of the "socialist" alternative to capitalism. So post-communism is not rendered redundant as a concept simply because the former communist nations have followed diverse paths of social development since 1989. The end of the bipolar world has been accompanied by a new but also fragile US hegemony along with the emergence of civilizational conflict and global terrors that, in contrast to the territorially based divisions of the Cold War, are partially "de-territorialized."

This constitutes a radical departure from the emergent social processes of the previous two centuries. For most of the nineteenth century socialism developed as a diverse body of ideas and political movements that presented an alternative to capitalism and colonialism. During the first half of the twentieth century it was possible to imagine or indeed expect that capitalism would be superseded by socialism in some form or another – a possibility that Weber and, following him, Joseph Schumpeter noted with some dismay. Socialist parties were attracting mass working-class followings and extensive support among intellectuals. As well as growing support in the industrialized countries socialism became increasingly influential among anticolonial liberation movements such as Indian Congress and the African National Congress. The bitter split between socialism and communism after 1917 damaged the movement, perhaps fatally, and the inability of Communists to form an alliance with Social Democrats in Germany eased the way for the Nazi victory in 1933. Nonetheless, the socialist and communist movements remained powerful forces in much of the noncommunist as well as the Soviet world during the twentieth century. Indeed, ironically, the Communist Party of Great Britain, that had never been a significant force in British politics, gained hitherto unprecedented influence on the intellectual Left through the journal *Marxism Today*, which during the 1980s was able to establish broad engagement between radical movements and issues. By the end of 1991 all this had gone along with the Soviet Union – communist and, increasingly, socialist ideologies, Eurocommunism, and the project of a post-capitalist order based on social justice and equality all consigned to history. With this passed an epoch in social and political thought and practice.

It is tempting to define postcommunist transition out of existence, suggesting that it is either essentially over, as many in East Central Europe would argue is the case in the parts of their states which interest them, or not yet seriously begun, as jaundiced observers of points further east often say. Either way, for this reductive view, the implications for the rest of Europe are seen as relatively limited and can be handled under the category of transitional arrangements, where "transition," like "convergence," now refers to European Union accession rather than the shift from totalitarian socialism to liberal capitalism. It is certainly true that the world-historical significance of the transition, rightly stressed by analysts like Andrew Arato, hardly seems to be reflected in the observable phenomena. Everything, so to speak, was tossed up into the air, but it fell down again into relatively familiar structures and patterns. As against this view, we start from the premise that "we are all postcommunist now," not in the sense of ideological demobilization or what Habermas, as early as 1985, called "the exhaustion of utopian energies," but in the sense that Europe, as well as the EU, are radically transformed by what has happened. It now makes sense once again, as in the period immediately after World War II, to think of a political Europe which in principle includes the whole subcontinent, but where East and West have experienced radically different trajectories over half a century.

There remains the crucial question of whether the social forces and structures that gave rise to socialist and communist ideas could yet be articulated in new visions of social justice in the twenty-first century, or alternatively whether these have disappeared? We cannot answer this here (not being in possession of a crystal ball), though we will address the implications of the fall of communism for thinking about global social movements and politics. The idea of postcommunism is neither bizarre nor redundant; we are still only beginning to see its manifestations working themselves through contemporary societies.

2

Class: Marx and Weber

The first main section of the *Communist Manifesto* opens with the sentence: "The history of every previous society is the history of class struggle." Accounts of state socialist societies can be roughly categorized according to whether they endorsed the Marxist assertion that class conflicts are central to all (or at least all developed capitalist) societies and whether, if so, they made the same claim about socialist societies. Official accounts of Soviet-type societies were tied to the orthodox view that there had been a history of this kind but it was now over. With minor variations, to do with the distinct status of collective farmers and intellectuals, these societies portrayed themselves as essentially classless or on the way to classlessness, and characterized by harmonious and cooperative, rather than conflictual, relations between their component strata.

Western Marxists with Trotskyist or Maoist leanings, however critical they were of Soviet-type societies, often argued that the nomenklatura elite was not a fully fledged (state) bourgeoisie and that the "degeneration" of these "workers' states" could be remedied by a merely political as distinct from a social revolution. Other Western theorists, such as Frank Parkin (1971) and Anthony Giddens (1973), along with some more unofficial accounts from writers based in or emigrated from state socialist societies (Djilas 1966; Ossowski 1963; Konrád and Szelényi 1979; Bahro 1978; Voslensky 1984) identified class antagonisms similar to, and/or different in various ways from, those in capitalist societies. Lurking behind all this was a broader question: was Marxism in general, and Marxist class theory in particular, appropriate to the understanding of state socialism, or should Marxism be understood primarily as a theory of capitalist society, going fuzzy at the edges when it attempted to analyze pre- or postcapitalist societies? Much Marxist theory, notably the state theory which flourished in the 1970s and 1980s, implicitly though never explicitly took the latter position.

The theoretical confrontation of these alternative models, which had become a central theme of comparative social science in the Cold War period, was interrupted by the revolutions of 1989. These were certainly revolutions, consigning to the dustbin the convergence theories that had predicted a gradual "Mexicanization"[1] of Marxist-Leninist parties and societies. Yet they were not so much Marxist-type social revolutions as Skocpolian[2] ones, marked more by regime collapse than by the modest social protests in Leipzig, Berlin, Prague, and eventually (and most theatrically) Bucharest. Marxists could join non-Marxist economists in telling a long-term story about the ultimate nonviability of centrally planned economies, given slowing growth rates, technological lags, and a poor climate for innovation, but these were essentially revolutions for (a certain conception of) democracy against (an attenuated form of) totalitarianism, with the paradigmatic political form a catch-all movement such as Solidarność in Poland or Civic Forum in Czechoslovakia, including pretty much everyone from Academicians to cleaners and from Trotskyists to monarchists. That many technocrats were also motivated by personal or collective economic considerations and that many ex-members of the nomenklatura elites subsequently found lucrative private sector occupations is true, but a secondary process – even in Hungary.

But if 1989 was widely, and with some justification, viewed as a further nail in the coffin of a Marxism which had failed to inspire either a successful postcapitalist economic and political model or even a convincing sociology of the regimes which had turned it into a state religion, it was less clear that the coffin's occupant was really dead. If the anticapitalist revolution had failed, with even China now firmly taking a kind of capitalist road, the Marxist critique of capitalism was in much the same state as at the time of Böhm-Bawerk (1896 [1949]), with a new experimental terrain to observe as capitalism was (re)introduced from Weimar to Vladivostok. What Giddens had called the *Class Structure of the Advanced Societies* could again be cast in a single model, without the dualistic refinement which he had needed when he wrote his book.

When Marx wrote *Capital*, he was right at the center of the industrial capitalist revolution which was sweeping through Europe and other parts of the world. The twentieth century allowed us to follow this process through into almost all the rest of the world; the twenty-first century that began in 1989 (see Hobsbawm 1995) affords the spectacle of the recapitalization of a third of the earth. What can comparative social science learn from this (so far as we can predict) unique experiment?

First, in a theme that we shall repeat throughout this book, Trotsky's so-called law of "uneven and combined development" applies *par excellence* here. Leon Trotsky's theory of combined and uneven development proposed in *Results and Prospects* (1905) served as an analytical foundation for "permanent revolution." Given the backward state of Russian society in the early twentieth century, due to structured unevenness, both bourgeois (plus nationalist or anticolonial) and proletarian revolutions could and must be telescoped into a seamless process, led by the working class. The concept re-emerged in Marxist social science in the 1970s, where it referred particularly to the way in which the capitalist mode of production depends upon earlier modes of production for an additional "super-exploitative" subsidy by reducing the costs of reproducing labor power (when for example global agribusiness buys cash crops produced on family smallholdings in the developing world). More recently David Harvey (1996: 295) has argued that the fulcrum of geographical unevenness is the differentiated return on investment that creation and/or destruction of entire built environments (and the social structures that accompany them) offer to different kinds of investors with different time horizons. Meanwhile, different places compete endlessly with one another to attract investment. In the process they tend to amplify unevenness, allowing capital to play one local or regional or national class configuration off against others. Uneven development can thus relate to differential growth of sectors, geographical processes, classes, and regions at the global, regional, national, subnational, and local levels. Brandenburg, to state the obvious, is not much like Belarus. To take two otherwise closely comparable postcommunist societies, Poland had a substantial private sector already; Czechoslovakia had virtually none. Theories of path-dependency, according to which past developments constrain current options (Hausner et al. 1995; Stark and Bruszt 1998) were one way of capturing these diversities. Some postcommunist economies were immediately thrown open to external investment (GDR, Hungary); others presented very considerable obstacles to it (most of Russia). In some, privatization was not much more than a slogan; in others it described a major revolutionary process.

A "modern" industrial bourgeoisie can develop in various ways. One path is via the conversion of agricultural property, as evidenced in early modern England and as described by Barrington Moore (1966).[3] Another is via the gradual expansion of existing artisanal and/or merchant activity; a third is by syphoning off resources made available by positions held in a state or church hierarchy. In postcommunist transition, the third of these has rightly attracted the most attention, under the slogan, which seems to have been invented in Poland, of nomenklatura privatization (Ray 1995: 452–7; Stark and Bruszt 1998). In a (for the beneficiaries) ideal scenario, existing state managers were able to reconfigure themselves as shareholders in newly privatized enterprises, in what in the West would be called a management buyout but was here often more of a hand-out. Even where, as in Russia, there was officially a more egalitarian distribution of shares, they were often bought up by existing management or local magnates. As the authors of a recent report (World Bank 2002: 72–3) put it:

> Navigating between continued state ownership with eroding control rights and a transfer to ineffective private owners with an inadequate institutional framework is possibly one of the most difficult challenges confronting policymakers in charge of privatization.

As in Western privatizations, there was a structurally inbuilt uncertainty as to what enterprises were "worth," and why: a massive industrial plant might turn out to be unsalable, or another valued for its site rather than its plant; many an East German or Eastern European supermarket has been built on the ruins of a factory. Soviet and Eastern European firms, with their traditions of vertical integration and self-sourcing of many of their needs, were well placed to shift their activities in creative ways; the name of an enterprise ceased to be much of a guide to what it actually produced. There were, of course, parallels in the West as, for example, tobacco and utility firms diversified their activities, but the Eastern variant displayed, as so often, a characteristically different degree of intensity, or in some cases desperation (Grabher and Stark 1997: v).[4]

Marx's class theory is of course grounded in his theory of modes of production, so in thinking about the relevance of Marxist class theory to postcommunism and vice versa we need first to ask whether there is a distinctive postcommunist form of production. Marx wrote in the *Grundrisse* of "forms which precede capitalist production," and perhaps we can identify at least a family resemblance between "forms which (also) come *after* state socialist production." More speculatively still, perhaps Marx and Max Weber's analysis of the emergence of capitalism in early modern Europe might help us to understand late twentieth-and early twenty-first-century capitalism in the postcommunist world.

Given the diversity of forms of capitalism as between, say, Canada and Kenya, the burden of proof is clearly on anyone who wants to make claims of this kind. Even in the West, there are clear differences between forms of capitalism. Michel Albert (1991) drew the now classic contrast between the US (and British) model, short-termist in both its pursuit of profit and its employment practices, and a "Rhineland" or "Rhenish" West European (and Japanese) model, more consensual and long-term (and, to its critics, sluggish) in its approach. Commentators immediately pointed out the differences within the Rhineland model, for example between Germany and Sweden (see Crouch and Streeck 1997). Postcommunist capitalism might have been expected to opt for the Rhineland model; to the extent that it did not – an approach exemplified by Vaclav Klaus's famous remark rejecting the social market economy in favor of the market economy *tout court* – this can perhaps be explained by a pendulum effect of full-hearted rejection of the old regime, and partly by the then dominant neoliberal and globalizing orthodoxy.

But capitalism as it has developed under postcommunist conditions does seem to have some characteristic features in terms of the kinds of resources that are mobilized and the ways in which this is done. David Stark's concept of recombinant property (Grabher and Stark 1997) is one of the most helpful. Following the Hungarian situation and its analysis in the late 1980s, Stark had already pointed to "hybrid mixtures of public ownership and private initiative" (1997: 37), and the post-1989 transition in Hungary and elsewhere in Eastern Europe, and the more subterranean transition in China, showed that "property transformation can occur without conventional privatization . . . [but also] . . . that property transformation does not necessarily clarify property rights." To the extent, therefore, that Marxist class analysis requires a clear concept of capital and clear principles of ownership, it may seem less relevant to this situation; more Weberian or Dahrendorfian reformulations in terms of control (Dahrendorf 1959) seem more attractive.[5]

More broadly, the Polish sociologist Jadwiga Staniszkis (1992, 1999) has outlined a model of "political capitalism," which she also grounds in the blurred property relations that marked the final stages of state socialism in many of the more advanced economies of the bloc. But this also, Staniszkis points out, parallels processes described by Marx and Max Weber in the early stages of European capitalism, in particular the "divided ownership" characteristic of late feudalism, "when the king, vassal peasant cooperative and direct users made claim to the same object (e.g., a piece of earth)" and a mercantilist policy "in which the state, in promoting the new economic mechanism, tried to use it for its own ends (stabilize the system, increase the pool of goods and services and in this manner satisfy needs which could not be satisfied by the state sector alone and decrease political pressure on changing the system" (Staniszkis 1999: 71). The "transfer from mercantilism to real political capitalism . . . [occurs] . . . where the actors of the enfranchising nomenclature . . . began at the same time to use their position in the mercantilist structures to promote their own ends" (1992: 72). Along with the growth of what she calls meta-exchanges such as those involving futures markets (the kind of process symbolized by Marx in the shift from $M-C-M^1$ to $C-M-C^1$) this led to "a point of no return accelerating the end of communism" (1992:73) and what she calls a "managerial revolution" at the level of "organized political capital," which itself becomes increasingly distinct from and antagonistic to small and medium private capital (1992: 80–1).

> It seems that not only the beginnings of the market economy were based on the combination of competition, cooperation, political redistribution and status-regulated interconnections. Similar characteristics appear also in organized mature capitalism with symptoms of state capitalism. The characteristic feature of capitalism that emerges from communism is the parallel existence of the early forms (when market rules are not universal, but aimed at the maintaining of the privileged position of one particular set of actors from the old regime, and when personal interconnections are a substitute for the still nonexistent institutional market structure) and the presence of mature forms of organized capitalism. (1992: 82–3)

As with the original development of European capitalism, some societies pass fairly slowly through the early stages while others start later and skip them (cf. Staniszkis 1999: 131). In a familiar rule of thumb, the further one goes East or South from the North Atlantic, the less economic relations correspond to an ideal-type of mature capitalism, and the more they are "embedded" in other social networks of personal acquaintanceship, political patronage, and so on. The political dynamic of EU enlargement in 2004 and subsequent years seems unlikely to remove these differences (we return to these issues in chapter 4).

Without looking in more detail at these processes at present, it should be clear that the capitalist class of postcommunist societies is going to be a rather different animal from that found in the West.[6] We turn now to look in more detail at processes of class formation. To anticipate our conclusions in this section, one should note, first, that what counts as capital or a productive resource is extremely unpredictable, and second that ownership and control of such resources, as we have seen already, are bound up with complex processes of justification and social valorization. As well as capital in the conventional economic sense, then, we should also be thinking of Pierre Bourdieu's concepts of cultural capital and social capital and the related concept of social capital developed by James Coleman, Robert Putnam, and others (Grix 2001).

Bourdieu (1983) distinguished three forms of capital: economic, cultural, and social. His concept of cultural capital has some analogies with the economic notion of human capital but this, Bourdieu argued, pays insufficient attention to the detailed structures in which it is deployed and to informal educational resources in the family and elsewhere, which largely determine the rate of return of educational investments. "The structure of the field, i.e., the unequal distribution of capital, is the source of the specific effects of capital" (1983: 49). Thus, for example, in the postcommunist context, the ability to speak or teach English may be a positional good of some importance in virtue of its rarity. Social capital Bourdieu defines as "the aggregate of the actual or potential resources which are linked to possession of a durable network of more or less institutionalized relationships of mutual acquaintance and recognition" (1983: 51). And in a sentence designed to illustrate the shift to ostensibly more meritocratic forms of social selection in Western societies but which also has relevance to the postcommunist context, Bourdieu wrote: "the more the official transmission of capital is prevented or hindered, the more the effects of the clandestine circulation of capital in the form of cultural capital become determinant in the reproduction of the social structure" (1983: 55).

To revert to the example just cited, an ability to speak foreign languages, acquired in special schools or through service in the tourist industry, security apparatus, etc., may be far more marketable than formal educational qualifications, and personal connections may carry more weight than ownership or control of formal economic or material resources. An ironical expression of this is the practice, quite common for a time in Russia, in which people got together, set a money value on their collective expertise, and asked banks to match this with loan capital. Once again, processes of this kind present in a somewhat crude and exaggerated form something which was by no means unknown in Western capitalism during the dotcom mania at the beginning of the twenty-first century. More optimistically, social capital can be viewed in a way which owes more to Putnam (1993) than to Bourdieu, as a collective resource rather than part of a competitive game. The point, of course, is that it is always both.

An approach of this kind is taken in one of the most important analyses of East central Europe, that by Eyal and colleagues (1998), discussed in more detail below. In this book, the authors continue a line of argument which one of them had first developed in the mid-1970s, that "in the industrially backward agrarian societies of Eastern Europe the intelligentsia, organized into a government-bureaucratic ruling class, has taken the lead in modernization, replacing a weak bourgeoisie incapable of breaking with feudalism" (Konrád and Szelényi 1979: 10). Thus despite the persecution of independent intellectuals, from which the authors themselves suffered, and the broader tensions between technically qualified members of the elite and the central authorities, which erupted from time to time in the 1950s and 1960s and eventually undermined the regimes, the intelligentsia could be seen, they argued, as the dominant class in state socialist societies.

Szelényi and Konrád (1990) suggested that the process to which they and others (notably Ludz 1972) had drawn attention, of the "intellectualization of the bureaucracy," had explained the weakness of the regimes in resisting pressures for reform, and even embracing these initiatives. But the intelligentsia had not yet succeeded, contrary to some Trotskyist analyses, in constituting itself as a fully fledged bourgeoisie, and was left holding the capitalist baby which, whether premature or overdue, certainly needed intensive care. Thus in opposition to theories of political capitalism and nomenklatura privatization, which they concede may better fit the situation in Poland and the former Soviet Union, Eyal et al. suggest that there was a considerable change of ownership and control from the old nomenklatura and that the new managerial elites of East Central Europe are defined more by their possession of cultural capital than by economic capital, diverted from the state and/or accumulated in the old "second," gray, or informal sector, or by social capital taking the form of "old" social networks deriving from nomenklatura positions. (New networks, based on membership of the opposition movements or on postcommunist NGOs or educational institutions, are a different matter.)

Without looking in detail at the empirical support for a model of this kind as opposed to one of political capitalism, since this would have to be argued out in a much more regionally and sectorally differentiated way,[7] and related to the broader discussion of elite continuity (Higley and Lengyel 2000), one can see in the critical responses to Eyal and colleagues a more

general tension between a Bourdieu-influenced model and a more orthodox
Marxist one. Michael Burawoy, who has conducted some of the most fundamental research on communist and postcommunist industry, brings out,
in an important review symposium in the *American Journal of Sociology*
(Burawoy 2001) the differences between an approach which focuses on the
strategies of class members, in this case of an elite class, and a Marxist class
analysis, which he favors, grounded in antagonistic relations tied to conflicts
at the point of production. The authors of the book reply, reasonably
enough, that there is little evidence of action by a "demobilized" working
class. On the other hand, survey evidence suggests a majority perception in
East Central Europe that there are "strong" or "very strong" conflicts between managers and workers and that income differentials are "too great,"
and a relation between the perception of conflict and objective inequality as
measured by Gini coefficient (Delhey 2001: 203–5).[8] And although many
managers may see themselves as managing enterprises under difficult conditions for the public good, this is not necessarily how their efforts will be
perceived. Once again, this is an area best left to further studies on the
ground.

This conflict of approaches leads, however, to a further point, in which
the analytical axis shifts in a sense from Marx and Bourdieu to Max Weber
and Bourdieu. Postcommunist entrepreneurs and managers, like those elsewhere, must have to some varying but never insignificant degree a belief
that what they are doing makes sense, has some point or value. State socialism was, of course, characterized by low levels of this belief, despite often
fatuous official attempts to sustain it. The shock years of postcommunist
transition often dealt a further blow to it, as previously valued goods lost
their markets overnight to the benefit of sometimes inferior but chic Western
imports. But, as in the early years of European capitalism, certain sorts of
motivation may require external sources of support; Weber believed this had
been provided in some parts of Europe by ascetic Protestantism. In postcommunist Europe, as in the developing countries, there was no substantive
doctrine of this kind, but that may not be the point. It has been argued with
some plausibility that what counted in, for example, the Japanese embrace
of Western capitalism at the end of the nineteenth century was the shock
effect of the opening up of the country and its rigid traditions to the outside
world, leading to a reorientation of traditional attitudes in a modernizing
direction (Bendix and Roth 1971). Something of this kind may have been at
work in postcommunist Europe in the 1990s, driven by normative conceptions of what is "Western," "modern," "European," or just "normal." Alternatively, one can simply argue, following Weber, that modern capitalist
practices have become essentially self-justifying, requiring no further legitimation from an external source such as the Protestant economic ethic:
"victorious capitalism, since it rests on mechanical foundations, needs its
support no longer" (Weber 1905: 181–2).[9]

It is possible to produce substantial amounts of evidence for both these hypotheses, and it is probably wisest to keep both in play as alternative interpretative frameworks, either of which will prove more explanatory in relation to particular states and regions. To give one example, it would have been unthinkable to write about "socialist entrepreneurs" in Czechoslovakia in the 1980s in the way Szelényi did about rural producers in Hungary, and whereas the rise of small and medium-sized businesses in the early 1990s in the Czech Republic was welcomed as "impressive" (Benacek 1997), a Hungarian commentator in the same volume was suggesting that the corresponding sector there was "becoming over-populated and over-fragmented" (Gábor 1997: 158) and talking about the need for "birth control" (1997: 170). Patterns of ownership are also diverse across the region, with banks, investment companies, and holding companies like the German Treuhandanstalt and its successor playing very different roles in different countries.

The authors of a study of new entrepreneurs conclude that "the creation in eastern Germany of a *class* of new entrepreneurs who will provide a social basis for capitalism still has a long way to go" (Koch and Thomas 1997). This may, of course, not be the right way to phrase such questions, to the extent that Russian and Eastern European capitalism is owned and even managed by foreigners. (In Germany, of course, the *Wessis* (Westerners) are not even officially or identifiably foreign.) The globalization and/ or Europeanization of Eastern European capitalism means that discussion of class relations necessarily takes on an international dimension which is more familiar in development studies than in the class analysis of advanced industrial societies. EU enlargement will undoubtedly give a further push to the Europeanization and globalization of managerial elites, though the German prologue of "enlargement without accession" (Spence 1991) suggests that the pace of such changes may not be particularly fast.

Once again we must labor the theme stated at the beginning of this chapter of unequal and combined development. The internal differentiation of the former bloc, to some extent papered over during the communist period, became a major theme as soon as the dust of 1989 had settled. The Visegrád group of Hungary, Poland, and Czechoslovakia, arising from a meeting in early 1991, had already grounded its original program of cooperation by stressing the similarity between the (then) three countries and by implication their distinctness from the rest of the former bloc (Declaration of February 1991). The GDR, one assumes, might also have been invited if it had not been incorporated into the Federal Republic, and Slovenia if it had not still been part of Yugoslavia. The first wave of EU Eastern enlargement included essentially the Visegrád group plus the ex-Soviet Baltic states (Estonia, Latvia, and Lithuania) and ex-Yugoslav Slovenia, based on an assumption that their economic and political development made it possible to fit them in (see Kaldor and Vejvoda 1999). It is interesting, however, to note how these clusters change over time; a standard reference book published in 1998 listed Slovenia and Estonia (but not Latvia and Lithuania) as likely members of the EU, and noted that Slovakia's then dictatorial political regime had rendered its application unviable.

The selection of these candidates for the first Eastern enlargement, with the prospect of membership for Bulgaria and Romania in 2007, may seem defensible or even obvious, but such global judgments about states conceal enormous internal differentiation. Scandals such as the Bulgarian one described below are perhaps more common the further East one goes, but they are by no means confined to the East and South of Europe. (In the Transparency International index of perceived corruption (Transparency International 2002: <www.gwdg.de>), which admittedly refers more to low-level bribery, Bulgaria appears around the middle of a scale of 101 states (the others excluded for reasons of inadequate data), and slightly less corrupt than Poland, Latvia, and the Czech and Slovak Republics.

It is in the nature of processes of criminalization and decriminalization of the kind discussed in some detail in the Bulgarian case that they are hard to estimate, but we should note that it is not just money that can be laundered, but also economic and other elites and entire branches of economic enterprise. It is easy to distinguish analytically between a virtuous spiral of decriminalization of previously criminal activities and personnel, as can be traced in the history of the United States and other advanced capitalist countries, and a downward spiral of increasing criminalization. What is less easy is to judge the relative importance of the two components of this double helix, and the overall trend. For Central and Eastern Europe (with the exception of parts of former Yugoslavia) we might be optimistic, whereas for Russia and most of the former Soviet Union the picture is a good deal less clear.

Finally, an approach which owes an often unacknowledged debt to Bourdieu can be pushed in a more radically culturalist direction. Malcolm Waters and others, in an extremely creative series of contributions, have developed a historical model of class societies which culminates in their supersession. Their model is based on three categories. First, a classical model of what they call "economic class society," in which economically based classes with strong subcultures conflict within the framework of "a weak or liberal state" (Waters 1997: 30). Second, an "organized-class society," in which classes are incorporated in political and other structures into a stronger state dominated by a political-bureaucratic elite. Their formal political and institutional representation in a sense compensates for their internal differentiation and the decline of strong occupational subcultures.

> Social classes take on a new lease of life despite market fragmentation and a progressing division of labor. The political–organizational superstructures of class, trade unions and political parties take over the dominant social-structuring role. (Waters 1997: 32)

Finally, in an emergent post-class or "status-conventional" society "stratification is sourced in the cultural sphere. The strata are lifestyle and/or value-based status configurations" (Waters 1997: 33). Intellectual property, mobile and fluid, tends to displace land and capital as the basis of social differentiation. Politics ceases to be class-based and identity, lifestyle, and issues politics become more important than the large blocs of left and right. Post-class societies remain differentiated, unequal and conflictual, but along shifting and unpredictable lines.

These three typical patterns could respectively be roughly identified, in Western Europe, with a short nineteenth century beginning in the 1840s, a social democratic/welfare-state twentieth century petering out in the 1980s, and a post-welfarist "third way"[10] twenty-first century just beginning.

Whatever one thinks of this overall conception, the model of organized-class society strongly recalls the world of state socialism. The nomenklatura elite, the officially defined and celebrated working class, its alliance with the collective peasantry and the mickey mouse political parties representing different classes and sometimes, in the people's democracies, approved ideological differences, fill out the picture of an organized-class society *par excellence*, or even one in which, as Pakulski and Waters (1995: 45) themselves argued, "political ranking displaced class division." The short-term volatility of postcommunist politics, its failure to settle into what had been, though was arguably ceasing to be, the left-right class-based Western European pattern of the earlier part of the century, can be explained by the removal of these organizing structures. At the same time, however, as noted above, postcommunist electorates remain more egalitarian in their attitudes than Western Europeans, to a degree more closely related than in the West to the actual levels of inequality in their societies (Delhey 2001). The traditional expression of egalitarian attitudes, in Europe and to some extent elsewhere, has been social democratic politics, but the scissor effect in the postcommunist countries of the local demise of socialist/communist political and economic policies and the general reorientation of Western social democracy into third way or "new" politics has perhaps prevented what would otherwise have been a natural development. However this situation changes in the coming decades, with EU enlargement again focusing attention on the issue (who will sit where, in which supranational groupings, in the enlarged European Parliament?) the postcommunist party landscape is of particular interest to students of class or post-class politics.

What, then, can we conclude about the continuing relevance of classical social theory to the analysis of processes of class formation and dissolution in postcommunist Europe, and what light does this massive reconfiguration of class relations have for our theoretical models? Very crudely, we should probably count the communist and postcommunist experience as supporting Max Weber, who had predicted a bureaucratized and sclerotic future for communism if it came about, rather than Marx. (The critique of Leninist and Stalinist bureaucracy was, however, also substantially driven by Marxists inside and outside the bloc.) Stratification patterns in communist and postcommunist societies, too, may seem more open to Weberian, Dahrendorfian or Bourdieusian models than to a simple opposition between exploiters and exploited grounded in the social relations of production. Weber's model of "classes, status groups, and parties" as phenomena of the distribution of *power* may seem particularly relevant in a context where, as a recent discussion of Russia argues, the relation to state power has been the principal source of privilege:

> Overall the shift from czarist to socialist planned economic and now to capitalist market economic power structures did not much affect the extraordinary importance of *authoritatively distributed privileges* as a central basic principle for unequal positions in the Russian social order. (Hölscher and Dittrich 1999, section 4.2)

Yet Marxism retains substantial explanatory power, both in general (Burawoy 2002; Burawoy and Wright 2002) and as a guide to understanding postcommunist social antagonisms. It may be that one requires a theory with the ambitous scope of Marxism to do justice to the world-historical ideological importance of the communist epoch (Lefort 1999) and to the way in which communism in Russia and much of Southeastern Europe was importantly a strategy for economic and social development. The concept of millenarianism, favored by some non-Marxist historians, had the merit of bringing out the similarities with religious movements, but at the risk of distorting the understanding of what remained in the end a secular belief system. More "realist" histories, grounded in short-run explanations in terms of interests, could hardly do it justice. And the democratic impetus behind the anticommunist revolutions recalls in some ways the early radical democractic Marx more sharply than Max Weber, for whom democracy was more of a (however desirable) political device.

The fact that no postcommunist proletariat has developed into a class for itself (even where, as in Poland in 1993 and 1995, there was something of a communist backlash) does not mean that class politics is dead or that East Central Europe has overtaken the West on the way to an American future. Theories of managerialism, originating in the early years of the USSR and often referring to it as well as to Western capitalism, clearly acquire a further dimension with the analyses of Szelényi and his collaborators (see Eyal et al. 2003). Whether or not one follows their *Bildungsbürgertum* (intellectual bourgeois) analysis all the way, it is clear that state socialist systems were essentially administered by professional cadres (Balla 1972) and that postcommunist managerialism is still strikingly more pronounced than in the West.

How far one can detect a shift to a more lifestyle-based pattern of consumption and social differentiation is still somewhat unclear. It has, however, formed a major emphasis of recent German work on Germany itself (Geissler 2000; Hradil 2001; Hradil and Schiener 2002) and on Russia (Hölscher and Dittrich 1999). The model of social milieus, based on value orientations and lifestyles, was developed by the market and electoral research institute Sinus in the 1980s (see figure 2.2) and taken up by a number of social scientists in the 1990s. In a comparison drawn in 2000, Sinus identified two specifically "Eastern" milieus, a conservative bourgeois-humanist one oriented to old Protestant virtues, and a "GDR-rooted" one, encompassing dismissed or retired members of the former East German elites whose attitudes remain strongly distinct from those of West Germans. Other Eastern milieus (such as left-intellectual, career-oriented, and traditional worker/peasant) were characterized as "converging" with corresponding milieus in the West. A more recent survey by Sinus itself (2002) still identifies nearly 4 million or 6 percent of "GDR-nostalgics" in the "traditional" (left-hand) side of their model.

Subjective representations of the class structure, which we discuss more fully in relation to issues of social solidarity in chapter 3, also display an interesting contrast, remarkably stable through the 1990s, between East and West. Eastern German respondents offered a sharply pyramidal model with a tiny upper stratum, while Westerners discerned a "spinning-top" model

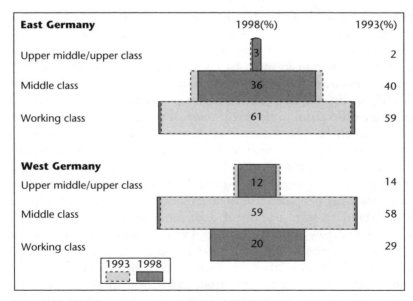

Figure 2.1   *Subjective class assignment, 1993 and 1998*
Source: Adapted from Roland Habich and Heinz-Herbert Noll: Soziale Sohichtung and soziale Lagen. In: statistisches Bundesarnt (Hg.): Datentepart 1999. Bonn 2000, p. 553.

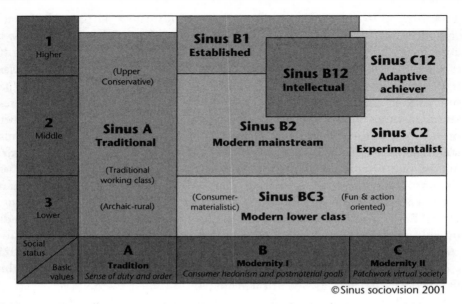

© Sinus sociovision 2001

Figure 2.2   *Multinational lifeworld segments: positioning according to social location and basic orientation*

with much larger upper and middle strata, the latter outnumbering the working class by 2 to 1 (see Figure 2.1).

So far in this chapter we have referred to Marx and Weber primarily as theorists of class and/or status, but Weber is, of course, well known as the leading theorist of bureaucracy – a topic of particular relevance to communist and also postcommunist societies. As we noted earlier, Weber's lack of enthusiasm for socialism was based on his fear that it would merely strengthen tendencies towards bureaucratization, which he saw as a dominant feature of the modern world. Soviet propagandists themselves sharply criticized bureaucratism in the early years of the Revolution and throughout the history of the USSR; a poster in the era of Gorbachev's perestroika in the late 1980s featured the ship of perestroika crashing though logs labeled, among other things, as "bureaucratism."

But the planned economy was inevitably bureaucratic in its operation and the same practices pervaded life in state socialism; "bureaucratic socialism" became a standard term in critical discussions inside and outside the bloc (Rizzi 1939; Hirszowicz 1980; Hodges 1981). Hodges's ambitious reformulation of Marxist analysis argued "that organization is a factor of production independent of both labor and capital, that corresponding to this factor are new social relations of production and a new mode of extracting the economic surplus from the direct producers, and that corresponding to these are a new working class, a new ruling class, and a new type of state" (1981: ix), and that the principal conflict would become that "between the central political bureaucracy and the administrative and technical experts at enterprise level" (1981: 136). But this prediction proved to be of rather little use in the late 1980s, when the intelligentsia deserted the regimes only where, as in Poland, society as a whole was largely doing so. More importantly, one can ask just what sort of bureaucracy ruled state socialist societies. In Weberian analysis, a charismatic bureaucracy, based on the real or perceived exceptional qualities of the bureaucratic official, is something of an oddity, yet Soviet party officials, especially but not only in the early years, were intended to be precisely this – animating the bodies to which they were assigned with no more concern for their existing expertise than that shown to Western cabinet ministers in a reshuffle. The career of Viktor Kravchenko (1947), who defected from the Soviet trade mission to the US, having managed activities from agriculture to aircraft production, illustrates this pattern, analyzed by the Hungarian writer Balint Balla (1972) in his classic and neglected work on "administration by cadre." A party cadre is by nature more like a soldier or a priest than a Weberian bureaucrat, though the inexorable processes of Weberian rationalization gradually effaced the differences.

As the bureaucratic or partocratic stratum mutated into what Djilas (1957) called a new class, it of course moved even further from Weber's ideal-type of bureaucratic administration, while illustrating his theorem of the objectification or routinization of charisma and, in a sense, the shift from a bureaucracy marked by charismatic forms to one owing more to traditional forms of rule. Weber had always been careful to distinguish between bureaucracy, which he tended to paint for the sake of illustration in what seemed like a positive light, stressing its technical superiority to other forms of rule, and "rule by officials." What emerged in the USSR and its subsequently acquired satellites and imitators was more like the latter.

As Weber insisted, once the process of bureaucratization is under way, it can be ended only by the collapse of the whole system. One of the major open questions in relation to postcommunist transition is how long it will take deeply entrenched bureaucratic and formal habits of work to give way to more rapid, informal, and flexible ones. The German case is again an interesting one in the intensity of the confrontation between Eastern and Western styles and of the resentments that resulted.

Before concluding this chapter devoted to Marxist and Weberian themes in communism and post-communism, we should look briefly at one of the most influential syntheses of the two paradigms. As we noted in the Introduction, the neo-Marxist "critical theory" of what came to be called the Frankfurt School, based around the Institute for Social Research in Frankfurt before and after World War II and mostly in the US during the war, is of particular interest for the imaginative and flexible way in which its members approached the authoritarian states which they found in the Soviet Union, in fascist Italy, and then Nazi Germany, and, incipiently, in their view, in the liberal democracies as well. Where more orthodox Marxists brought out a wholly different theoretical toolkit for the analysis of the Soviet Union and of the fascist regimes, and the post-World War II theorists of totalitarianism tended to assimilate them all too crudely, the Frankfurt theorists were struck by similarities and continuities between these authoritarian regimes and their predecessors, and between the psychological processes operating in both. The philosopher Herbert Marcuse, for example, produced brilliant analyses of the slide from liberalism into totalitarianism (1934) and of authoritarian family structures (1936), followed after the War by a critique of Soviet Marxism (1958) and of *One Dimensional Man* in advanced industrialism (1964). Of later critical theorists, Jürgen Habermas has written relatively little in this area, apart from important essays on what he called the "catching-up" or "rectifying" revolution (Habermas 1990). Thinkers influenced by him have, however, produced important analyses of communist and postcommunist societies. Andrew Arato noted that "from the very beginning his [Habermas's] reconstruction of Marxism has sought to make possible a thoroughly autonomous treatment of what was previously relegated to the superstructure (politics and culture), with the unintended consequence that . . . two . . . major factors necessary for the genesis and reproduction of Soviet society (the heritage of the bureaucratic state and of cultural traditionalism) could now become accessible to analysis" (1982: 197). Arato went on to advance an analysis of state socialism developed from some ideas in the work of Habermas and Claus Offe which is still worth reading today. More recently, Offe has worked substantially in this field, with an important volume of essays (Offe 1994/1996) and a major collaborative venture with Jon Elster, Ulrich Preuss, and others (Elster et al. 1998). Other studies with a background in critical theory include those by Guldimann (1984), Deppe and colleagues (1991), Meuschel (1992), and our own work on the public sphere (Outhwaite 1986, 1996) and on state socialism more generally (Ray 1996). None of these can be seen as in any simple sense an application of critical theory, yet all are in one way or another informed by it.

Finally, we might ask what, if anything, critical theory has to learn from the fall of communism and its aftermath. First, to the extent that it is committed to strong notions of communicative action, civil society, and the public sphere, the importance of civil society as a slogan and an organizing principle in the late 1980s was an initial encouragement, followed by a more substantial let-down as these movements and principles largely disintegrated. Nor does there seem to be anything quite comparable to the democratizing after-effects of the 1968 movements on the political culture and values of Western societies (see Sica and Turner forthcoming). Secondly, Habermas (1992) and others have drawn pessimistic conclusions from the experience of state socialism and its end about the very possibility of political communities organizing production on the basis of agreed social needs.

Habermas's concept of socialism as radical democracy and the related language in other analyses of social responsibility, stakeholders, and so on suggests a narrowing of horizons which we are not yet wholly resigned to. Finally, however, whatever the degree of demoralization and demobilization in many parts of the postcommunist world, one can still find egalitarian attitudes which, while hardly radical socialist, align East Central Europe on some dimensions with Scandinavia and afford some support to intellectual and political movements of social criticism. The next chapter explores some of these issues.

3

Society, Solidarity, and Anomie: Durkheim

The question of social solidarity, or "how is society possible?" is *the* central problem for sociology, to which most social theories attempt to provide an answer. We cannot in the space of one chapter deal with every aspect of solidarity, but we wish to indicate how the postcommunist experience and its diverse outcomes might influence our thinking about this issue. This chapter will identify some issues in social solidarity and in the course of later discussion in this book we will return to the issues raised here. The term solidarity is of course a central element of the Marxist and, more broadly, socialist tradition, but we have tied it here to Emile Durkheim, who established its use in the late nineteenth century as a theoretical category of the emergent discipline of sociology.

Despite the limitations of Durkheim's theory (of which there are many) this is an important statement of a central sociological problem – how people strive together and act as a coherent force. Marx by contrast had a limited and largely implicit theory of social solidarity. In his early writing on alienation he counterposed the division, misery, and objectification of capitalist society to a non-alienated communist future. Whereas in capitalism producers are separated from other producers, the products of their labor, and indeed their very humanness (species being), a communist society will represent a return of humanity to its social being (Marx 1977: 89) and hence to solidaristic social relations impossible under capitalism. Indeed, Marx and Engels assumed that the global triumph of the "cash nexus" hastens capitalism's demise since it destroyed all old solidarities but was incapable of creating new ones.[1] This inability to understand how, despite inequalities and conflicts, societies can cohere and reproduce themselves weakened their understanding of capitalism. Further, the formation of working-class solidarity was clearly crucial for Marx and Engels, but they also acknowledged that class solidarity was not an inevitable outcome of people having class interests in common. As Crow (2002: 25) argues, this "highlighted the need to explore what precisely solidarity is founded upon and what sustains it." The subsequent development of capitalist and state socialist societies suggests that the bases of social solidarity are complex and operate on multiple formal and informal, state, non-state, and familial levels. Within this mix, social welfare is particularly important in attempting to reconcile conflicting claims of self, family, and community.

Writing against the background of a political doctrine known as solidarism,[2] which dominated French political thinking in the second half of the nineteenth century (Zeldin 1973, ch. 21), Durkheim devoted his first major work, on *The Division of Labour in Society* (1895) to an ambitious contrast between the "mechanical solidarity" of simple societies, based on their homogeneity, and the organic solidarity of more complex and differentiated societies, based on the mutual dependence of individuals. Durkheim differed from orthodox economic theory, Herbert Spencer's sociology, and Hayek's later notion of catallaxy in arguing that this solidarity was not an automatic product of self-legitimating commercial exchanges. Rather, it was grounded in deeper moral sentiments and ties reaching "far beyond the short moments during which exchange is made" (Durkheim 1984: 227; Ray 1999c: 97; Crow 2002: 12ff.).

Culture and Economy

A great deal of Durkheim's work attempted to demonstrate that social solidarity was secured by moral/religious bonds, a view underpinned by his belief that all major social institutions and shared values have religious origins. Thus,

> in the beginning everything is religious. . . . No one has yet shown under what economic influences naturalism developed out of totemism, by what series of changes in technology it became in one place the abstract monotheism of Jahwe, and in another Graeco-Latin polytheism . . . it is indisputable that at the outset, the economic factor is rudimentary, while religious life is by contrast, luxuriant and all-pervading. (Durkheim 1976: 161)

Durkheim wished to avoid claiming either that the economic factor was an epiphenomenon (since once it exists, it exerts influence) or that it is a substratum, since the malaise of European society does not originate only in industry (1976: 102). Durkheim's explanation of social order lies in the ways in which the need for discipline (regulation) is balanced against the need for attachment to groups (attachment). These two processes, regulation and attachment, refer to general features of social relationships and contribute to social solidarity in variable ways, e.g. in ascriptive vs. consensual solidarity, which will be historically variable and determined in part by other social forces. One of the core problems for modern societies is to resolve the balance of regulation and attachment in a context of unprecedented complexity organized across vast social spaces.

Although he is often regarded as a social or structural determinist,[3] Durkheim was aware that outcomes of crucial social transformations are uncertain and contingent on political forces – which was the case, for example, in the Dreyfus Affair in which he was actively involved. The transition from mechanical to organic solidarity potentially allows for increases in social complexity and integration through the establishment of civil and legal rights grounded on a "cult of individualism" that has binding, quasi-sacred force.

However, Lockwood (1992) poses what he sees as a "Durkheimian dilemma" – that the concepts used to define and explain order or solidarity entail two quite different conceptions of disorder, neither of which is tenable. These are: (1) order or disorder is defined by the degree of moral consensus, solidarity and anomie being the limiting cases; (2) shared values are ultimately the only major source of stable regulation of social interaction and of structuring of wants or interests. If this is so, then what are the limiting cases? At what point does solidarity break down, and why? One is where consensus and moral regulation are lacking – the Hobbesian scenario (anomie). But there is also the (unacknowledged) possibility of polarization of society around two competing and internally solidaristic value and belief systems (schism). The first is the termination of society; the second requires that some social force other than morals disunite common value systems. Both are antithetical to Durkheim's scheme, which aims to regard moral-religious bonds as primary.

This critique is only valid, though, if one insists that any reference to non-moral influences renders the theory inchoate. Regarding the first issue, the possible "absence" of society, the Hobbesian limiting case, this was even for Hobbes an extreme state that could not in reality exist (though it could come close during civil war). Regarding the second issue, social schism, Durkheim did implicitly acknowledge the possibility that non-moral processes could disrupt solidarity by explaining anomie in terms of unregulated economic change creating class polarization. It is true that these (as economic processes) are not in themselves moral forces, but they intrude into the moral realm, which is insufficiently regulating egoistical desires. Durkheim does thereby shift from suggesting that the cultural (moral) is primary to a more dialectical view of culture and economy in symbiotic tension. But this may not be the most serious difficulty for his theory of anomie. Rather, this may be the way it overly polarizes solidarity and disorganization (a view Lockwood also advances). The symptoms of social disorganization – class conflict, abnormally fluctuating rates of crime, and societal conflicts – are not the work of atomized individuals with disordered desires but require organization, networks, and common purpose like any other collective activity. Thus we reach the important if paradoxical conclusion that social disorganization is compatible with social solidarity. It all depends on the level of designation of "society" at which solidarity is articulated and raises the question of negative consequences of social solidarity rooted in parochial sentiments creating exclusion as well as inclusion (Bauman 1999). This will be pursued further in chapters 7 and 8 in discussions of civil society, memory, and modernity.

The discussion so far points towards a theory of the codetermination of cultural (moral) and economic forms. Durkheim himself argued that apparently foundational processes or systems, such as the market, were dependent on the existence of shared values – hence his comments on the "non-contractual basis of contract." Thus from Durkheim arises a core sociological insight that "one cannot be a self on one's own" (Taylor 1989: 36). Social bonds have value in themselves and are never just pursued instrumentally or purely egotistically. Thus there is no necessary conflict between individualism and social solidarity, a point that seems to have been missed by more recent work on individualization (e.g. Beck and Beck-Gernsheim 2001). However, Durkheim's main interest was to develop this view against utilitarian and contract theories (such as Spencer) on the one hand and Marxist materialism on the other. The consequences of differential embedding of economic and institutional systems in cultural and moral life are not greatly developed in his work – though they have been by subsequent theories such as Polanyi's notion of embeddedness and the constructive role of the state in economic development (e.g. Polanyi 1944). Indeed, a great deal of sociohistorical political economy emphasizes, in opposition to economic formalism, that market exchanges are embedded in supportive but constraining social, organizational, institutional, and normative frameworks.

The collapse of communism and emergence of postcommunist capitalism(s) demonstrates the importance of the economy/culture configuration and the extent to which they are codetermining. Thus the different outcomes in postcommunist countries have been more diverse than neoliberal reformers envisaged. Early programs of privatization and marketization were underpinned by the naive view that, according to Jeffrey Sacks, an advisor to several postcommunist governments, "markets spring up as soon as central planning bureaucrats vacate the field" (Sacks 1993). However, in economic exchanges no individual preferences are formed in isolation from knowledge of what is available and desired by others. Interdependence of actors in pursuit of economic objectives will depend on wider interdependencies of families, localities, and civil society. Bryant and Mokrzycki (1994) and Skapska (1994) stress how economic systems emerge organically from particular historical and cultural contexts and, in Durkheimian fashion, point to the non-contractual elements of contract that are ignored by neoliberals. Similarly, Hans van Zon (1993) questions the neoliberal assumption that free markets and parliamentary democracy are natural and optimal states, since they both depend on trust, stability, and institutional regulation, which have to be carefully developed. Markets presuppose trust between participants, confidence that promises made will be kept, which implies the restraint of self-interest by civic virtue (Smart 2003: 109). Again, there are arguments about the need to limit the extent of markets to protect the public good – for example to mitigate poverty, prohibit unethical trade such as trade in body parts and trafficking of people. This raises questions about the extent to which markets are foundational for civil society and to what extent they undermine it. This classical dilemma between self-interest and social cohesion is being played out again in postcommunist societies. These arguments have featured in discussions of "embeddedness." That is, the ways in which exchanges such as markets are embedded in supportive but constraining social, organizational, institutional, and normative frameworks (Jessop 2002), which involves the constant formation and dissolution of social relationships in ways that presuppose conflict as well as cooperation between those involved. Thus there is nothing automatic about either market formation or its particular mode of embedding in wider cultural relations.

But the notion of "embeddedness" is somewhat loose (Sayer 1995: ch. 4) and different types of markets can be "embedded" in different ways. This can be illustrated by contrasting two ideal-typical market situations. One, similar to Okun's (1981) notion of consumer market prices, might be described as "embedded," while another, like Okun's auction-market prices as "disembedded." The former envisages economic exchanges as embedded in community networks, which constrain the circulation of money and thereby reduce risk. Rules tend to be situationally specific and govern behavior within well-established networks, where trust is dependent on face-to-face interactions or reputations, and generalized or systemic trust (Luhmann 1982) is low. In this model credit tends to be limited by mutual obligations rather than mediated impersonally by banks. By contrast, in "disembedded" systems of exchange, ties of community are progressively replaced by impersonal, arms-length, connections, and money acts as a symbolic store of value and a steering medium. There is a high degree of risk and fluidity (rapid entry and exit) and behavior is governed by abstract rules and high levels of institutionalized, systemic trust. Here credit expands via a well-developed banking system, and as Luhmann puts it, money becomes self-expanding and reflexive (1982: 208). The more fluid and disembedded are exchanges, the more complex systems of impersonal trust and regulation need to be.

Fligstein (2001) and Fligstein and Sweet (2002) identify two strands of thought on the embeddedness of markets. The first emphasizes market processes and the social structures that appear in markets, typically conceived as networks. The question remains, though, as to how networks emerge and how relations between government actors, legislators, and markets are constituted. The second approach (which they adopt) tries to link the development of markets more explicitly to questions of political and legal governance. This approach tends to emphasize how markets depend on rules and cultural understandings that are in turn structured by state institutions. Again, this challenges neoliberal accounts of economic action that minimize or ignore entirely the central role of the state in market formation, since state-building and market-building go hand in hand and there is no evidence that rising social inequality is a stimulus to productivity. This issue is of crucial importance for understanding the process of economic reform in postcommunist societies. We can therefore move from general considerations of solidarity to look at modes of embeddedness and their effects on social cohesion.

Welfare and Solidarity

Welfare systems are a means of securing the reproduction of capital in non-capitalist forms of reproduction. Though associated with the left and its critique of capitalism, welfare systems in industrial societies were promoted by conservatives (such as the German Historical School, including Friedrich List, Adolph Wagner, and Gustav Schmoller) for whom social security was a means of limiting the destructive power of the market and preserving patriarchy and absolutism as a social shell for a capitalism without class struggle. This concept of the "monarchical welfare state," which would guarantee social welfare, class harmony, loyalty, and productivity, was embodied in the German Bismarckian system introduced in the 1870s and 1880s. In this model, an efficient production system comes not from free-market competition, but from discipline and an authoritarian state that harmonizes the good of the state, community, and individual (Esping-Andersen 1989). By contrast, the later, Western welfare state was an integral element of the Fordist circle of growth based on mass production and mass consumption, which offset tendencies to social polarization and class conflict. Although Western systems were grounded in Atlantic Fordism and the Cold War, the Western social democratic concept of welfare was also one in which risks were pooled and individuals no longer faced uncertainty alone but as part of a group. Moreover, concerns that had once been individual became political (Baldwin 1990: 2). In the process was developed a new concept of citizenship in the West that developed the principle of "full membership of a community" (Marshall 1992). In state socialism, however, systems arguably remained "Bismarckian" in that social policy was tied to an authoritarian and disempowering order of statutory paternalism. This is expanded below. With the passing of the bipolar era a new concept of the state emerged and core social democratic voters moved away from an ethos of collectivism and solidarity (Inglehart 1990).

Solidarism was connected in complicated ways to the politics of mutual aid, friendly societies, and what became the welfare state. While the Durkheimian tradition, like Marxism, was not particularly enthusiastic about the welfare state,[4] it is still the case that one index of the degree of social solidarity is people's willingness to contribute to meeting the needs of others, whether through individual or collective charity or through some state-based system of redistributive taxation. Welfare systems were, according to Habermas (2001: 108) made possible by the existence of pre-political communities of fate that presupposed particular collective identities. However, Beck (1992: 95) argues that welfare systems in some ways made redundant Marx's ideas about class solidarities based on shared economic adversity because they empowered people by creating "comprehensively insured individualization" (Beck 1997: 101). Although this is contentious (see for example Crow 2002: 31–7), there is wide agreement that postwar welfare systems in capitalist societies were part of a new social settlement that regulated capital and labor (Jessop 2002). Western welfare systems represented acknowledgment that laissez-faire capitalism was incompatible with social solidarity and that governments had responsibility at least to provide for collective goods and services; subsidize or provide social goods such as health, education, and criminal justice; redistribute goods and outcomes (e.g. through social security).

The Western systems then went beyond the Bismarckian concept of welfare without effective citizenship, although it could be argued that state socialist systems did not. Here benefits tied people into an authoritarian redistributive state in which there was no role for democratic articulation of needs or debate about the scope and purposes of welfare. This has been described as a system of "covert legitimation" (Markus 1982) that rendered people dependent on, and acquiescent to state agencies for their material well-being through redistributive policies, full employment, wide access to education, income maintenance, housing subsidies, health and welfare, social mobility, and social security.[5] Similarly Staniszkis (1992: 101–2) referred to "functional legitimacy" and the idea appears in Pakulski's (1986: 35) notion of conditional tolerance. However, it is also suggested that in the East, as in the West, welfare developed into an implicit social contract between the Party and people (e.g. Jowitt 1978; Cook 1992; Bunce 1983). Increasingly, by the 1970s and 1980s, Soviet systems attempted to strike an instrumental bargain with the people – welfare and security in exchange for political acquiescence – but the bargain was giving rise to two kinds of strain. First there was the process whereby the state and Party was increasingly held responsible for failures and irrationalities in the system. Second, the expenditure burden of social goods became more difficult to sustain in a context of falling productivity and for some countries (such as Hungary and Poland) rising foreign currency debt.[6]

In the East and West, by the late 1970s welfare systems were in crisis. In the West a taxpayers' backlash, both real and carefully hyped by neoliberal governments like Thatcher's in the UK, was a key element behind the attempts to run down welfare provision in many of the advanced capitalist societies. This was underpinned by increased globalization of economic exchange, labor market flexibility, and the decline of traditional industrial sectors. Bauman (1998) argues that welfare systems contributed to social solidarity so long as all citizens believed themselves to be engaged in collective endeavor and enjoying common entitlements, but that this has broken down as people calculate whether they are winners or losers. He writes of a marginalized "new poor" in a system that works against solidarity and promotes division. In the state socialist countries, as always, the process of decline of welfare was shorter and more explosive than in the West: it seemed that massive universalistic systems of health, education, and welfare provision (Therborn 1995, ch. 5), predicated on an assumption of full employment, sometimes collapsed overnight or withered away, turning their former beneficiaries loose to face rising unemployment, devalued or collapsing currencies, and other forms of social dislocation. These are widely held views but the evidence from Western and postcommunist societies suggests a more complex picture. Welfare systems are inherently like Alice, who had to run fast in order to stay in the same place. Confronted by open-ended demand functions, they apparently need to grow in absolute and relative terms in order to deliver a constant level of provision, except where restructuring produces genuine economies.

The ideology of solidarity in state socialism was double-edged: it carried with it the implication that the state would provide a basic minimum for anyone in need. Mutual aid came into play at the margin, as consumers (and of course producers as well) helped one another get round the endemic shortages of goods by a mixture of direct exchange and gifts to be reciprocated at some time in the future. In an article originally published in 1993, Claus Offe (1996: 237–8) provides a useful balance sheet:

- State socialism . . . provided a free and universal system of health, education, and vocational training to its citizens;
- it also provided heavily subsidized housing, which, however, remained scarce and qualitatively deficient in most places;
- formal unemployment was virtually unknown . . .
- childcare services were generously provided in order to free female labor for employment, and also in order to maximize state control over the political socialization of children;
- many mass consumption items were heavily subsidized . . .
- income inequality was significantly smaller than in market societies, but disposable income was also lower;
- but many quality consumption items were unavailable in the market . . .
- retirement incomes were extremely low . . .
- health and other services were of poor quality in many places;
- enforcement of positive rights and claims was difficult.

Further, statistics that may appear positive – for example the higher numbers of doctors per head of the population in socialist as opposed to capitalist countries – could conceal more negative comparisons such as inferior medical technology (Holmes 1997: 234; Kornai and Eggeston 2001). In fact, already before the fall of communism there had been an internal critique of this economy of guaranteed employment and welfare (*garantirovannost'*); see for example Zaslavskaya (1989, esp. ch. 6).[7] One element of the anomic (to use another Durkheimian term) confusion of ideas accompanying the collapse of communism was an uncertainty about what aspects of the old order were worth preserving. The term "socialist achievements" (*Errungenschaften* in German) had been worked to death in the old regimes, and in the East, as to neoconservatives a decade earlier in the neoliberal west, "social" in the sense of social policy sounded too much like socialist. "Shock therapy," some thought, might be more effective without anaesthetic.[8] But more important probably than any intentional demolition of welfare structures was their inadvertent destruction through the loss of the infrastructure that had preserved them. Much provision was through enterprises which were no longer able to sustain it. Factories and firms that could barely keep afloat were not going to prioritize their childcare or health facilities.

The picture however is an uneven one. Despite the horror stories coming from Russia and Poland, reflected most strikingly in the collapse of life expectancy figures, which had already begun to decline in the 1970s,[9] studies based on other countries of Eastern and Central Europe stress the continuities in welfare provision. The two new problems, nonexistent or unacknowledged under communism, were unemployment and poverty. Other areas of provision, such as pensions, sick pay, health care, and family support, were often substantially preserved, albeit against the background of a general shift towards continental/German, as opposed to Scandinavian or British, modes of provision (see figure 3.1). In other words, the pattern described by Therborn (1995: 96), in which state-supplied provision in the North and East contrasts with insurance-based systems in most of the other EU countries,[10] has changed as the East looks more to the continental West for its social policy and to the Atlantic West (UK/US) in its more liberal form of capitalism. As the Czech prime minister, and later president, Klaus put it, they wanted a market economy without the (social) predicate. This is not the place to explore in detail the reasons for these ideological and organizational preferences, but in the choice of general capitalist models, as mentioned in chapter 1, the prevalence of neoliberal ideology suggested imitating Thatcher's Britain or Reagan's US, where these policies were followed most wholeheartedly. These countries, rather than the Nordics, were at the forefront of attention, and there may have been a certain reluctance to follow too slavishly the alternative German (and of course also French) model. In the case of welfare regimes, however, only the most fanatical neoliberal would advocate the US system or the manifestly failing, though admittedly cheap, UK one.

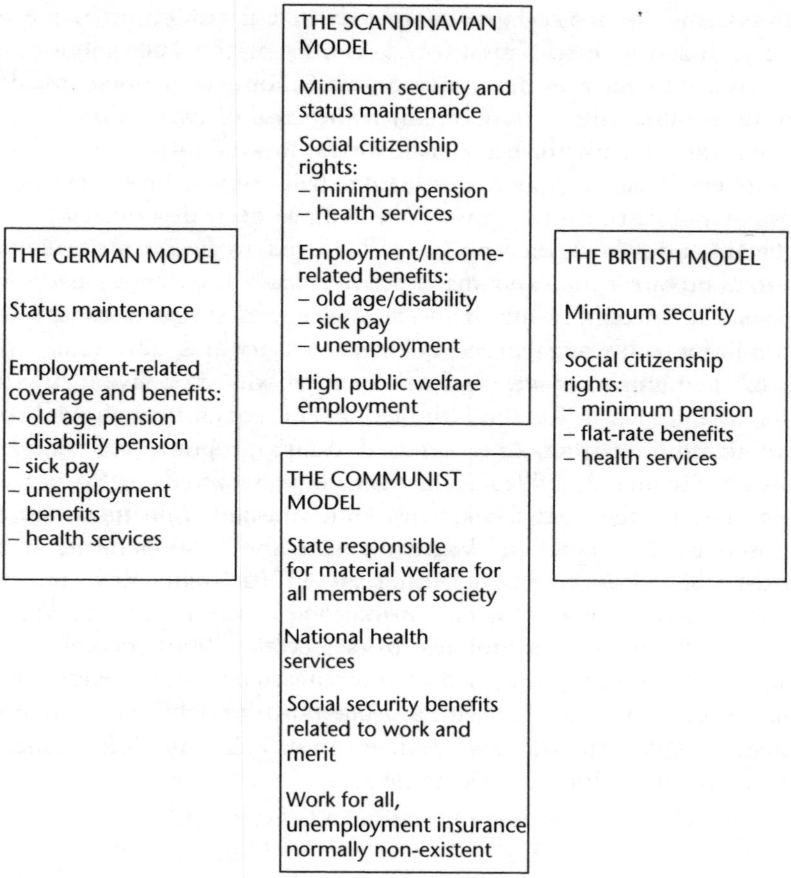

THE SCANDINAVIAN
MODEL

Minimum security and
status maintenance

Social citizenship
rights:
– minimum pension
– health services

Employment/Income-
related benefits:
– old age/disability
– sick pay
– unemployment

High public welfare
employment

THE GERMAN MODEL

Status maintenance

Employment-related
coverage and benefits:
– old age pension
– disability pension
– sick pay
– unemployment
  benefits
– health services

THE BRITISH MODEL

Minimum security

Social citizenship
rights:
– minimum pension
– flat-rate benefits
– health services

THE COMMUNIST
MODEL

State responsible
for material welfare for
all members of society

National health
services

Social security benefits
related to work and
merit

Work for all,
unemployment insurance
normally non-existent

Figure 3.1   *Major European welfare state models since 1945*
Source: Budge et al. (1997: 46).

Postcommunist Solidarity Crisis

With the end of communism divergent economic and institutional arrangements developed in a context of protracted transition recession that has
affected most postcommunist countries (Kolodko 2002).[11] According to the
World Bank (2002: 5):

> The magnitude and duration of the transition recession was, for all countries,
> comparable to that for developed countries during the Great Depression, and
> for most of them it was much worse. . . . The CIS had an average of 6.5 years
> of declining output, resulting in the loss of half the initial level of measured
> output. Even at the end of the decade, the CIS had recovered only 63 percent
> of its starting GDP values.

Welfare systems did not collapse completely or uniformly; rather the region shows a mixed bag of reforms (Kornai and Eggleston 2001). But in many places – especially most of the former Soviet Union – development is dominated by unregulated illegal economies, high levels of corruption, and rising inequality. The Marxist theorists of historical inevitability were replaced by new social engineers such as Yegor Gaidar (Minister of Privatization in the 1991 Russian government) whose policies have been described as "market Bolshevism" and "shock therapy." This involved swift and far-reaching liberalization, privatization, and marketization with the consequences of increasing social inequality and undermining social supports of the former system, all of which was regarded as both necessary and inevitable.

Unlike communism, however, shock therapy was short-lived. By 1994 it had been abandoned in Russia, although its consequences for social solidarity were already apparent. The core of Gaidar's program had been freeing prices – on January 2, 1992, price controls were lifted on 90 percent of traded goods. By the next day queues had vanished from most shops and prices risen by 250 percent. Wages rose by about 50 percent, so living standards dropped enormously. During the 1990s Russia saw startling increases in income inequality, with distribution of income more unequal than most advanced capitalist economies. Rosser et al. (2000) present decile ratios and Gini coefficients for 16 postcommunist countries.[12] Russia has the greatest measure of inequality with a decile ratio for 1992 of 6.84 and Gini coefficient of 0.393 (the US has a decile ratio of 2.25 and Gini coefficient of 0.189) (Rosser et al. 2000).[13] See Table 3.1.

Table 3.1   *Gini coefficients for postcommunist countries*

	1987–8	1993–4	Variance	
Bulgaria	0.23	0.34	0.11	48%
Czech Republic	0.19	0.26	0.07	37%
Hungary	0.21	0.24	0.03	14%
Poland	0.26	0.31	0.05	19%
Romania	0.23	0.29	0.06	26%
Slovakia	0.20	0.20	0.00	0%
Belarus	0.24	0.28	0.04	17%
Estonia	0.30	0.39	0.09	30%
Kazakhstan	0.26	0.33	0.07	27%
Latvia	0.23	0.27	0.04	17%
Lithuania	0.23	0.36	0.13	57%
Moldova	0.28	0.36	0.08	29%
Russia	0.28	0.48	0.20	71%
Ukraine	0.24	0.31	0.07	29%
Uzbekistan	0.30	0.31	0.01	3%

Source: Rosser et al. (2000).

Theories of social solidarity claim that there are two divergent equilibrium patterns – one in which social solidarity is achieved through horizontal linkages, mutual aid, and trust – the other marked by class conflict, vertical hierarchies, and general mistrust (Putnam 1993). Inequality threatens social cohesion in at least two ways – detaching disadvantaged and excluded people from the labor market and institutions of civil and political society, and encouraging withdrawal of elites from the social mainstream (Giddens 1998: 101). Thus a sharp increase in inequality can undermine confidence, trust, and social solidarity – replacing them with envy, mistrust, and a desire to beat the system (undisclosed economic activity to criminal organizations) which feed into an expansion of informal activities. As a result, declining tax revenues undermine official social safety nets – creating more inequality and stimulating further informal activity (Rosser et al. 2000).

Registered unemployment, of course, shot up in the 1990s from rates of 1–2 percent to 10–20 percent, with the Czech Republic, separated from Slovakia in the "velvet divorce" of December 1992, a prominent exception. The increase in unemployment and the dramatic rise in prices in most countries of the bloc mean that figures suggesting continued or increasing provision should be treated with caution. As in the West, constant or increased resources directed at social welfare could and did coincide with what were perceived as worsening conditions on the ground, given the natural tendency of costs to increase. Conversely, attempts at retrenchment, such as those in Reagan's US and Thatcher's UK (Pierson 1996) and even in Sweden (Budge et al. 1997: 354–5), produced only marginal reductions (Marmor and Okma 1997). Even in postcommunist conditions of "transformation recession" and drastically falling living standards, welfare costs remained high. In Poland, for example, in the early postcommunist years, "Public social expenditures from 1989 to 1992 diminished in real terms, but their share in national income increased from 15.3 percent to 22 percent" (Budge et al. 1997: 356).

Even in the best circumstances, it was still the case that postcommunist citizens had exchanged social security, in the sense of relatively certain employment at poor but predictable rates, and somewhat austere but again predictable conditions of life, for social security in the narrower sense of a conditional and uncertain entitlement to state-provided benefits. As Offe (1996: 239) put it, "a highly *integrated* social policy must be replaced with a *separate* institutional system." The European welfare state, from its beginnings in the late nineteenth century, had been in large part an oblique answer to "the social question," responding to political demands for democracy and/ or socialism with the consolation prize of welfare regimes. Bismarck's social legislation of the 1880s was initiated in the middle of a twenty-year period during which the socialist party was banned. In democratic France, in the aftermath of the 1848 revolutions, conflicts such as that over the "right to work" pointed up potential challenges to the state. As Tocqueville pointed out, this would entail, if taken seriously, that the state either itself become an employer or that it impose rigid controls on independent entrepreneurs (Don-zelot 1984: 44). The question, then, for the Republic, was how to give rights to those whose social condition did not match their political status, "without these rights giving them rights against the state" (1983: 71). As Donzelot argues, it was the rise of the social sector with social legislation, an ideology of solidarity and an institutionalized practice of negotiation, which answered these dilemmas. Similarly in Britain, the more protracted development of social policy legislation, from the restriction of night work for children in 1802 to the full-fledged post-World War II welfare state, was in part a re-sponse to the challenge of radical democrats inspired by the French Revolu-tion or, later, socialists radicalized by the two world wars. "Initially, the policy of integration was directed exclusively at the working class, whose militancy against the system was to be restrained and channelled" (Flora and Heidenheimer 1981: 343). In France, in particular, "solidarity" has been the organizing slogan for social policy, and to some extent for state ideology as a whole, from the late nineteenth century to the present.[14]

The postcommunist deal was in some ways the reverse of this: one gave up a certain kind of security in exchange for freedom and political democ-racy. Gender issues are important here: men, who had tended to be more active in dissident and counter-cultural movements, were also better pro-tected against unemployment in the postcommunist transition (see Einhorn 1993, 2003). This marks something of a contrast with Western Europe, where in the final decades of the twentieth century, despite continuing de facto gender discrimination against women, it was often "their" jobs which survived, as traditionally "male" jobs in mining and heavy industry were lost. Western societies have displayed a striking correlation between female participation in the paid labor force and the percentage of women in na-tional parliaments (OECD 1992), and the shakeout of women from employ-ment in postcommunist countries, either through dismissal or from forced or voluntary return to childcare as nurseries were closed, paralleled their exclusion from parliaments, where their numbers had previously been boosted by quotas. Different pension regimes, for example, can also gener-ate different, gendered, configurations of winners and losers (Ferrera et al., in Giddens 2001).

Through the early 1990s there was a growing awareness of the socialist "world we have lost," and opinion surveys in a majority of the "new dem-ocracies" saw the transition as a political but not an economic success. This majority view can be distinguished from the optimists (East Germany, Czech Republic, Poland, and Slovenia), where it was seen as a success in both dimensions and the pessimists (Hungary, Ukraine, Belarus, Russia, and Cro-atia), who saw it as a double failure (Delhey 2001: 150–1). The Eurobarom-eter time-series data are particularly interesting on this dimension, displaying quite dramatic variations from one year to another. Thus al-though no country in Jan Delhey's presentation of the data saw the transition as an economic success but a political failure, measured satisfaction with democracy and the human rights situation was actually a good deal lower than that with the market. The 1998 figures[15] showed a wide variation in support for a market economy as "right for the country's future." Over all the countries surveyed, half of respondents supported it, with a third against, with Estonia and Bulgaria roughly in this modal position. Romanians and Poles were solidly pro-market, with two-thirds in favor and respectively only 26 percent and 19 percent against, while in Lithuania, Slovenia, Latvia, Hungary, Slovakia, and the Czech Republic there was less than 50 percent support, which dropped to barely one-quarter of Czech respondents, where half were opposed. Given that Czechoslovakia was one of the most prosperous countries before and during the communist period, and that the Czech Republic was in the lead in postcommunist development, these results are somewhat surprising. In both Slovakia and Hungary, the latter another transition success story, net support plummeted to near zero in the early 1990s and remained constant thereafter. In Bulgaria, by contrast, the decline was reversed in the mid-1990s. Better-educated respondents were solidly pro-market: three-quarters of those with higher education and two-thirds of those with secondary. Those with only elementary education were evenly divided. Age had little impact for those in the 15–40 group, after which people became less favorable (53 percent of those aged 40–54, 41 percent for over-55s).

But solidarity, if it is a useful concept, means more than a toleration of redistributive taxation – itself, of course, something which mostly took place in a relatively hidden form under communism through state subsidies rather than direct taxation. It must also mean some kind of identification with other members of the imagined community. So far as one can generalize about postcommunist societies, it seems that such sentiments are relatively muted, in a context where the rhetoric of togetherness and unity had been discredited through over-use. The relative egalitarianism of postcommunist public opinion seems to be less based on positive feelings of solidarity and more on suspicion of those who have stolen a march on the rest. The fact, for example, that egalitarian attitudes are particularly strong in Bulgaria may in part reflect scandals such as the one discussed in chapter 4.

This returns us, of course, to the broader issue of why postcommunist Europe has tended on the whole to look to Anglo-American rather than Scandinavian models of capitalism and to continental European rather than Nordic models of the welfare state. It is tempting, and perhaps in the end unavoidable, to turn to simple explanations in terms of pendulum swings, the desire for a clean break, the rejection of "third ways" (in the pre-Blair sense of the term where it means an alternative between capitalism and socialism), and so on. One way or another, the welfare regimes of postcommunist Europe no longer look particularly distinctive except in the severity of the problems they confront and in the residues of their communist structures. Claus Offe's pessimistic assessment, formulated at the beginning of the 1990s rather than at their end, but one which many, including perhaps their author, would still advance, sees a situation characterized by the weakness of social democratic political forces on the one hand, and on the other an "associational wilderness which . . . must today be described as a pluralist-syndicalist-populist hybrid that is a far cry from Western European patterns." Such conditions, Offe (1996: 240–1) points out, form "the worst possible structural background for the emergence of social policies and social policy institutions." In a somewhat less negative vein, Graham Crow (2002), whose book on *Social Solidarities* includes a useful discussion of Solidarność in Poland, looks comparatively at the problems of social solidarity in what he calls "unsettled societies," including those in postcommunist Europe. His analysis, following Beck, of the decline of traditional solidarities and their replacement by more contingent and chosen ones (a shift which, in terms of classical social theory, could be compared with that from Tönnies's *Gemeinschaft* to Schmalenbach's *Bund* or voluntary association) has particular relvance to the postcommunist condition, where old solidarities resulting from a shared condition, a widely shared, if more rarely openly expressed, opposition to the system, and mutual aid with the necessities of life in a shortage economy have lost their relevance.

Let us look a little more closely at the notions of social and political solidarity. In political theory, it has become standard to contrast liberal with republican and communitarian conceptions of the political community. In liberal thinking, political legitimacy arises directly out of the self-interest of the individual members of society who support economic, social, and political institutions which enable them to fulfill themselves in more or less noble ways. It is not the job of the state or the political community to judge between alternative methods of self-fulfillment, so far as these are legal. In communitarian thought, political legitimacy derives out of the substantive will, to paraphrase Tönnies's account of *Gemeinschaft*, of a real and vibrant human community. In republican conceptions, by contrast, such as that of Hannah Arendt, the political community is seen in more voluntaristic terms as in some sense self-constituting, formulating its own substantive goals in an active process of collective will-formation. (This division is paralleled in nationalist discourse between economically based theories of nationalism, seeking the best political shell for individual or collective prosperity, and more explicitly nationalist theories of an ethnic or civic form, respectively.)

This, however, is a difference of emphasis. No plausible theory of political legitimacy, whether normative or, as in the example cited below, empirical, can avoid some reference to the notion of solidarity. As Claus Offe (2000) puts it:

The "horizontal" phenomena of trust and solidarity (linking citizens to each other) are preconditions for the "vertical" phenomenon of the establishment and continued existence of state authority, manifested in effectively ensuring the performance of civic duties. In simple terms, this means that before citizens can recognize the authority of the state, they must first mutually recognize each other as being motivated by – and hence reciprocally worthy of – trust and solidarity. It is precisely when this abstract but resilient trust in "everyone else" as the collective co-author of the obligating norms is undermined, or when citizens' active interest in each other's well-being is successfully discredited that liberal notions about curtailing the scope of the state's authority flourish. Trust in one's fellow citizens provides the cognitive and moral foundations for *democracy*, the risks of which no one would reasonably accept otherwise. The solidarity citizens feel toward one another, or to which they allow themselves to be obligated through their representative institutions, is the moral basis of the *welfare state*. Thus, both democracy and the welfare state are dependent upon the prior existence of binding motives, which in turn are tied to the form of political integration found in the nation-state.

For Offe, liberalism in the particular sense in which he uses the term in the above quotation represents a danger for the political community. And Peter Wagner (2003), following a line of argument that can be drawn from Arendt and others, has suggested that the totalitarian identification of individual interests with those of the state can go in either direction. In other words liberalism, if it claims that collective interests are nothing more than the sum of individual interests, that there is nothing but what Rousseau called the "will of all" (*volonté de tous*) as distinct from the general will, may undermine the political community no less disastrously than in the more standard version of totalitarianism in which people are told that their interests are identical with those of the party, state, or leader. Political freedom can disappear in either way.

The revolutions of 1989 were palpable evidence that the forms of solidarity that maintained the old regimes had been dislocated – in particular, they undermined the political clientage of the Party and the extensive system of nomenklatura privileges. However, the period of diverse anticommunist social movement activity, during the 1980s, provided new forms of communal, *Gemeinschaft*, or *Bund* solidarity for those who participated in them. In many cases this was essentially confined to groups of intellectuals and students, but in Poland the Solidarność movement at its height (1980–1) recruited 10 million people – almost one-third of the population, with a much wider basis of more informal support. But within a few years after the fall of communism this Gemeinschaft solidarity had fragmented into competing political parties, secularists vs. Catholics, neoliberals and their opponents, generational divisions, those for and against membership of the EU, and so on. This is indicative of the fractured *Gesellschaft* solidarity of complex societies, in which people are bound together not by an immediate sense of "we-ness" so much as shared national or state-based identity and common procedural rules for the conduct of public life.

However, within these frameworks the balance between solidarity/security and inequality/growth still had to be worked through. The new postcommunist democracies initially confronted neoliberal regimes such as that of Thatcher and Major in the UK on the one hand, and more traditional social or Christian democracies in most of the rest of Europe. In the second half of the 1990s, however, a further model came into prominence, anticipated by Bill Clinton in the US and known as the "third way" in the UK, where Tony Blair's New Labour came to power in 1997. It was widely imitated elsewhere, notably in Germany under Gerhard Schröder's "new centre" (*neue Mitte*).[16] Anthony Giddens's classic presentation of the argument for the third way defines it as "an attempt to transcend both old-style social democracy and neoliberalism" (Giddens 1998: 26). Social democracy he sees as bound up with the bipolar world, and tending to lose its ideological as well as its social base in the post–Cold War world. Not only is it ideologically associated with a discredited state socialism, but it arguably shares its failure to further economic innovation, with large-scale bureaucratic welfare states discouraging enterprise. Neoliberalism, for its part, dissolves the traditional values to which conservatives like Thatcher were also attached.

> The dynamism of market societies undermines traditional structures of authority and fractures local communities; neoliberalism creates new risks and uncertainties which it asks citizens simply to ignore. Moreover, it neglects the social bases of markets themselves, which depend upon the very communal forms that market fundamentalism indifferently casts to the winds. (Giddens 1998: 15)

Third way politics, by contrast, aims to empower people "to help citizens plot their way through the major revolutions of our time: *globalization, transformations in personal life* and *our relationship to nature*" (Giddens 1998: 64; emphasis in original). [And while] "Third way politics should preserve a core concern with social justice" (1998: 65), [these issues] "are not about social justice, but about how we should live after the decline of tradition and custom, how to recreate social solidarity and how to react to ecological problems (1998: 67).

One can, of course, ask whether the basic orientation of third way politics is as new as the issues to which it is now presented as a response, given that the transformation of social democratic parties began with the German SPD in the late 1950s. In the East, of course, it *is* new, because social democracy is new: there had been no explicit social democratic alternative to communism since the enforced fusion of social democratic and communist parties in the late 1940s. The texts grouped together in Giddens (2001) are remarkably silent about postcommunist Europe, even those concerned with the European region. It seems clear, however, that third way ideas have had some attraction in many states, whether as a coherent strategy or as a convenient veil for the reduction of state provision.

It is worth stressing, though, that these social and institutional changes have not resulted either in the end of welfare or in a collapse of support for solidaristic values. The patterns are highly differentiated across the postcommunist region. Moreover, the polarity between marketization and social solidarity needs to be refined. We have seen how market exchanges presuppose solidaristic networks, ties, institutional structures, and cooperative activity. We have also seen that these are institutionalized in different ways depending on the particular nature of the culture–economy fix. So this may provide a way out of Durkheim's dilemma – the extent to which social solidarity is successfully stabilized and the degree to which societies are polarized, or on the other hand, relatively integrated, depends on the mode of this institutionalization.

Anomie and Networks

We turn now to the issues raised by another classically Durkheimian concept, that of anomie. In Durkheim's analysis, anomie is principally a matter of lack of regulation, specifically of desires or passions, which is why he associates the anomic type of suicide with economic booms as well as crises, and also with divorce. (Robert Merton (1938) rightly pointed out that these desires are not so much inherent as socially generated.) Although anomie in Durkheim's sense is certainly an aspect of the postcommunist condition, as borders were opened to travel and imported goods, we should broaden the focus to a more general state of normlessness and uncertainty. Communist societies, though lacking the rule of law in an ultimate sense, since law was in practice subordinate to the political regime, were marked by a very high degree of regulation and self-regulation.

Whatever the psychological consequences of these restraints, their discrediting and/or removal was also traumatic. One of the best studies, by an East German psychiatrist (Maaz 1990), argues that the pervasive repression in every area of life in the GDR led to a state of emotional blockage (*Gefühlsstau*) and suppressed rage. Yet an initial satisfaction at the removal of the old system gave rise within a year to a whole new set of real and neurotic anxieties. Behind real anxieties about jobs, social security, savings, crime, ecological crises previously concealed, and so on, neurotic anxieties appeared more directly than before: fears of freedom, independence, and change (1990: 160ff.). And Germany was, of course, at the relatively ordered end of the transition spectrum; in the former Soviet Union there was not only the loss of a state, as in the GDR, but a widespread collapse of economic and legal structures. It was chilling, though not perhaps surprising, to hear Russian intellectuals talking in very Hobbesian terms about the need for a new dictator. One response, with origins in Tocqueville's classic analysis of mid-nineteenth-century America and Durkheim's of late nineteenth-century France, is to rely on the growth of intermediate associations between the individual and the state. But communism had precisely destroyed or incorporated such independent associational life and the habits which sustain it. The civil society called forth in the anticommunist revolutions seemed rather flimsy (see chapter 6).

For a Durkheimian analysis, crime and suicide rates are important (negative) indicators of social cohesion. The development of crime in postcommunist transition is a topic in itself; the conditions and opportunity structures were so fundamentally transformed that it is probably unhelpful to generalize about them here. We should, however, point briefly in particular to what Marxist dialecticians might call the unity of criminalization and decriminalization. On the one hand, much private economic activity, previously stigmatized (in much of the bloc) as speculation, was legalized; on the other hand large areas of enterprise fell into criminal control, as in the Bulgarian example discussed in detail in the next chapter. Secondly, the opportunity structures of crime were radically transformed by increased transborder traffic of legal and illegal commodities – including people. Finally, widespread unemployment and the collapse of wages for those in employment, combined with the lure of newly available goods, generated classic conditions for Mertonian anomie. How far this, rather than the other factors mentioned above, explains the increased crime in postcommunist Europe is a matter for more detailed specialized research. An interesting overview by Killias and Aebi (2000), based on the Council of Europe's *European Sourcebook of Crime and Criminal Statistics*, notes that property offenses rose between 1990 and 1992 and decreased again in the years to 1996. The authors suggest that opportunities rather than anomie are the most likely explanation.

> Within a few months [of the opening of the Iron Curtain], a substantial market for stolen consumer goods . . . emerged in eastern Europe . . . it may not be necessary to turn to abstract theories (like Durkheim's theory of anomie) in order to understand the rapid growth of trans-national large-scale theft and fencing industries . . . It is not clear why theft and burglary decreased after 1992. It could be that the Eastern black markets stopped growing after an initial boom. (Killias and Aebi 2000: 47)

Suicide provides a more immediately promising indicator of social dislocation. Suicide rates are, of course, marked by two features: their regularity over time, which so impressed Durkheim, and their dependence on local variations in classifying practices, which has been[17] a main theme of critical discussions ever since. Within Europe, including postcommunist Europe, the most striking feature is the north–south difference. Southern Europeans, including postcommunist and predominantly Muslim Albanians and Eastern Orthodox Romanians, though not Catholic Croats and Slovenes, are relatively well protected from suicide, while Northerners average more than twice as many deaths, with Russia and the Baltic Republics way out in the lead, followed by Belarus and Hungary. After that, the charts show a gentle slope, with Eastern and Western countries regularly succeeding one another.

It is of course the year-on-year variations which are of most interest. Although one must always allow for the possibility of changes in reporting practices and definitions, it is striking to note the rises in, for example, Belarus between 1990, when a gradual decline was reversed, and 2000, by which time the male figure was nearly twice as high. (Female rates, always much lower except in China, also rose, but by only around 12 percent.) In Croatia, affected, of course, not only by postcommunist transition but also by war, rates varied little, and the Czech Republic and Slovakia show a similar pattern. Estonia, by contrast, like Belarus, shows a sharp increase for males, but followed by an equally strong downward trend. Germany was static, with a slight downward trend. In traditionally suicidal Hungary, both male and female rates peak in the mid-1980s, just before a transition from a system that had long been more market-based than anywhere else in the bloc except Yugoslavia. In the Former Soviet Union, Kazakhstan, where there are also as many Russians as Kazakhs, shows a postcommunist male surge, while Kyrgyzstan, with a much smaller Russian minority, does not. Rates also rise sharply in Russia, Ukraine, Latvia, and Lithuania, with a downward trend strongest in Latvia. Poland and Romania show only a slight increase. In Slovenia, as in Hungary, rates are actually lower in the 1990s than in the previous decade, and in the rest of Former Yugoslavia they are static. The detailed evaluation of such statistics is of course a matter for experts (see, e.g., Sartorius 1996), but there seems to be a fairly clear relation between the magnitude of the transition shock and social dislocation as indicated by these figures. Most local experts seem to endorse this.[18]

For Durkheim, of course, society was both a constraining (and enabling) social fact and a collective representation; his theory of religion, we should recall, is essentially about the self-representation, not to say self-worship, of society. Recent (and more modest) defenses of the concept of society have retained this double focus on facticity and representation (Dubet and Martuccelli 1998). More skeptical authors, such as Baudrillard and Urry (and, in a very different way, Luhmann), have questioned whether we can or should be representing society in this way, especially in the light of globalization and the alleged marginalization of the nation state. For Urry, we should be thinking in terms of flows (of migrants, capital, images, and ideas) rather than static containers such as societies and social structures.[19]

While we do not share this approach at a general level, and wish in particular to stress the diversity of the socially and politically determined forms taken by postcommunist transition, we would not deny that the radical transformation of state forms and structures and the discrediting of communist appeals to society have drastically reduced people's capacities to represent "their" society to themselves. At the most radical, the state has ceased to exist (USSR, GDR, CSR, and Yugoslavia), with varying and unpredictable consequences in each case (Bunce 1999). For Soviet citizens, whether or not they supported the regime, the USSR was a quasi-imperial frame of reference comparable to that of the US (Filippov 1992). The breakup of the empire, even if it was welcomed by many of the newly independent nations or ostensibly a matter of indifference to many Russians, cannot fail to have destabilized social frameworks of representation. In Germany, a residual or remembered GDR identity (*Ostalgie*) coexists uneasily with an all-German one. In Yugoslavia too, attachments to the former Federation compete with those to the new states with which many Yugoslavs feel uncomfortable, since their ethnic origins and geographical location often do not fit into neat national boxes. In other states, such as Poland, Hungary, and Bulgaria, the national frame of reference is less problematic, though the intension, as distinct from the extension, of national identity may still be unclear. As studies since the time of *The Civic Culture* (Almond and Verba 1963, 1980) showed, citizens of different states think their national identity differently, using different combinations of ethnic, civic, religious, and other elements, and thinking their relations to their history, to neighboring territories and to larger entities such as Europe in very different ways (see Hjerm 2003).

The crucial issues here are the levels of identification of the object of solidaristic integration and the legitimacy of force establishing internal pacification. Three postcommunist patterns can be identified. First, the continuity of the former national state (e.g. Poland and Hungary), where despite social dislocation and rising conflict there was a continuation in national and societal identity. Second, subnational schism (former Yugoslavian and Soviet Republics), in which a collapse in legitimacy of the state apparatus combined with local identities and solidarities. Third, there is irredentism – the emergence of reunified or enlarged states such as Germany and Greater Serbia. A crucial variation within the latter forms is between violent and nonviolent transitions. Here crucial factors will be modes of state decomposition, mobilization of memories and communicative systems, and the formation of mutually exclusive identities.

If anything, and despite the qualified sovereignty of the states in the Soviet bloc and the rhetoric of the socialist community of states, the nation-state frame of reference was stronger than in Western Europe, where a substantial degree of economic (and, for most states, political) integration was a fact of life. Communism, though theoretically internationalist, was national (in the sense of referring to the national state) in its form and in its self-legitimation. Romania was a particularly crass example, but even in Germany there were increasing attempts in the 1980s to reappropriate elements of the (East) German past such as Luther and Frederick the Great, which would previously have been deemed politically incorrect. It was not only West German ideologues who practiced what Habermas (1986, ch. 6) called "the public use of history." Opposition movements, too, were substantially shaped around the nation; Polish Catholicism in the 1970s and 1980s was in many ways an anti-regime civic religion, disconcerting many supporters when in the 1990s it pursued a more conventionally reactionary and misogynistic Catholic agenda. The years 1989/90 also, of course, meant the liberation of historiography from communist constraints and the reopening of important national issues such as the Katyn massacre in Poland.

As always, however, nationalism was a source of division as well as of solidarity, perhaps most strikingly in the Baltic Republics, where a civic nationalism which had been tolerated and sustained up to a point even under the Soviet regime immediately raised complex ethnic issues when the Baltic States became really independent. Estonia had a one-third Russian minority and Latvia even more; only in Lithuania were Russians no more numerous, at 10 percent, than other minority nationals taken together. Resulting issues of minority rights have been problematic, and only resolved (or at least papered over) under the pressure to prepare for EU membership. Aside from any national sentiment, however, the Baltic States had powerful economic reasons for breaking away from the Soviet empire, and the same motivation can be seen in the Czech regime's desire to dump Slovakia in 1992 and in Slovenia's secession from Yugoslavia in 1991. The consequences were, of course, drastically different in the last case, since although Slovenia escaped successfully it was the first domino in the disastrous Yugoslav sequence which has continued into the present century.

Yugoslavia was the bad surprise of the postcommunist decade. Its disintegration had been widely predicted to follow Tito's death (which occurred in 1980), but in the event came ten years later and was far bloodier than most observers had expected. Conversely, the break-up of the Soviet Union was more peaceful than expected (Pryce-Jones 1995), and the separation of the Russian Federation and the other Republics did not, as many had anticipated, lead immediately into further balkanization.[20] Issues of nationalism are discussed more fully below.

After nearly fifteen years of a distinctly cool engagement, the most economically and politically advanced of the former communist states were incorporated into the EU in 2004, raising new issues of who "we" are and for whom we may be co-responsible. Civic state nationalism has been the *de facto* basis of social solidarity for Western Europe since the beginnings of the welfare state, and it is not clear what, if anything, will take its place. Within the established welfare capitalist democracies of the West, this may not matter so much, with an EU policy regime perhaps gradually replacing the national one, just as the federal level has gradually displaced the state level in the US. But where "national" independence is relatively new, as it is *de jure* for most of the postcommunist accession states and *de facto* for all of them, the intrusion of a European frame of reference may be a complication too far.

The lessons of communism and postcommunism for our reflection on social solidarity are therefore ambiguous. If solidarism was conceived as a moderate alternative to socialism and communism, early twentieth-century Marxism was the real thing, positing a society in which solidarity would be the organizing principle of production rather than a communitarian background and emollient to the workings of capitalist market societies. With the collapse of communism, we are pushed back, for the present at least, to looking at ways of nurturing and developing social solidarity within capitalist societies. Touraine's question, "Can we live together? Equal and Different," means essentially the same thing in East and West. Expectations of employment, housing, health care, etc., which were automatically satisfied, if often at a poor level, under the old regimes, have now largely been abandoned.

Nation and Solidarity

We close this chapter with some reflections on nationalism, which perhaps owe more to Max Weber than to Durkheim. Nationalism, whether spontaneous or manipulated, has accompanied and driven the demolition of the USSR and Yugoslavia and the separation of the Czech and Slovak republics, as well as being an important force behind anticommunist movements, notably Solidarity. The proliferation of new nation states and the rise of nationalist ideology and, in some cases, warfare, looks like support for Max Weber's nationalist realism, rather than Marx's internationalism, though globalization and European integration suggest that the boot may end up on the other foot. It is also interesting to note what has *not* happened in the postcommunist world. Contrary to predictions of universal balkanization (Mestrovic 1994) and, in particular, the expectation that the former Soviet Union would fragment more or less to infinity (the war that did not happen), one of the most striking features of the postcommunist period has been the relative stability, if one excepts Yugoslavia and Chechnya, of postcommunist borders. However much decentralization (to put it mildly) there has been *de facto* in Russia, no one much has found it necessary or desirable to attempt to secede. Even if, to take two relatively likely future examples, Bosnia-Herzegovina splits apart or the Kaliningrad area attempts to break away from Russia, this seems unlikely to set off a chain reaction. To the extent that a defense of the concept of society relies on pointing to the "stickiness," the tendency to persistence, of social formations, the postcommunist world paradoxically appears as a witness for the defense, or at least as an illustration of the power of a state-based civic nationalism as against a more ethnically based form. At the same time, of course, it counts against a naive version of liberal or Marxist voluntarism that stresses the malleability of social formations and the possibility, as the Internationale puts it, of making a *tabula rasa* of the past.

The Eastern Enlargement of the European Union, which began in 2004, is a further element in the "urbanization" or taming of Eastern European nationalism. Just as the new members' currencies will be locked into the euro, before finally disappearing into it, so their existing political structures will remain in the form of member states of the union, their previously international relations becoming increasingly matters of a kind of European-level domestic politics. Already, as we show in the discussion on convergence in the next chapter, they are beginning to adapt to this changed reality (Jacoby 2002), with some at least of the members of the 2002–3 constitutional convention seeing themselves as European politicians at least as much as representatives of their home states. At a more grassroots level, too, there may be grounds for the optimism expressed by Kaldor and Vejvoda (1999[2002]: 168) at the end of their review of *Democratization in Central and Eastern Europe*:

> The most positive finding of this study has been the energy and initiative to be found throughout the CEECs at a local level. Individuals have sought ways to change their situations through forming NGOs, setting up small businesses or getting involved in local politics. Often they make links with similar individuals and groups in Western Europe, thus acting as harbingers of a possible future European civil society.[21]

Enlargement is undoubtedly a major challenge, but it seems likely that the EU will rise to the occasion, in its usual messy, uneven, but ultimately effective manner.

One of the reasons why the EU should be an object of major theoretical as well as practical interest to sociologists is that it relies on forms of solidarity which are not grounded in the traditional European national state. This reliance on what Mark Granovetter (1973) called "the strength of weak ties" is probably unprecedented in the history of Western social policy, which has always taken the national state as its frame of reference, with "overseas aid" tagged on as a more or less marginal extra. European (in the sense of EC/EU) social policy has always been peculiarly incoherent and fragmented, dressed up as a combination of support and structural reform in the Coal and Steel Community and the Common Agricultural Policy, with social and regional funds playing a very marginal part and welfare policy basically left to the member states. As Scharpf (2002: 645–6) has shown, this pattern was set in 1956, at the very inception of the EC, when a French proposal to harmonize social protection and taxation regimes was defeated. As a result,

> the course of European integration from the 1950s onward has created a fundamental asymmetry between policies promoting market efficiencies and those promoting social protection and equality. In the nation-state, both types

of policy had been in political competition at the same constitutional level. In the process of European integration, however, the relationship has become asymmetric as economic policies have been progressively Europeanized, while social-protection policies remained at the national level. (Scharpf 2002: 665–6)

The unclear relations between the EU's own development aid and that provided unilaterally by member states, and the somewhat incoherent attempts to justify European aid (see Karagiannis 2004) are further examples of this. The replication of even a rather cold, Bismarckian welfare state on a European level seems both essential and unlikely – unless, that is, it achieves the mobilization of bias (Bachrach and Baratz 1970) in the same way that the Common Agricultural Policy, substantially supported by farmers, was grudgingly accepted by urban Europeans. In Scharpf's view, a Europeanization of social policy is unfeasible, and the best alternative is a legal framework setting minimum standards for member states, and as Joe Weiler (2002: 569–70) argues in the same issue, although "Europe prides itself on a tradition of social solidarity which found political and legal expression in the post-war welfare state . . . the consensus around the classical welfare state is no longer as solid as before."

This is, of course, to assume that solidarity, even if intangible, is important. An alternative view would be that what count are systematically interlinked mechanisms which secure the same outcome, just as markets may be understood as more or less closely simulating genuinely social production for socially agreed needs via the operation of the individual profit motive. System integration, in other words, matters more than social integration. Many aspects of the development of modern societies may be seen to support this latter view. On the other hand, there are also increasing demands for what Habermas would call communicative justification of societal policies. The European Union, like the national states which gave birth to it, started off as, and is still, an elite project, marked by a "democratic deficit (Marquand 1979; Mény 2003); it remains to be seen whether it can grow the sort of roots which national states were able to stimulate or simulate through banal (Billig 1997) and not so banal nationalism.

4

Three Types of Convergence

There were traditionally two principal organizing concepts for discussion of communist societies in the second half of the twentieth century. One of them was "totalitarianism": the other was "convergence." The former, of course, stressed the anomalous character of communist societies, along with the newly defeated fascist ones, while convergence models stressed their allegedly growing similarities and hence the (at least incipient) normality of post-Stalinism. Put like this, they seem to be polar opposites. In practice, however, the concept of totalitarianism, with its emphasis on state terror, tended to become an ideal-type from which later divergences were measured. Though few commentators were naive enough to believe that everything had changed after Stalin's death in 1953, or with Khrushchev's "secret speech" of 1956, there was a growing consensus in many Western countries that the term totalitarianism could no longer be applied in a strong sense, and that something else was needed to explain a "post-totalitarian" reality – at which point the idea of convergence took up the strain.

General and Specific Theories of Convergence

As with relativity theory, there was a special and a general theory of convergence. The special theory asserted the increasing similarity of capitalist democracies and state socialist societies, based on a variety of observable phenomena. The general theory was more speculative in character and offered an explanation of observable similarities, based on some notion of the logic of industrialism. An economic variant, developed by Tinbergen, was cast in terms of convergence toward an optimal form of economic system (see Ellman 1984). The imperatives of industrial production made demands on other sectors of modern societies (we were in something like a functionalist universe of discourse) leading to educational expansion, bureaucratic state and corporate organization, urbanization, the primacy of nuclear family models, and so on. As the British sociologist Ron Dore sometimes represented it in a useful diagram, the image was one in which the centripetal force of the core industrial institutions of advanced societies pulled the other sectors into regular and parallel circles around them.

Dore's *British Factory: Japanese Factory* (1973) was an important demonstration of the empirical weakness of the general convergence thesis,[1] while a number of commentators pointed out its theoretical difficulties. Another British sociologist, John Goldthorpe, pointed to its historicism, in Karl Popper's sense of the term: a historical prophecy based, in this case, on a thesis of technological determinism. Raymond Aron, who had done much to popularize both the notion of industrial society (Aron 1962) and that of totalitarianism (Aron 1965), was explicitly skeptical about convergence. Krishan Kumar, too, while accepting the fact of some substantial convergences among industrial societies, criticized

> the evolutionist mode of explanation, and the historical abbreviation of the course of industrialization . . . the idea of a technologically-determining "logic of industrialism" . . . proved a poor predictor of the future development of western societies . . . and of the important differences that continued to characterise their political and social structures. (Kumar 1978: 153–4)

Kumar and others were more favorably disposed to what we have called here the special theory of convergence, that between "actually existing socialism" and Western capitalism. He cites with approval an article by Dunning and Hopper (1966: 181–2) which pointed to the trend away from laissez-faire capitalism toward greater political control and, in the socialist countries,

> the re-introduction of certain market mechanisms of a limited kind. Perhaps even more important, however, are the ways in which capitalist and socialist societies have become more similar both in their high degree of centralization and bureaucratization of the economy and of the polity, and in the patterns of conflict which have emerged between bureaucratic interest groups within and among organizations.

Both advanced capitalist and advanced or developed (*razvitoye* in Russian) socialist societies, as they were beginning to describe themselves in the 1960s, were "Fordist"[2] in their industrial structures, oriented to large-scale production and with a heavy emphasis, especially in the USSR and US, on military production. The more US and other capitalist corporations grew in size and in their degree of vertical integration (in-house production of components and ancillary products), the more their internal transactions resembled those of a planned economy, where barter was common and prices for transactions between enterprises were ultimately irrelevant. Conversely, "USSR Inc." or "DDR GMBH" could be seen as operating like super-corporations. Theories of managerialism, which had been developed already in the 1920s, enjoyed a new prominence, in books such as *The Red Executive*

(Granick 1979) and *Soviet Prefects* (Hough 1969). Party apparatchiks were becoming more technically skilled – a process documented for Germany by Peter Ludz (1972).

The partial opening up of the state socialist societies to world trade and foreign investment in the 1970s and 1980s, documented for example in the popular book *Vodka Cola* (Levinson 1978), reinforced many of these tendencies, and even in the late 1980s there was a serious intellectual case to be made for the likelihood of convergence in this sense. Some of the more critical literature coming from Eastern dissidents and emigrants, as well as from Western observers, suggested that the stakes might be higher than they had appeared in the somewhat bland and sociologistic discussions which had predominated hitherto. On the other hand, perestroika in Russia and its analogues elsewhere in the bloc suggested that things were more open to change than they had seemed earlier. There were discussions, as there had been earlier, of a possible "Mexicanization" of the USSR and its ruling party. (The Mexican PRI had developed an impressive expertise in keeping opposition parties out of power by a variety of more or less disreputable devices, but it was not, nor had it ever been, totalitarian.) Both politically and economically, then, there seemed some prospect that these systems were reformable.

Heteronomous Convergence

By the beginning of 1990, the special theory of convergence was dead in the water – one element of the binary opposition starting points or paths having ceased to exist, at least within Europe. The general theory, however, was immeasurably strengthened, with somewhat speculative triumphalist assertions of the coming of a "new world order" (George Bush I) or even the "end of History" (Fukuyama) resting on a more sober realization that capitalism was now "the only game in town." We must, however, be careful to distinguish between a perceived inevitability and one grounded in the nature of things, between an alleged "logic of industrialism" and a more concrete logic of the real pressures of global capitalism, moving into an economic and political vacuum in the East (Hausner et al. 1995; Sidorenko 1999). This suggests a third concept of convergence, closer to the European Union's notorious "convergence criteria" for economic and monetary union; we might call this heteronomous convergence, since it is imposed by outside or local elites as an explicit policy objective. Convergence was always conceived as a process taking place behind the backs of human actors, but in this third sense it occurs via policies formed in newly democratized polities, but against a powerful background of TINA ("There Is No Alternative") arguments.

How far the postcommunist states were free to act is of course a question that has to be posed against the background of broader discussions of globalization,[3] but for the moment it is worth looking in a little more detail at the early postcommunist years. One of the first policy options, universally adopted, was a negative one: the demolition of central economic planning mechanisms – the Soviet state plan (Gosplan) and its homologues in the other states. This was a principal arena for TINA arguments, and one where they were perhaps best founded. There was a more or less universal consensus that central economic planning, which had been subject to repeated reform attempts in one country or another more or less since its inception, or at least since its implementation across the bloc in the early 1950s, had failed catastrophically and definitively. Yugoslavia had long abandoned it; in Hungary and Germany it had been substantially marginalized; in Poland private agriculture and much other enterprise existed without reference to it.

The second key policy, practiced with varying degrees of determination and haste, was price liberalization and the removal of state subsidies – the key element in what came to be called "shock therapy." Again, there was a consensus that much economic activity was unsustainable in its current form, often involving the subtraction rather than the addition of value, as when perfectly good cotton was turned into unsaleable clothing, or food was produced only to be left to rot or plowed over again. The third major plank of policy was privatization. Here again there was a consensus on its desirability, though divergence on how it should be carried through. And what British social democrats had called the "commanding heights" of the economy when they nationalized them after World War II, turned out once again to be less commanding than one might expect.

It is clear that these three policies had what Wittgenstein would have called a family resemblance, but less evident that they entail one another. Western capitalist economies, as noted in chapter 1, display wide variations in levels of state economic activity, and postcommunist states continue to do the same. But, as with Thatcherism in the UK, TINA arguments were successfully deployed despite the manifest existence of alternatives not far away.[4] We are dealing, then, not only with liberalization from above (where else would it have come from in such systems?), but also, and less obviously, with privatization from and often to "above" (into the hands of the existing nomenklatura). Some of these practices of what has been called "recombinant capitalism" (Stark 1996; Ray 1996) may, as we shall suggest later, be seen as alternative forms of "embedding" – ways in which organizations can mobilize existing social and cultural resources in the absence of those, such as organized capital markets, supply networks and so on, which are taken for granted in other advanced European economic systems. But if one is looking for theoretical models to describe this process, it is hard to choose between Durkheim and Gabriel Tarde – the former looking for a massive social fact working its way out in accordance with a strong state of the collective consciousness, the latter seeing processes of imitation.

Wade Jacoby (2000) has made impressive use of an imitation model in analyzing Western Germany after 1945 and united Germany after 1990. Such an approach, he argues, suggests important modifications to existing rationalist, culturalist, and structuralist approaches to change in comparative politics, by opening up areas of contingency in the ways ideas and structures are adapted as well as adopted. Jacoby (2000: 216) notes that future Eastern EU members have had even less say than Eastern Germans in adapting to common patterns: "As East European policymakers look to imitate EU-approved structures, it is important to note that institutional transfer has a different character where a universal standard has been established." In a more recent paper (in Bönker et al. 2002), Jacoby analyzes the role of the EU, and specifically the Commission, in relation to the accession countries, in terms of a religious analogy of confession and absolution. The future members increasingly have to analyze and document the areas in which they fall short of the *acquis communautaire*, accept the need to reform, and share in the task of monitoring their own progress in doing so. In a process beginning in 1998, the EU, in the form of the Commission, nominated 31 "chapters" of legislative and institutional arrangements for "screening."[5] By the end of 2002 all 31 had been closed for all the new member states due to join in the first wave in 2004. Several remained open in Bulgaria, and nearly half in Romania, whose membership is currently envisaged for 2007 (see table 4.1).

As Jacoby (2002: 138) puts it,

> The expectation of remedial action – penance – is built into the structure of the screening. The key tool of the screening process is the "harmonogram," a complicated grid listing for each area to be screened . . . the relevant EU directives and the applicant counties' existing legislation pertaining to each directive. Depending on the gap that results, the harmonogram goes on to list a set of legislative and institutional tasks needed to meet the directive fully, and a description of the appropriate ministry personnel tasked with completing this action by a specified date.

While it was possible for accession states, as in the Czech example discussed in some detail by Jacoby (2002: 141–2), to evade some of these pressures by creative presentation and accounting, this freedom was gradually reduced. The impression that administrative tidiness had somewhat obscured the political excitement of Eastern Enlargement[6] was probably reinforced by the tendency to use "Europe" as a shorthand for "the EU," with the implication that the new members were only now joining it. The French President Jacques Chirac's threat in 2003 to the new prospective members that they should not step out of line and support the US/UK war against Iraq was a further source of annoyance. In any case, however, in the alleged remark by Commissioner van den Broeck, the bottom line was that "the CEE states are joining us; we are not joining them" (cited by Jacoby 2002: 135). The EU's intransigence and arrogance on a number of issues to do with Enlargement[7] is in striking contrast to the incoherence so far of its so-called common

Table 4.1   *Accession negotiations: state of play*

Chapter no.	Bulgaria	Romania
1 Free movement of goods	X	X
2 Free movement of persons	X	*** 0
3 Free movement of services	X	**** 0
4 Free movement of capital	X	X
5 Company law	X	X
6 Competition	* 0	0
7 Agriculture	*** 0	**** 0
8 Fisheries	X	X
9 Transport	X	*0
10 Taxation	X	X
11 EMU	X	X
12 Statistics	X	X
13 Social policy	X	X
14 Energy	X	*** 0
15 Industry	X	X
16 SMEs	X	X
17 Science and research	X	X
18 Education and training	X	X
19 Telecommunication	X	X
20 Culture and audiovisual	X	X
21 Regional policy	** 0	*** 0
22 Environment	X	*** 0
23 Consumers and health protection	X	X
24 Justice and home affairs	*0	*** 0
25 Customs union	X	X
26 External relations	X	X
27 CFSP	X	X
28 Financial control	X	*** 0
29 Financial and budgetary provisions	** 0	**** 0
30 Institutions	X	X

0:      Chapter opened, under negotiation
X: Chapter provisionally closed
(X):   Chapter for which the provisional closure proposed in the EUCP has not been
        accepted by the candidate country
*:   Chapter opened to negotiations under the Swedish Presidency
**:   Chapter opened to negotiations under the Belgian Presidency
***:   Chapter opened to negotiations under the Spanish Presidency
****:   Chapter opened to negotiations under the Chapters opened (1), Chapters closed (2)

Source: European Commission, Enlargement DG
(<http://europa.eu.int/comm/enlargement/negotiations/pdf/stateofplay_dep_june2003.pdf>).

foreign policy. This matters, of course, if it reinforces hostility to EU membership among populations such as that of Poland, initially favorably disposed to it. Without going further into the details, we should note two
essential points: the primacy of external influences over domestic ones
(Jacoby 2002: 141) and a politically driven convergence process coming on

top of a process of marketization which had already been substantially driven by states.

On the latter point, Kazimierz Poznanski (1992: 56) has convincingly argued that

> the postcommunist transition has to be viewed as basically a state project and not a market project. Though the market is the ultimate objective of the transition, the process of getting there is mainly in the state's hands.

Poznanski's overall analysis may be unduly pessimistic, but it is hard to argue with his basic characterization of postcommunist transition as "a process in which markets are formed by a crisis-ridden state." Similarly, writing about a "Russian-style capitalism," Gustafson (1999) argues that as a result of nomenklatura privatization the state retains ownership of the economy through stock holdings. Yet the state sector is shrinking because of massive tax evasion that undermines revenue collection. Detached from civic life, with undeveloped political parties, a weak state presides over an incomplete transition to market institutions. The transition process thus offers a further illustration of the explanatory power, even in a context (for the more advanced parts of the bloc) of globalization and European integration, of a state-centered approach.

We still lack an adequate sociology of privatization, either in a Western or in an Eastern context. The issue has tended to be discussed either in narrowly political or economic terms, or with reference to a political philosophy of anti-statism derived from neoliberals such as Friedrich von Hayek. Both in the West in the 1980s and the East in the 1990s, the privatization process throws up interesting issues to do with property claims, and in many ways confirms earlier managerialist theses about the relative unimportance of ownership, as distinct from control, of enterprises. Against a bewildering background of mergers and break-ups, Western consumers have largely lost any sense of who is the ultimate owner of the corporations with which they have to deal; in the postcommunist world, it was often astonishingly difficult even for experts to find out information of this kind. Nor would this information necessarily tell one much about the fine detail of the operations of those enterprises, however important it might have seemed both to those who retained a traditional Marxist assumption of the importance of property rights or the neoliberals who saw privatization as a panacea (cf. Sakwa 1999: 43). As the editors of a volume which otherwise pays little attention to postcommunist capitalism note in their introduction,

> in some respects the move from state socialism to pure capitalism . . . is among the easier transitions for that part of the world to make. While in the past people in those societies were told that economic success came from the state, all that has changed now is that the state has been replaced in the

message with the market – again leaving out the crucial role played by social institutions. (Crouch and Streeck 1997: 8)

As in the West, though in a much more acute way, it was hard to value previously public enterprises;[8] many were of interest, if at all, mainly for the real estate they occupied and their buildings were quickly demolished to make room for supermarkets. As often, the German case illustrates this in a particularly acute manner; West German executives rushed across the newly opened border to inspect the premises of their Eastern counterparts, and rushed as quickly back home, demoralized by the technological backwardness even of leading Eastern producers. Locally, consumers too showed a tendency to abandon local goods in favor of imports, though often returning to them after a year or so.

One of the great counterfactual questions in this area is what would have happened if state socialism had imploded either ten years earlier, before the rise of neoliberal economic theory and politics, or ten years later, after its partial eclipse. Would economic advisers less committed to neoliberal orthodoxy and more sensitive to institutional issues (to put it crudely, less American and more Scandinavian), have implemented different policies? One fairly plausible answer is that in the long run it might not have made so much difference; that the rapid but uneven transitions, accompanied in many countries by abrupt swings back and forth between radical liberal and more "conservative" (often former communist) political leadership, ended up in much the same position as more measured policies would have done.[9] Shock therapy was of course brutal, as was the "dental" philosophy which accompanied it: "Of course it will hurt if you haven't been to the dentist for forty years." Many people's lives were wrecked by the collapse of employment and welfare structures; the catastrophic decline in life expectancy in Russia and elsewhere is a stark indicator of this (Mesle, in Coleman 1996). Once again, however, our thinking is inevitably shaped by the fact that the postcommunist societies have, after all, somehow survived. Yugoslavia, despite everything, did not become the rule, and the former Yugoslav republics are making uneven but discernible progress.

If, then, we have seen the early stages of what looks like a capitalist future for postcommunist Europe and Russia, and it sort of works,[10] even where it doesn't work at all well, we must ask to what these societies might be converging, and why? Is there anything distinctive in the long term about the postcommunist countries other than that they were once communist, or perhaps we should say pre-postcommunist?[11] The German case, despite everything, suggests a negative answer. The area of the former GDR will remain distinctive for at least another generation, but probably not much longer than that. This is, of course, a special case, where "Westernization" was most thoroughgoing and many of the badges of semi-national distinctiveness remain only in architecture, museums, and nostalgia-themed bars and cultural events (*Ostalgie*). This seems like the future for the more prosperous parts of the postcommunist world. But if there turns out to be something like an economically and socially integrated European Union, covering much more of Europe but with income disparities gradually moving to levels no greater than those between its existing members, it is far from clear that all parts of the continent will be inside. On the other hand, there is no natural stopping point – even as far as Anatolia or the Urals.[12]

Once again, then, the general theory of convergence intersects inevitably with conjectures about the likely evolution of what we have called heteronomous convergence – convergence guided from "Brussels." Whether or not convergence is over-determined in this way, however, there seems no reason to expect East Central Europe, at least, to continue to differ drastically from the "West" – itself, of course, a geographical abstraction encompassing a wide variety of economic and social emphases (Therborn 1995; Fitoussi, in Crouch and Streeck 1997). It cannot be denied that the legacy of communism is, on the whole, a massive short-term handicap. Even its positive aspects in such areas as health, education, and childcare have sometimes become a mixed blessing: the education was often more than usually irrelevant to modern industrial life; the Russian language less use than English or German; the traditionally high rates of female participation in the workforce of no immediate benefit to economies with massive unemployment. This is, however, a short-term disadvantage, probably of less significance than the encouragement of more secular attitudes to life. Attitudes to work were of course shaped by the communist principle of "we pretend to work, and they pretend to pay us," but these are again modifiable, as proved by Japanese employers in the UK (who, admittedly, have been known to insist on hiring young workers only). Similarly, the ex-nomenklatura elites who dominate many areas of economic life in postcommunist countries and give it some of its particular flavor will give place in time to young bourgeois who may or may not have had nomenklatura grandparents – something which will interest only students of social mobility.

The issue of convergence tends, then, to resolve itself into broader questions of whether there is something like a distinctive European social model which will persist in an increasingly regionalized global economy. Here, opinions are divided, but there seems no reason to believe either that the currently fashionable US "model" will become the world standard or that East Central European newcomers to the European Union will be able, even if they wished, to push it into such a position. Even a hypothetical end state of EU-40 or so would be more or less evenly balanced in terms of population between old "East" and "West" (cf. Coleman 1996: viii), and with a Western majority for the foreseeable future – though this is not to say that the Eastern tail might not exercise a good deal of leverage on the Western dog. Whether it wags to the left or the right is of course a further open question.

The 1993 European Council in Copenhagen laid down criteria for eligibility to join the European Union: stability of democratic institutions, a functioning market economy, ability to cope with market forces, and commitment to union and to the other basic principles of the EU. It is, of course, the third which is likely to prove the most problematic in the enlargement process. While the existing member states have, ever since the accession of Greece in 1981 and Spain and Portugal in 1986, coped with widely diverse income levels between states as well as within them, the Enlargement in 2004 involves countries only two of which, Slovenia and the Czech Republic, have a per capita GDP comparable with some of the existing members, and even theirs is not much more than half of the EU average. These disparities are not of, course, a barrier to trade, as witnessed by the flood of foreign goods into Russia from around 1991, but they have serious implications for agricultural price and support regimes and for social security and migration policies.

In other words, the Eastern Enlargement of the EU is "Not Just Another Accession" (Eatwell et al. 1997). As the authors of this pamphlet stress, there are at least four important differences with earlier EC enlargements. The Eastern applicants for membership, and other potential applicants, are relatively backward, often cut off from world trade and financial institutions for historical reasons, and also numerous and diverse. Whereas the EC/EU has previously incorporated one or two relatively poor states at a time, the Eastern Enlargement will of necessity take place in several stages, with consequent destabilizing or, at the least, disturbing effects on those aspiring to join but not yet in. Moreover, the EU has now become a more tightly integrated entity, with the common currency now acting as a powerful symbolic, as well as real, force for unification. New members will not be able to adopt a wait-and-see policy in relation to the common currency as the UK, Sweden, and Denmark were able to do in the past. For an illustration of the worst-case scenario for the economies of East Central Europe, it is enough to look at what happened in the former GDR and then imagine what it would have been like without the massive transfers of funds which the Bonn government had the political will to carry through but the EU clearly would not. As the former Chancellor Helmut Schmidt put it rather dramatically in 1996, with the German example of course in mind:

> If I were a Polish entrepreneur I would be very alarmed. Within six months of joining the EU Poland will be wiped out, because in the fields of marketing, productivity, and so on it is far from being able to compete. (quoted in Eatwell et al. 1997: 28)

Eatwell and colleagues go on to outline two alternative futures for Poland, which can serve in this context as a model for most of the more advanced economies of the region.

For Poland . . . there are a wide range of possibilities. On the one hand it could become a dynamic part of the EU, like Ireland, as a result of low costs, high domestic investment, foreign direct investment, fiscal discipline, and relatively competent human capital. On the other hand, it could become a burden on the Union, like the Mezzogiorno, as a result of low productivity, unproductive fiscal transfers, a relatively small number of competitive firms, inadequate public administration, and the cost-raising effect of membership of an economic union with more advanced countries. (Eatwell et al. 1997: 46)

It is not our aim in this book to add to the specialized literature dealing with the possible futures of the various states and regions of Eastern Europe and Russia. It does, however, seem to be clear that what is developing is not so much a radically distinct form of capitalism as a wide variety of forms responding to, and reinforcing, local peculiarities. Cox and Mason, for example, bring out the differences between the three most advanced major postcommunist countries, Hungary, the Czech Republic, and Poland, arguing (1999: 201–2) that

the character and direction of the transformation process was strongly influenced both by the context of the existing institutional framework and by the contest between different social interests within each society. . . .

Although the three countries discussed here have developed further and more clearly than most of their European neighbours in the direction of a capitalist system based on market regulation of the economy and private ownership, the contest over the meaning and forms of transformation has resulted in a slower pace of change than policy makers had hoped for, and the persistence of complex and hybrid forms and patterns of social group relations.

As we stressed earlier, one should also not overemphasize the homogeneity of the "Western" model, which looks very different in different parts of Western Europe (Albert 1991; Hausner et al. 1995). As one of us has argued, against Habermas's concept of a "catching-up" or "rectifying" revolution, there is no one single model to be imitated or modified (Ray 1996). But Habermas's conception can also be understood in a slightly different way, as pointing to the ways in which postcommunist capitalism is responding to absences, whether of resources, skills, or legitimacy, in the contexts in which it operates.[13] There seems little evidence that these are evolutionarily more advanced forms of capitalism, however well adapted they may be to current local circumstances. As Staniszkis puts it:

An analysis of the emerging infrastructure of the market led me to the assertion that this does not differ too greatly from the other historical examples [she cites early twentieth-century Japan and postcolonial Africa] of institutionalization . . . in *conditions of high risk* (high transaction costs, incomplete market infrastructure, unequal competition with capital from more developed markets) and with *the existence of a social foundation of networks based on social statuses.* (Staniszkis 1999: 349; emphasis in the original)

Here an argument which we examined in relation to the EU has another area of application. Many of the characteristics noted in East Central European organizations (persistence of traditional attitudes and connections, orientation to local and national markets as opposed to those further afield, and so on) would have seemed less out of place in the Europe of the 1970s, let alone the immediate postwar years, than they do now.

Social Context and Institutional Formations

Much of the discussion of Eastern European economies has focused on their specifically economic performance or, at best, the impact of economic restructuring on employment, social security, and so forth, but we need also to consider the broader social consequences of the reconstruction of economies which are now again for the most part in private ownership. Ever since the early Trotskyist, managerialist, and Yugoslav dissident critiques of state socialism, there had been discussion about whether the nomenklatura could be appropriately described as a bourgeoisie or a ruling class (Voslensky 1984); after 1989 the question could only be what sort of bourgeoisie it had become or been replaced by. A nouveau riche, ex-nomenklatura and/or substantially criminalized bourgeoisie (see the example at the end of this chapter) is of course something very different from a typical Western European established bourgeoisie, but managerialist theories are probably right to stress the similarities between "old" state managers, at least in the more advanced countries and sectors of the bloc, and "new" managers in residual state, privatized, or new private enterprises. With EU enlargement, the full incorporation of Eastern European senior managers and owners into an increasingly transnational capitalist class (van der Pijl 1998, 2000) is probably only a matter of time.

There is, then, convergence, but in a way that is more one-sided and less endogenous than originally envisaged, and in which theories of colonialism on the one hand, and regional integration on the other, are more use than the original convergence theory. The only partially predictable rise and fall of regions with the opening up of the bloc can perhaps best be understood by looking at the comparative positions of cities and their increasing and often unpredictable polarization into "winners" and "losers." Positional attributes – being the first entrant into a new game or entering it at an optimal point – become more important than long-standing natural or human resources.

The passing reference above to a criminalized bourgeoisie raises an important issue for much of the postcommunist world. Under communism, much private economic activity was of course illegal (black market) or semi-legal (gray market). This varied substantially between countries, with Poland retaining, in particular, a substantially private agricultural sector once it became clear that collectivization would meet serious resistance. (Elsewhere in the bloc, so-called collectivized agriculture was in practice little different from that in the state sector.) Poland, even discounting agriculture, and Hungary had much larger private sectors than Czechoslovakia and Germany, while Yugoslav self-management tended to blur the differences between the state and private sectors. With the transition, it ceased to be illegal to buy goods for resale (a practice previously known as speculation) or to employ more than a very low number of wageworkers. A private sector mushroomed, often, as in Russia, under the euphemistic label of "cooperatives." Some operations, however, remained underground, either because the commodities which they produced or traded were still illegal (drugs, armaments, illegal migrants, etc.), or because they were more profitable that way. As in the Bulgarian example discussed below, the partial rundown of the security services provided additional encouragement for gamekeepers to turn poacher.

Finally, it is inherent in the process of privatization, whether in postcommunist Europe or in the "old Europe" where neoliberal administrations tended to predominate in the1980s, that the values attached to state assets are "essentially contestable"; the commodification of something not previously commodified cannot but be contentious. In the postcommunist context, where there was not an established system of private commercial law to govern such transactions but where new legal provisions were being drafted on the hoof, it was often hard to know whether one was operating legally or illegally, and not surprising that many budding capitalists hoped for the best. As a result, there was a tendency for the relatively innocent communist corruption networks, based on low-level conspiracy to defraud the state and on the exchange of favors, to mutate into more grandiose networks of what rapidly came to be called "Mafia" (with or without direct participation from the Italian homeland).[14]

Any model of convergence has to consider whether, where, and how quickly, the relatively highly criminalized capitalism of much of the postcommunist world will settle down to the levels of criminality considered normal in the West. The latter is, of course, a shifting target, with increasingly tight formal restrictions on, for example, "insider dealing," the use of privileged information sources for private profit, coexisting with increasingly spectacular scandals such as those of Enron and Halliburton (the latter still *sub judice*) in the US in 2002–3. Optimists point to the decriminalization in the nineteenth and twentieth centuries of what are now highly respectable US companies; pessimists stress the size of organized crime worldwide and by implication the unlikelihood that postcommunist Europe would avoid full participation in its further development. The example of Italy, a founder member of the European Communities, is enough to show that, although a more than usually criminal reputation may be an embarrassment in accession negotiations, EU membership *per se* is not incompatible with the existence of a major criminal sector, reaching right into the state elite.

Bulgaria: A Case of Fuzzy Institutionalization?

This chapter has raised the questions of whether and how postcommunist countries might undergo "convergence" with Western European market economies and the institutional and cultural logics involved in these processes. It was noted in chapter 2 that Fligstein (2001) argues that large-scale market building relies heavily on embedded networks that emerge through institution building and the establishment of rules and legal procedures (hence, given the importance of the state to these there will continue to be different national forms of capitalism). The example of Bulgaria[15] (not atypical in many ways of the European postcommunist transition[16)] illustrates two points in particular. First, that a path-dependent pattern of emergence into postcommunism can create a fuzzy institutionalization of markets where boundaries between state and economy, public and private are unclear. Second, that the space for a more rule-following institutionalization requires democratic political processes in which NGOs can operate, although the goal of EU membership (i.e. heteronomous convergence) is likely to be an important stimulus to this. Even so, the path to publicly accountable regulation is uncertain and capitalist economies are sustainable with fuzzy institutional forms.

In Bulgaria, as we noted earlier, Soviet influence was less resented than elsewhere in the bloc and the country experienced a "Gentle Revolution" in 1989. The other side of its gentleness was a certain degree of incompletion highly favorable to members of the former elites. This provides a good illustration of problems of partial reform allowing informal and illegal practices to become embedded in institutional practices to contribute to the formation of an alternative form of capitalism to those of western Europe and the US (Lotspeich 1995; Varese 1994). Bulgaria experienced a slow, or arrested process of decommunization during the 1990s partly because the Bulgarian Socialist Party (the former communists) retained power in the 1990 general elections and were in and out of government over the next decade.[17] Difficulties of creating a democratic culture and constitutional system were exacerbated by lack of decommunization of administrative, police, and security apparatuses, and enabled communist networks to persist in an atmosphere of weak regulation. Former communists were given preference in official positions, especially in the reorganization of the state broadcasting and security services in 1993 (Holmes 1993: 323). At the same time there were a series of constitutional disputes between the government and the Constitutional Court in the late 1990s that resulted in further erosion of the authority of the judiciary.[18] Relations between the government and the Constitutional Court subsequently improved but the judiciary remains "weak" (*East European Constitutional Review*, 11/12, 4/1 (2002/3): 13). Although a multi-party system and constitutional rights had been established relatively quickly after 1989, there were considerable difficulties with recognition of boundaries between the government, state, public sphere, and "private" activities. Indeed, it is often alleged that the state is at the mercy of former State Security–run corporations that can effectively block attempts to regularize their activities.

One manifestation of this during the 1990s was the problem of organized crime (as in many postcommunist countries) that took many forms – protection rackets, illegal international movement of finance and commodities, organization of illicit drugs and prostitution, laundering of illegal profits, and corporations that appeared to be trading legally but concealed illegal organizations. Organized "Mafia" crime was particularly prominent in the tobacco and alcohol trades, gas processing, "insurance," restaurants, and entertainment including nightclubs and casinos.[19] Along with more general privatization after 1990, there was also a privatization and diversification of criminal organizations. Organized crime has its origins in decades of illicit dealing, falsification of records, informal arrangements between enterprises, complex maneuvers with state planners, and the extensive informal economy, which left a culture of illegality shared by state officials and private entrepreneurs. Many of the old networks that facilitated criminal activities in the old regime survived into the present, but this does not mean that there was necessarily *collusion* between former Party and state officials and new entrepreneurs. On the contrary, the state and the new private sector are in competition for access to resources from the communist system (Ganev 2001). In the process the way may be open for NGO activity that increases transparency and regulation, although this is a highly uncertain process.

One example of the expansion of former networks into new private activities was the formation of "insurance companies" linked to "security companies" that organized protection rackets. Many of those involved in this kind of organized crime were formerly part of the police and communist security services. These groups routinely engaged in violence, threats of violence, and kidnapping in pursuit of extortion (*Ikonomichecki Zhirot*, May 15, 1996). As elsewhere in the world, these included threats and vandalism, beating, kidnapping, and assassination unless regular "insurance" payments were made. Protection rackets were disguised as insurance companies and almost everyone in business had to show that they were "protected" by one of the large firms, such as "VIS-2" (thought to be the largest), "SIK," "Apollo," "Spartan," and "Pirin Invest." These were known as "wrestlers" (*borets*) because of the alleged involvement of former Bulgarian wrestlers and other sportsmen, often with connections to the former security services. Following extensive adverse press publicity, the government began to regulate and license the insurance business in the late 1990s, but "outlawed" companies found a way back in by finding brokers and selling portfolios to "legitimate" companies. It was reported that the successors of VIS-2 (Planata Ins) negotiated with legal companies and, in order to conceal their former connections with "wrestler" companies, re-named themselves several times after the non-licensed company had gone into liquidation (*Kapital*, May 19, 1998).

Allegations and an official inquiry into their activities centered on Multi-group, a powerful corporation registered in Bulgaria in 1992, with diverse financial and industrial interests such that there is hardly a branch of the economy in which it is not involved. It was run by former party cadres, including (the subsequently assassinated) Ilia Pavlov (a former wrestler), married to the daughter of the then director of Military Counterintelligence, who subsequently traded in the sale of former Soviet military equipment. Of twenty directors, twelve were from the former state industries and commun-ist government (Ganev 2001). Described by Interior Minister Bogomil Bonev as having a "Mafia structure," Multigroup has since 1990 allegedly intertwined political influence and shady business. It is claimed in the Bul-garian press that this has ranged from stolen car contraband to intricate financial operations and international contracts for gas and electricity. Mul-tigroup has been linked with corruption scandals including those involving the role of the secret services transferring state assets out of the country.

After the assassination of Pavlov in March 2003 *Kapital* (March 10, 2003) commented:

> If there is a company or a person, which best characterizes the Bulgarian postcommunist model, these are undoubtedly Multigroup and Ilia Pavlov. The history of the group is to a large extent the history of Bulgarian transition – with the unclear origin of the capital, the draining of money from state funds, the domination of both the input and the output of state-run companies, the draining of state-owned banks, and the corruption of politicians, magistrates and journalists. . . . the group had the structure of a state; with nearly 20 holding companies and a host of subsidiaries the group covered practically all sectors of the economy. In the early years of the transition Multigroup's power came from its symbiosis with the state.

The group's biggest triumph was its strategic cooperation with Gazprom, the former Soviet Gas Company. Money from Multigroup allegedly funded political parties – the Bulgarian Socialist Party and then the campaign of Simeon II National Movement (*Kapital*, March 10, 2003) and according to press reports was connected with bribing MPs (*Kapital*, July 25, 1998). Again, the Multigroup subsidiary, SIC, allegedly attempted to block Sam-sung's bid for the Kremikovksi steel plant, which would have deprived them of much of their control of the Bulgarian economy, and it was claimed that intimidation and violence were used to gain information about the Samsung bid (*Kapital*, August 22, 1998). In the event, the plant was divided, part retained by the state and part sold to a Turkish company, Erdemir.

These are good examples of the development of closed networks as a means of protecting the local economy against global competition. The 1997 OECD Economic Overview for Bulgaria concluded that a culture of officially sanctioned irregularity and lack of legality has become one of the most important impediments to reform and a cause of its ineffective macro-economic policy. A study of bribery and corruption in Eastern Europe (Grødeland et al. 1998) suggested that in Bulgaria low-level and high-level corruption were widely accepted as a fact of everyday life and were on the increase. Respondents in this survey claimed that in the (communist) past control was more rigid and officials showed more responsibility to the public, but that now corruption is widespread. Bulgarian respondents blamed low salaries among the police and other officials for this situation. The police, it was reported, "demand bribes in an extortionate manner . . . they demand money directly, [with] no scruples." Almost all Bulgarian respondents in the survey thought that connections were necessary to solve a problem and that the former nomenklatura, in the police, judiciary, and new businesses have the best connections, from the past. Similar results have been found in studies conducted by Vitosha Research Group (2001), which found that 43.3 percent of companies surveyed reported that they had made "additional payments" (bribes) in order to win contracts.

Syndicate crime is dependent on networks of corrupt officials extending into the police and security services. Police officers, civil servants, and members of the state administration may leave their careers and go on to establish industrial enterprises, shops, brokerage agencies, etc. In so doing they do not break their former connections or friendships; on the contrary, they usually count on the support and protection of former colleagues. These types of symbiotic relations developed on a wide scale in the 1970s and now form the basis of much private economic activity. They have been important to the process of "nomenklatura privatization," in which large quantities of state assets passed illegally into the ownership of the former political elite, the nomenklatura. It is often claimed that "the Mafia" exercise control over the courts and the judicial process (*Novinar*, April 17, 1996).

It is not that the new entrepreneurs simply controlled the postcommunist state. Rather, there was competition between the state and organized crime for control of resources in the new economies. There has been a sustained attempt by governments to bring criminal organizations under control. Arrests are occasionally made and some criminal leaders are successfully prosecuted and sent to prison, although many attempted prosecutions are unsuccessful. Successive postcommunist governments, both the Bulgarian Socialist Party and the Union of Democratic Forces, have acknowledged the extent of the problem, and a framework of legislation has been put in place intended to tackle organized crime.[20] The Interior Ministry once acknowledged that it was "powerless" against the ability of the Mafia to interfere in politics and the legislative process by threatening parliamentary deputies (e.g. *Struma*, July 30, 1997). However, a public scandal, "Sugargate," arose when between 1994 and 1998 Multigroup directors illegally imported 300,000 tonnes of sugar refined at subsidiary refineries (Bartex Trading), losing the state 52 million levs in excise duty. Multigroup directors were prosecuted (*Kapital*, August 22, 1998). This signaled a change of style in Multigroup, which in due course reinvented itself as a legitimate company, launching itself as an international operation. But its origins lie in a network of local and highly embedded markets that were protected against global competition. This kind of insider privatization creates powerful interests that profit from imbalances created by partial reforms – firms that oppose trade liberalization, bankers who oppose economic stabilization to preserve profits from distorted financial markets, Mafiosi undermining the creation of the stable legal foundations of a market economy (Hellman 1998). The result is a partial reform equilibrium that in turn prompts a popular backlash against reform and global integration – evident in the common pattern for former communist parties to be returned to power under a social democratic label during the 1990s.

Fuzzy institutionalization is illustrated by the evolution of parallel systems of management in a gray sector of unofficial channels that has been estimated to control about a third of economic turnover (Coalition 2000, 2001). This is especially apparent in cross-border trade where possibly 25–35 percent of imports and exports move through illegal channels. This has been stimulated particularly by the entry of foreign retail chains, in response to which some local suppliers attempt to circumvent competition and provide cheaper goods. Possibly 50 percent of imported alcohol has an illegal origin (Coalition 2000, 2001).

Competition between the government and the private sector opened the way for NGO activity especially through Coalition 2000,[21] a campaigning anticorruption movement that was backed by the OECD and EU. Coalition 2000 conducts research, builds coalitions with national and local organizations, campaigns and lobbies for transparent government and anticorruption legislation in Bulgaria. The prospect of EU accession was an important lever through which they have been able to exercise influence. By 2001, amidst deepening public sensitivity and criticism of corruption, the success or failure of political parties could depend on their stance on this issue. The platform of anticorruption measures is crucially dependent on the institutionalization of democratic government and cultures of openness. Hence recent developments and recommendations include:

- reform of public administration;
- judicial reform and freedom from political dependence (which began with the 2001 Strategy for Judicial Reform in Bulgaria);

- reform of the party system (which began with the 2001 Law on Political Parties);
- increased transparency in procedures for divestiture of pubic assets (e.g. the 2001 Law on Privatization and Post-Privatization Control), with open auctions, public registers of privatization deals, a new Privatization Agency and equal treatment of potential buyers;
- customs administration reform to reduce illegal trafficking (ongoing);
- increased role for civil society and civic involvement, and independent media that openly scrutinize government and the private sector.

There is no guarantee that these and other measures will be successful in reducing corruption and organized crime in the longer term, partly because as well as institutionalized rules this program requires a cultural shift – without the will to be transparent actors will find ways of continuing illegal practices (Coalition 2000, 2001: 44). Nor is increased regulation in itself a solution; rather it can exacerbate the problem – licensing regimes themselves generate economic interests for evasion of control while increasing the risks and therefore the returns from so doing and creating a spiral of control, evasion, and further control. Recent state initiatives have limited Multi-group's activities – these include the new privatization regulations, breaking of monopolies, the creation of a currency board and stricter bank supervision, the liberalization of markets, and the entry of foreign competitors. At the same time, the murder of Pavlov highlights the problems of Mafia-founded businesses – when the business grows too big its founders want to become legitimate but true legalization actually presupposes their elimination. Whether Pavlov was killed because he wanted to legitimate the company or in order to clear the way for it, the history of Multigroup illustrates the difficulties of making a transition to institutionalized regulation. The conclusion of this case study is that there is no *necessary* process of convergence around a particular configuration of economic and political institutions. Market logics are geared to private gain, not public good, and there is no necessary reason why the latter should arise from the former. Institutional regulation within a democratic polity is a public good but will require, to be effective, the active participation of NGOs, civil society, and probably some measure of external, transnational constraint, or heteronomous convergence.

Neo-convergence?

Convergence theories were part of an evolutionary perspective in social theory and since we have at times used evolutionary language in this chapter, it is important to ask how far this can be justified. Our position here is probably close to that defended over many years by Anthony Giddens: that while one can make meaningful comparative judgments about relative degrees of adaptation to circumstances, one should beware of what Giddens neatly characterized as an "unfolding" model of endogenous and prepro- grammed development. Learning models of evolution, of the kind favored by Habermas and a number of other German theorists (Habermas 1973; Eder 1985), are less problematic in this regard, if we remember that learning is also a matter of forgetting what is no longer needed – something in which postcommunist citizens have had to become especially expert. Postcommu- nist Europe is rich in human capital and, to varying degrees, rich in what may be the most important current denomination of political capital: ac- ceptability in principle within the EU.

Another theoretical model, which is evolutionary in a moderate and, in our view, defensible sense, is the classic analysis by the US historical sociologist Barrington Moore. Moore argued that the way in which the transition from agrarian to capitalist and industrial societies took place had crucial conse- quences for their political structures. Roughly speaking, early and spontaneous capitalization of agriculture and subsequent processes of industrialization con- duce to political democracy (the English and North American model), while top–down industrialization under state guidance, found in societies which made the transition to capitalism and industrialism at the same time, and later in the nineteenth century or even in the twentieth, tended to lead to authoritar- ian patterns of political rule (Italy, Germany, Japan). Moore did not discuss Russia at length in *Social Origins* (1966), since he had done so elsewhere, but his model also offered an explanation of the political accompaniments of late Tsarist and of Leninist and early Stalinist industrialization. Both involved the imposition of state policies on backward and extended territories and the revolutionizing of established social structures.

Moore's model seems also to have some application to the export model of Stalinism imposed on Central and Eastern Europe after World War II. By and large, this was more readily accepted in the more backward territories, where industrialization and economic development had the most tangible benefits. In Czechoslovakia, by contrast, where communism had had a stronger indigenous presence in the immediate postwar period, opposition was stronger in the Czech lands than in Slovakia. Bulgaria was particularly receptive to Soviet hegemony, though partly of course for historical reasons of a different kind: Russia was perceived as the liberator of the nation from earlier Turkish rule. National communism in its very different forms in Romania, Albania, and Yugoslavia also enjoyed considerable support, of a kind not found in the rest of the bloc, where there was significant resistance in Germany (1953), Hungary and Poland (1956), and Czechoslovakia (1968). Here, Moore's model requires significant adaptation to local circum- stances. There might have been good economic reasons for Poles to support Stalinist industrialization and the collectivization of agriculture, or at least better reasons than for Czechs, but historically deep-rooted hostility to Russia and the strong ideological counterforce of the Catholic Church made opposition stronger and prevented, for example, the collectivization of agriculture in the 1950s. In Germany, opposition was correspondingly weakened by the residual antifascist legitimacy of the GDR regime and the opportunity, until the final closure of the Berlin frontier in 1961, of emigration to the other German state.

In the postcommunist spectrum, we can again see what Moore might want to cite as supporting evidence in the greater strength of democracy in the north and west of the region (including Hungary) and of authoritarianism in the south and east. Offe et al. make considerable play of implicitly Moorean arguments. Moore was, however, thinking very much within a nation-state framework, and supranational and global influences of the kind discussed more substantially since 1989 suggest a further relativization of his analysis. Whereas it was possible through the 1980s to discuss the relative importance of factors internal or external to the nation state, not least in the relatively closed states of the Soviet bloc, in the 1990s and since it has become hard to decide even in principle what counts as external and what as internal (issues that are explored further in chapter 6).

Convergence theory reflected the vicissitudes of East–West relations in the second half of the twentieth century. Early theories predicted a bipolar convergence around social welfare, state interventionism, democratic representation, and technocratic planning. These were dominated by theories of the managerial revolution and the logic of industrial society that would bring common organizational forms to previously radically different systems. This theory further presupposed the post–World War II form of the state that was sovereign within its borders and followed a largely endogenous path of development. Since 1989 we have seen the emergence of a monopolar convergence theory in which the East abandons the Party, central planning, communist ideology, industrialism, and social welfare in favor of neoliberal social and economic policies, political and cultural pluralism, and global trade. The autarkic authoritarian state is to be replaced by the regulatory state that creates the legal and institutional conditions for the growth of markets, a private sector, and global and regional integration. But the discussion in this chapter indicates that this process is highly path-dependent and the idea of transition to an idealized version of the "West" is an illusion. Path-dependence plus differential modes of integration into the global economy (see below, chapter 6) may structure significantly different socio-economic outcomes that are belied by a common language of governance-speak. The Bulgarian case illustrated the potential for fuzzy institutionalization of marketized and privatized enterprises within a framework of regulation that allowed Mafia-like organizations to emerge. The extent to which these can be eradicated and replaced by transparent and regulated markets depends upon the robustness of democratic politics, social movement activity, and a culture intolerant of illicit dealing.

5

Socialism, Modernity and Beyond

Comrades, we tell you now that the triumphant progress of science makes changes in humanity inevitable, changes that are hacking an abyss between those docile slaves of tradition and us free moderns who are confident in the radiant splendour of our future.

Umberto Boccioni et al., *Manifesto of the Futurist Painters* (1909)

All fixed, fast-frozen relations, with their train of ancient and venerable prejudices and opinions are swept away, all new-formed ones become antiquated before they can ossify. All that is solid melts into air.

Marx and Engels, *Manifesto of the Communist Party* (1969[1848])

Underlying theories of convergence was a view of modernity as an inexorable process of social development – a view that is echoed in different ways in theories of modernization, reflexive modernization, and postmodernism. This chapter examines these complex and contested views more closely. Modernity and its futures have been a focus of extensive dispute – not only in the social sciences but also in literature and the arts. Movements of heroic modernism, such as the Futurists, have clashed with Romantics, who predicted the eventual nemesis of modernity's vain attempts to vanquish the forces of nature and myth. These debates are pertinent to interpreting the fall of Soviet socialism, an event that has been claimed both as a vindication for postmodern skepticism and the beginning of a more thorough modernization. Marx and Engels's *Manifesto of the Communist Party* has often been cited (notably by Berman 1985) as a celebration of modernism, although the dialectic irony of their thesis is often missed. Marx and Engels used hyperbolic language echoing the Romantic critique of modernity ("drowning ecstasies of heavenly fervour in the icy waters of egotistical calculation," etc.) in order to turn it on its head. They sought to show that capitalism was not, as Romantic critics thought, based on reason and science; on the contrary it was founded on the rule of money, as a power divorced from human will, that would in due course become a fetter to further development. Nonetheless, Marxists have not generally had much sense of Marx's (nor anyone else's) irony and by the twentieth century, if not before, Marxism understood itself straightforwardly as a modernizing movement whose program was to intensify industrialization, urbanization, efficiency, centralization, and sweeping away the "idiocy of rural life." Not surprisingly, perhaps, understandings of Marxism and socialism have been caught up in the critique of the cultural, social, and theoretical underpinning of modernity associated with postmodernism, which contrasted modernism's commitment to linear development through scientific knowledge with fluidity, irony, and deconstruction.

More generally, this debate is relevant to theorizing social change and its future trajectories. Theories of social change have always been central to sociology, which itself emerged during the unprecedented changes of industrialization and the rise of capitalism. However, theorizing social change is problematic since there is a difficult balance to strike between generalized abstraction, such as a theory of world development, and historical concreteness, where general processes risk being lost from view. Much of Weber's work, for example, attempted to steer a pragmatic course between the German Historical School, for whom the cultural sciences were idiographic, concerned with specific and nongeneralizable forms of social organization, and the positivists, for whom general laws of historical change were possible. This debate is not much talked about now, and its terms of reference have changed considerably: it was noted in chapter 1 that few sociologists would now wish to develop causal theories of change based on naturalistic principles. Nonetheless, there is likely to be a tension in any theory of social change between universal claims on the one hand, and giving proper attention to local detail and specificity on the other. We will see that this problem arises particularly with theories that are explicitly or otherwise based largely on Western experience.

Moreover, theories of social change are not simply about the past and the present. Despite the fact that we have no idea what our historical possibilities will be, these theories usually contain projections of alleged current developments into the future. Generally, moreover, theories of social change have not been neutral toward these developments; on the contrary they have contained positive or negative evaluations of the direction of contemporary society. On the one hand, for example, Marxists and theorists of evolutionary modernization projected positive (though radically different) concepts of future society founded on theoretical models of contemporary developments. On the other hand, theories based on a pessimistic reading of Weber's concept of rationalization have projected a future of progressive enclosure within the "steel shell" of bureaucracy and formality. For both, optimists and pessimists, however, there were discernible tendencies within the present that were universal and present in all societies, pointing toward a common future. More recently, theories of postmodernity claimed to overcome the "chronophonism" of temporal theories of social change, although there has been a lapse in some such theories into notions of developmental sequence and universal stages. Indeed, some of these work with crude notions of temporality that are oddly reminiscent of modernization theories. Even more recently, following the waning of postmodern theory, there have been attempts to resuscitate modernization theory in various guises.

Within this fraught terrain, Soviet and post-Soviet systems have been incorporated into several prevailing theories of social change as alleged instances of their central claims. This reflects the way in which sociological theory has been largely grounded in the experience of modernity in North America and Western Europe, and has regarded state socialist systems as variants, albeit deviant ones, of familiar forms such as "industrial society."[1] For modernization theories the Soviet systems were a version of modernity that was incomplete and therefore prone to instability. For theorists of postmodernity the Soviet systems signaled the exhaustion and failure of modernity, at least in its "heavy," industrial mode. From this point of view, the fall of the Soviet Union demonstrated the hubris of modernity that overreached itself in its attempt to build a planned and rational society through the control of people and nature. This is a theme on which we have commented in the past (e.g. Ray 1993, 1995, 1997; Outhwaite 1992) and this chapter will not recapitulate these arguments, apart from providing brief summaries. Our intention is to re-examine the debate about modernization, modernity, and postmodernism in the light of the end of communism. This chapter, then, examines the vicissitudes of the relationship between socialism, modernity, and postmodernism and argues that we need to move beyond increasingly tired and overgeneralized theories.

Modernization Theory and the Future of Soviet Civilization

Classical modernization theory, developed in the 1950s, was primarily concerned with the problem of underdevelopment – how regions that subsequently came to be known as the "Third World" could develop levels of social, economic, and cultural organization comparable to those of industrialized nations. Soviet socialism represented an alternative path of development the potential appeal of which had been demonstrated by the spread of communism among developing nations – notably the Chinese Revolution (1949), the Cuban Revolution (1959), and various forms of "Third World socialism." The wars in Korea (1950–53) and Vietnam (1956–75) illustrated that these had become arenas of bitter conflict. Modernization literature during this postwar period lost Weber's stress on the specificity of the Western model of development and assumed that the experience of the West "constituted the apogee of the evolutionary potential of mankind" (Eisenstadt 1987: 3).[2] It tended to assume that modernization was a more or less linear process with a teleology in that it led toward an optimal set of organizational arrangements that in some versions (e.g. Parsons) was guided by the evolutionary universals. By this he meant any organizational or institutional development in society that was important enough to advance (or "upgrade") the evolutionary process. The modernization literature was divided as to whether alternative routes to modernity (other than the predominant US model) were viable, but generally a somewhat idealized view of developed Western capitalism was held up as the model for the rest of the world. On this basis some theorists, such as Parsons and Rostow, predicted, correctly, if vaguely, that Soviet systems would experience internally generated pressure to change, especially to democratize and increase internal functional differentiation. This process would be driven by systemic needs and arise from the adaptive capacity of the system.

For modernization approaches Walt Rostow's (1979) concept of stages of growth was influential. He set out what has become the most famous model of development of human society within this paradigm, claiming that progress to societal and economic modernization entails a number of stages. First, "traditional society," by which he meant feudal societies based primarily on agricultural production, were constrained by limited agrarian technology. However, they did contain within them the potential for further development. Based primarily on the case of England in the seventeenth century Rostow argued that a second, "transitional stage" followed, in which the preconditions for modernization were established. The important preconditions were increases in scientific and technological discoveries that were then used to improve the production processes. Also there developed a group of individuals who saw the advantages in investment in new factory-based production along with the growth of "lateral" relations of world trade between nations. Then follows the gradual growth of a modern state, which uses "rational" ideas. Rostow's third stage is the "take-off," which occurred in England in the 1780s, in the US in the 1840s, in Germany in the 1870s, in Russia in the first two decades of the twentieth century and in China and India in the 1950s. In this way Rostow pinpointed the importance of the unevenness of the processes involved and further suggested that for all examples, save that of England, the first to modernize, they have been propelled in modernization by the external influence of nations that have already modernized. Sixty years after the take-off stage there is the fourth, maturity stage, in which countries consolidate their production process based on investment and the factory. Rostow then points to a fifth, "mass-consumption" stage in which all the benefits of the production process are diffused throughout society as a whole.

Influenced by Rostow, Talcott Parsons's model of modernization (1964) as a universal social process is probably the most famous and ambitious. He proposed four features of human societies at the level of culture and social organization that had universal and major significance as prerequisites for sociocultural development. These were technology, kinship organization based on an incest taboo, communication based on language, and religion. Primary attention, however, was given to six organizational complexes that develop mainly at the level of social structure. The first two, particularly important for the emergence of societies from "primitiveness," are stratification, involving a primary break with primitive kinship ascription, and cultural legitimation, with institutionalized agencies that are independent of a diffuse religious tradition. Fundamental to the structure of modern societies are the other four complexes: bureaucratic organization of collective goal-attainment, money and market systems, generalized universalistic legal systems, and democratic association with elective leadership and mediated membership support for policy orientations. Although these have developed very unevenly, some of them going back a very long time, all are clearly much more than simple inventions of particular societies.

Perhaps a single theme tying them together is that differentiation and attendant reduction in ascription has caused the initial two-class system to give way to more complex structures at the levels of social stratification and the relation between social structure and its cultural legitimation. First, this more complex system is characterized by a highly generalized universalistic normative structure in all fields. Second, subunits under such normative orders have greater autonomy both in pursuing their own goals and interests and in serving others instrumentally. Third, this autonomy is linked with the probability that structural units will develop greater diversity of interests and subgoals. Finally, this diversity results in pluralization of scales of prestige and therefore of differential access to economic resources, power, and influence. Modernization involves increasing levels of complexity both at the levels of the system as a whole and within its subunits.

Clearly, some of the features identified by Rostow and Parsons existed in the Soviet Union by the 1960s, and by the mid-twentieth century some argued (though perhaps not amounting to the "conventional wisdom" suggested by Pye 1990) that communism had advantages over democracy in speeding economic development.[3] This view was apparently supported by a long historical trend that favored strengthening and centralizing the power of the state. For some, the Soviet Union represented a return to an eighteenth-century Enlightenment vision of a rational, educated, and scientific society based on the maximization of resources and the steady improvement of human nature (Caute 1988: 264). Since the 1930s and 1940s Soviet communism had been viewed by foreign admirers as a new civilization (e.g. Webb and Webb 1936) in which the Party exercised its will by persuasion, ultimate authority rested with the Central Committee but everything was decided by groups and committees. Such enthusiasm was enduringly captured by Lincoln Steffens's comment, on returning from the Soviet Union, "I have been over into the future and it works" (Caute 1988: 26). Examples of the Soviet modernist vision are Leonard Sabsovich's anti-urbanist architecture, which envisaged agro-urban settlements powered by a nationwide hydroelectric grid, or Okhitovich's linear socialist cities, which provided the basis for Magnitogorsk (Starr 1978).[4] Soviet Marxism glorified the machine, technology, and science and waged an aggressive war against all forms of traditionalism, at least until the German invasion in 1940, when Stalin encouraged a return to some forms of traditional practice, notably religion.

Between 1917 and the end of the Soviet Union in 1991 Russia had been transformed from a predominantly rural, illiterate, and technologically un-developed society into a highly industrialized, urban, and literate culture. But Berman (1985) does make the important point that modernization in Russia, from Peter the Great building St Petersburg on the marshes of the Neva estuary to Stalin's industrialization, was founded on forced labor, the existence of which presupposed a premodern society (Berman 1985: 173ff.).

However, influenced in part by the Cold War, modernization theorists were not convinced that the Soviet Union really represented a stable form of mod-ernity. Communism was "a kind of disease which can befall a transitional society if it fails to organize effectively those elements within it which are prepared to get on with the job of modernization" (Rostow 1979: 164). The missing element for Rostow was a substantial and enterprising middle class, which for classical and contemporary modernization theory has been an es-sential precondition for stable development. Recent neomodernization theor-ies have returned to this theme when considering the conditions for successful postcommunist democratization. The most likely development within the Soviet Union was, he argued, that "the increased right of individual dignity and privacy, higher levels of consumption," and the adoption of modern science would change the form of power and military organization in a more open and democratic direction.[5]

Again, in the course of his discussion of evolutionary universals, Parsons comments on "modern socialist societies," which, he says, "appear excep-tional because they achieve high productivity with relatively minimal depend-ence on market mechanisms." He will have been aware of the experimentation with increased use of markets (for example in agriculture) during the 1960s and noted that the negative consequences of "radical de-monetization" were being acknowledged. However, what he says about dem-ocratization is particularly interesting in retrospect. From the theory of evolutionary universals in complex societies, he argues that "no institutional form other than democratic association can mediate consensus" among people and groups. In relation to the Soviet Union, he says,

> I do indeed predict that it will prove to be unstable and will either make adjustments in the general direction of electoral democracy and a plural party system or "regress" into generally less advanced and politically less effective forms of organization, failing to advance as rapidly as otherwise may be expected. (Parsons 1964)

Legitimacy will be undermined, he continues, if the Party proves unwilling to trust the people it has educated. One could argue that the system's hesitant reforms in the early 1960s were pointing, not toward a multiparty system, but in the direction of increased public participation in the political system and more reliance on expertise than political ideology in policy formation

(Hough 1969). It could further be argued that when these ended after 1968 and the invasion of Czechoslovakia, the system did begin to "regress" into a less advanced form – ruled by a gerontocracy exercising power and patronage through a patrimonial bureaucracy, which therefore assumed increasingly premodern organizational forms (Fehér 1982; Jowitt 1983). However, whether these outcomes that were anticipated by Parsons serve as support for a theory of evolutionary universals is less clear. The demise of the system could have occurred for reasons other than those anticipated by Parsons and modernization theorists.

There were a number of problems with modernization theories, not least their assumptions about linear temporality and the idea that different parts of the world existed at different stages of development. Further, there was the problematic notion of progress toward an optimal form of social organization as the goal of all social systems. This was a normative theory that valorized the institutional structure of the West while paying little attention to the costs of modernization. The latter included the impoverishment of much of the Third World, neocolonialism, military and political domination, dislocation of stable communities. and expropriation of profits by transnational companies supported by often authoritarian governments that ignored basic rights and needs. Issues of power and conflict, while not ignored by modernization theories, were not central either since the process was (and still is, for example, in Rostow 1991) largely one of social change driven by increasing technical efficiency. Further, the idea of universal evolutionary adaptation assumes that long-term survival of social systems is dependent on their hitting on efficient organizational forms that are stabilized into sociocultural reproduction. There is no reason to suppose this is so – on the contrary, non-functional practices (like the QWERTY keyboard) might be stabilized because they become embedded and changing them would be too costly. An alternative approach, as noted above (pp. 4, 45–7) is that of path-dependence, in which organizations do not adapt to an optimal state but follow a developmental logic along a path already begun. As Andrew Sayer puts it:

> Fitness does not guarantee survival, nor does survival imply fitness. Organisms/organizations may be able to set in motion positive feedback which helps them survive but which closes off the development of other, possibly superior forms. . . . Change is therefore frequently path dependent, so that what survives depends on the nature of the initial state as well as competition, and geographically specific lock-in effects may restrict developments along particular lines. . . . Development should not therefore be seen as an optimal path chosen from a range of alternatives. (Sayer 1995: 141)

This is more promising as an explanation of the different postcommunist trajectories than appeal to ahistorical theories of necessary development. In the years following 1989 neoliberals recommended the adoption of a highly stylized version of the institutions of prices and property (allegedly) found in the West. The neoliberal agenda had itself emerged in response to the crisis of the Fordist-Keynesian model of socio-economic regulation in the West from the 1970s, and would not obviously export well to a radically different context. Moreover, there is evidence that an organization that learns too quickly sacrifices efficiency and loses the flexibility that arises from diversity (Grabher and Stark 1997). Rather than view social development in terms of increasing approximation to optimal forms of organization which involve destroying the legacies of old, "inefficient" practices, it is better to view legacies as resources for the future.

Further, strategic decisions will never be made simply on technocratic criteria – that is, an assessment of the most optimal outcome – but through conflict with values and political goals. For example, in the years immediately following the end of communism there was extensive debate about the formation of new property rights. One principle of ownership, that was reflected in restitution laws, such as those in the Czech Republic, was grounded in the view that property is a natural right and legitimately allocated according to a principle of justice, namely historical proprietorship. According to this view, communist nationalization was illegitimate and justice demanded that property be restored to pre-1948 owners or their descendants. By contrast, a more technocratic concept of legitimate proprietorship tied claims to allocative efficiency, suggesting that the appropriate owners are those who will use their assets most efficiently and creatively. The latter view tended to accept the postcommunist status quo as a fait accompli and that the former communist elites had acquired the education and skills suitable to acquiring and managing former socialist property (a view taken, for example, by the Russian Minister for Privatization, 1992–6, Anatoly Chubais). In support of this view Mal'kov (1992) distinguished what he called the "conspicuous rationality" of Western market economies from the "disguised rationality" of Russian economic agents, whose behavior is intelligible from the standpoint of Russian cultural traditions of collectivism. Different views prevailed in different transition economies (see, for example, World Bank 2002), but these outcomes reflected particular contests of values and forces each played out within national contexts. There is no essential process of "modernization" but there are adaptations based on cultural, economic, and political structures as people engage in different ways with global systems to differing degrees of efficacy.

Modernity's Discontents

Widespread rejection of modernization theories during the 1970s accompanied a politicization of the discipline and a revival of Marxism and other radical theories. As the influence and explanatory power of these, too, subsequently declined, the postmodern turn in sociology re-posed questions about "modernity," though now understood in more negative terms. The collapse of Soviet socialism got caught up in these debates and was sometimes seen as itself evidence of the arrival of a postmodern condition. This section reviews these arguments.

Critique of modernization

"Sometime in the mid 1960s," says Alexander (1995), "between the assassination of President Kennedy and the San Francisco 'summer of love' of 1967, modernization theory died." Modernization theory held a positive view of modernity as a Western ideal, even though this could be a conflictual and uncertain process. Amidst a general revival of Marxist theory in the 1960s, the first wave of critiques of modernization theory came from the ECLA[6] group and then from world systems theory. In the mid-1970s Immanuel Wallerstein announced that "we do not live in a modernizing world but a capitalist world" in which it was the need not for achievement but for profit that made it tick. Intellectual work was then needed to understand how we were living through a transition from capitalism to socialism (Wallerstein 1979). The details of these approaches need not concern us here, but there are a few points worth noting. The premise of world systems theory is that the world order has a patterned unity in which it is possible to weight the relevance of different components of the system. It proposes that levels in the system are integrated and claims to show how the global system impacts on locales and the reciprocal effects of these on each other. World systems theory claims better (potential) explanatory power than modernization theory since neither its liberal nor Marxist varieties can explain why large regions of the world are not (fully) urbanized, proletarianized, or commodified. In particular:

- The concept of "modernity" was undifferentiated and lacked a focus on capitalism as distinctive and transitory phase of development.
- Dependency and world systems approaches broke with the temporal linearity of evolutionary modernization theories, arguing that the world system contemporaneously generates "advanced" and "underdeveloped" sectors.
- Where there are repetitive cycles within the system these are time-bound and the system is undergoing historical transformation. One example of this is the theory of the Kondratieff cycle (K-wave) which identifies a series of long waves of economic activity and is associated with major social upheavals.[7]

- There are no sequences of development, so one cannot say that Europe was the first industrialized region and others "followed" because the whole system undergoes change at the same time but in different ways at different locations (Chase-Dunn 1983, 1989).
- There have been phases in the development of the world system: (i) world empires (based on political/military domination, e.g. Ancient Rome); (ii) European colonialism; (iii) postcolonial modern capitalist economy and political and economic integration of nation states. Phases should be explicable in terms of a theoretical dynamic that refers to a logic of accumulation and competition among nation states. The theory should further explain differences in the mode of subsumption of peripheral economies to the core (e.g. smallholder production and latifundia).

The international division of labor and dependence of noncapitalist social relations on exchange with capitalism define the spatial boundaries of the world system. The boundaries of the components (core, semi-periphery, and periphery) are specified in spatial and logical terms with criteria that link characteristics of the system with outcomes. For example, during the 1980s there was extensive debate among sociologists and economists of development about the persistence of small-scale family farms in much of the developing world. Many Marxist and modernization theories predicted the disappearance of precapitalist forms of production with the global spread of transnational agribusiness and more efficient forms of cultivation. However, further research argued that, on the contrary, capitalism encouraged the survival of small-scale agriculture in parts of the world (e.g. Currie and Ray 1986), because global capitalism "fossilizes and insulates pre-capitalist modes" (Sklair 1991). Thus global capitalism is not universally modernizing but preserves precapitalist forms where firms can harness cheaper inputs (such as family labor) by doing so.

Although world systems theory is not an integrated set of theoretical propositions and has been eclipsed partially by globalization theories (see chapter 6) it offers an analysis of social change that is often lacking in subsequent modernity theories. However, world systems approaches were weakened by a number of developments. First, there was the emergence during the 1970s and 1980s of the newly industrialized countries of Singapore, Taiwan, South Korea, and Malaysia, whose success in breaking through dependent development appeared to strengthen the model of capitalist rather than socialist development. This further challenged the claim of dependency and world systems theorists that entry into the developed core region of the world was virtually impossible. Second, the theory was heavily economistic and was eclipsed by more culturally inflected theories of globalization and postmodernity. Third, despite being global in focus, world systems approaches remained within a territorial concept of the social contained within nation states, which were understood to form the relatively unalterable three-tier hierarchy of core, semi-periphery, and periphery.

A wider failure of radical theories of social change became apparent by the later 1970s, and the wave of heroic optimism that had informed the renaissance of Marxist and other radical theories of revolutionary change subsided. One upshot of this was a radical rejection of modernity, which had the paradoxical effect of re-establishing the idea of "modernity" as a diffuse cultural and social phenomenon. The evident crisis fermenting in the socialist world, the decline of Western social democracy, and the increasing power of a US-led neoliberal hegemony were accompanied by the decline of theoretical Marxism and any remote prospect of the transition to socialism that Wallerstein had confidently predicted. In particular, new theoretical developments emphasized domination as a feature not just of a particular set of social arrangements, but of the modern *per se*. One example of this was Foucault's theory of Panoptic surveillance, which placed both capitalist and socialist systems within a critique of carceral societies. Again, revived Critical Theory (harking back to Adorno and Horkheimer) drew on the Weberian theme of rationalization within which the emergence of science and technology, indeed enlightenment in itself, held the core of modern systems of domination. Differences between particular social systems became less important than the overall tendencies toward bureaucratic control and surveillance.

Disenchantment with modernity and its promise of a better future was central to postmodernism, in which the exhaustion of the project of modernity was sometimes approached with comic detachment, as for example in Baudrillard. The postmodern turn in social theory was closely tied to the collapse of communism in at least two ways. First, many of the exponents of postmodern theory had at some time in the past been associated with Marxism and especially the French Communist Party, and this was part of a process of individual and collective self-examination. Foucault (1980), for example, was concerned to force communists and Marxists to confront what it was in their texts and practices that "made the Gulag possible" (1980: 135). For Lyotard, disenchantment with the modernist project was closely bound up with a rejection of Marxism as the prime example of a grand narrative of historical justification. Second, the fall of communism could then be taken as confirmation of the crisis of the modernist project in general, heralding a new form of social and political organization.

Postcommunism/postmodernity?

The fall of communism coincided with disenchantment with Marxism and radical politics and the rise of postmodern skepticism about the possibility of progress. This did not signal an eclipse of radical politics and theory but rather its fragmentation into particular identities and subjects – in the process abandoning socialism's belief in emancipation through the action of a collective subject. The radicalism and self-confidence of the neoliberal right mirrored this crisis for the left as the success of neoconservatives in the US continues to do. Since the 1980s the right had been engaged in radical projects of social restructuring that were dismantling the postwar settlement of social democratic Fordist and Keynesian management. Both the triumphal neoliberals and disenchanted postmoderns found in the collapse of communism support for their political and theoretical projects. For postmodern theorists the Soviet Union was the epitome of modernity and its collapse signaled the end of the modernist project in a wider sense. Lyotard's postmodern manifesto had pronounced incredulity toward meta-narratives of historical justification – especially Marxism – and the end of communism appeared to embody modernity's final bankruptcy as an intellectual and political project. This view of the Soviet system resonated with the critical pessimism of the times and drew on Weber's warnings about increasing bureaucratization and the steel-hard cage (*stahlhartes Gehäuse*) of rationality. Weber's model of bureaucratic organization is open to various interpretations (Clegg 1989, 1994; Chalcraft 1994; DiMaggio and Powell 1983; Ray and Reed 1994), but a central theme is that "bureaucratization offers above all the optimum possibility for carrying through the principles of specializing administrative functions according to purely objective considerations" (Weber 1984: 215). Insofar as bureaucratic procedures epitomize the modern, its appearance is marked by the decline of what Simmel (1990: 457) called the old social obligations, which promotes an atomization of society and the colorlessness of modern life, a cool reserve, and anonymous objectivity. From this point of view, socialism embodied the complete calculability of life and would therefore represent the logical conclusion of modernity rather than its negation: the dictatorship, as Weber put it, of the public official not the proletariat (Weber 1978, II: 1402). The converse was also then true – the collapse of the system indicated the crisis of modernity. To what extent are these claims justified?

Postmodernism, of course, is notoriously hard to pin down as a set of theoretical propositions and while "no area of either academic life or popular culture is untouched" by its influence, there is confusion about its nature (Best 2003: 227). This is a debate that will be difficult to resolve, since as Lemert points out, "It cannot be proven . . . that the world has become postmodern . . . one of the central tenets of postmodern philosophies is that nothing can be *proven*" (Lemert 1997: 31). Nonetheless, there are grounds for thinking that the certainties associated with modernist culture are being undermined. There is the challenge to political and scientific orthodoxies posed by feminist, gay, anti-globalization and race-based social movements. There is the politics of identity that influences contemporary society in complex and contradictory ways. There is the reappearance of traditionalist cultures and "fundamentalism" as a challenge to the hegemony of Western modernity. Finally, there is the experience of uncertainty and fluidity which weaken stable social relationships and communities. Whether we call these changes "postmodern" or not, they point toward a transformation and increasing diversification of everyday life. So, let us examine the debate, with a view to trying to move beyond it.

Bauman in particular has argued that communism, along with fascism, was the epitome of modernity, albeit in one of its most nightmarish forms the collapse of which portends a crisis of modernity *per se*. Bauman depicts modernity in Promethean terms which are contrasted with the fluid, differentiated, and aestheticized cultural forms of postmodernity, or latterly "liquid modernity" (Bauman 2001). Modernity, he says, "was a long march to the prison. It never arrived there (though in some places, like Stalin's Russia, Hitler's Germany or Mao's China, it came quite close) albeit not for the lack of trying" (Bauman 1992: xvii). Similarly, Berman (1985) interprets Goethe's *Faust* as an allegory of modernity's destructiveness, which was reflected in Stalinist projects such as the White Sea Canal.[8] According to this view, Marxism-Leninism was the archetypal grand narrative of domination (Lyotard 1979) and communism was modernity in its most determined mood and most decisive posture (Bauman: 1992: 166). Soviet modernism was associated with gigantism, Fordist mass production, and consumption; an extensive, corporatist, and rationalized state; a secular, etatist ideology; cultural homogeneity governed by the ethos of technology and the culture industry (cf. Murray 1992). Moreover, central to this view of modernity is the development of increasingly subtle systems of control and their incursion into everyday life, particularly through institutions and social technologies, such as Foucault's (1975) carceral or Panoptic society. The less coercive, visible, and imposing power becomes through the centralization and mobilization of administrative control, the more pervasive, internalized and "normal" it appears. It is true that surveillance was crucial to the Soviet apparatus, which intruded into most areas of everyday life, through networks of informers, eavesdropping, monitoring, and so forth. The discovery of massive Stasi (East German secret service) archives following the fall of the Berlin Wall illustrated the extent to which the state agents pried into the minutiae of everyday life – even if much of the data were useless since they could not be analyzed or acted upon.[9]

With the postmodern turn the differences between capitalism and communist modernization, emphasized by modernization theory, were played down. Crook et al. (1994: 42n.) argue that Soviet-type societies were variants of an industrial society which is now converging with the West in a "crisis of corporatism," marked by decentralization, new social movements, privatization and a "shrinking state," deregulation and globalization. They explain the crisis of communism as part of the global crisis of the Fordist regime of accumulation, which they in turn associate with the emergence of postmodernism. Further, Bauman argues that, confronted by a postmodern consumer society in the West, the obsolete steel-per-head philosophy proved no match for the lure of the narcissistic culture of self-enhancement, self-enjoyment, instant gratification. This accords with commentators who see in the broad Civic Forum–type coalitions that eased communists out of power, a "postmodern politics" of "unrestrained recycling of archaic and unorthodox concepts within pluralist frameworks" (Ost 1990: 16–17). One claim made in this context is that politics has undergone "culturalization," and is now less governed by instrumental goals and more oriented to identity and recognition. Examples of postmodern politics can be found especially around the collapse of communism. These kinds of protests, deploying techniques of parody and irony, can be found among some social, especially student, social movements prior to 1989. For example in Poland in the late 1980s, "Orange Alternative," part theater, part sociopolitical movement, practiced "socialist surrealism," which aimed to offer a distorting mirror to everyday life in Poland. It described its politics as socialist surrealism, or "how to be curious orange," on the basis that any collective nonconformist action, such as everyone wearing orange, would undermine public order. An example of their operations was the "Eve of the October Revolution" (a parody of Christmas Eve) which was advertised through leaflets in bombastic text:

> ПРАВДА will set us free. Comrades it is time to shake off the indifference of the popular masses! Let us begin to celebrate the Eve of the October Revolution!

At 4:00 PM on November 6, 1988, several groups gathered in the center of Wrocław with cardboard models of the cruiser *Aurora*, the battleship *Potemkin*, dressed as Red Army soldiers, banners demanding the rehabilitation of Trotsky, prompting a German reporter to cite this as the largest demonstration of Trotskyists in Eastern Europe! They were joined by hundreds of passers-by wearing red clothing (as requested on the leaflets) and demanding (with double irony) that the working day of militiamen and the secret service be limited to eight hours. Nonetheless, the militia broke up the demonstration, breaking under batons hallowed symbols of communism such as the *Potemkin* and *Aurora*.[10] This kind of activism can also be found in other forms of "situationalist" politics of street protest manifest in ecological, anti-war and anti-globalization protests. In this sense the fall of communism was part of a wider shift in understandings of the "political" away from formal organizations with strategic agendas to fluid networks of protest and spectacle grounded in what Maffesoli (1996) describes as tribe-like but temporary groups and circles that condense out of the homogeneity of the mass.

Such networks and events confronted the powers that be not with an alternative vision and strategy (as with conventional parties and movements) but with spectacle, irony, and the politics of parody. Even so, the "postmodern" always lacked sufficient coherence to designate a social movement. For some, postmodernism releases new energies and subversive forces, although not all writers share Bauman's and Ost's "affirmative" postmodernism (Rosenau 1992: 15). In marked contrast for example, is Mestrovic's (1994) bleak vision of an anti-modernist convergence between a "balkanized" amoral, Western, postmodernism and violent, Eastern, postcommunism. Nonetheless, for both affirmative and negative postmodernists, the collapse of communism signals a decisive break with the modernist project of which it was a part.

One can only argue that postmodernity and postcommunism are part of a common process insofar as postmodernism is understood as a trend or process that renders some social arrangements, in this case centralized and autarkic systems, less viable than other, more decentralized and globally integrated ones. Some do suggest this. Macnaughton and Urry, for example, claim that the Soviet system was unable to cope with the "combined consequences of instantaneous and glacial time" (1998: 15). Stuck in modernist clock time, in a time-warp of forced modernization, the surrounding pressures from media-driven instantaneity became overwhelming, hence the systems fell. Despite their antipathy to "chronophonism" (historical time) Krishan Kumar (1995: 137) notes how postmodernists suggest that this is a stage beyond the modern. Crook et al. (1994: 36–41) define the new epoch in terms of processes such as semiotic pastiche, decentralization of state power and decoupling from economics, the erosion of class and gender divisions, the growth of ephemeral and informal social movements, flexible work specialization, and the erosion of established scientific disciplines. These, at least, are open to empirical evaluation, and it should be possible to determine where and why such generalizations hold true and when they do not.

On the other hand, Baudrillard's use of the end of communism to claim that history is running backwards and the twenty-first century cannot begin is ironic allegory. He says that progress has disappeared yet is continuous – the lifting of the blockade around Eastern Europe now inaugurates a dazzling mobilization of a final process – a postmodern remake of the original version of modernity which "wipes the twentieth century by undoing the Cold War and World War 2." Further, much postmodern theory eschews notions of historical development, since "chronophonism" belongs to the exhausted "imperative of productivity" (Rosenau 1992: 67), and since "everything has already happened . . . nothing new can occur" (Baudrillard 1993). For these theorists, then, postmodernism is not a stage beyond modernity so much as the exhaustion of modernity, or as Bauman puts it, "modernity coming to terms with its own impossibility" (Bauman 1992).[11]

Whatever the particular take on socialism and postmodernism, there is a body of argument that the collapse of communism is part of the wider cultural, social, and economic transformation of the West – that as Kumar (1995: 151–2) suggests, the end of communism and the end of modernity perhaps possess an "elective affinity." However, there are several counter-arguments to this view. First, it can be argued that the Soviet system was at most a partial modernization of premodern social relations and still contained premodern elements, such as a patrimonial bureaucracy. In this case, its collapse opened up the possibility for more thoroughgoing modernization, or modernization according to the Western pattern. This has prompted a re-examination of some earlier modernization theories that will be considered in the next section. Second, there is the argument that the fall of communism was symptomatic of the crisis of a particular phase or type of modernity – one that was associated particularly with industrial society and centralized state structures – rather than modernity *per se*. However, both these views assume that there is a temporal sequence of stages in social organization that each society is destined to travel, as does Bauman's later formulation of the transition from "heavy" to "liquid" modernity (Bauman 2001). A third approach would take the view that there are no more stages or sequences to social development and that thinking in terms of temporal transitions ignores the way in which particular outcomes are the product of configurations of global and local circumstances. In these terms neither the view that the fall of the USSR represented the triumph of postmodernity nor the view that it offers hope of renewed modernity are adequate. The post-communist world is one in which the play of modernization, modernity, and otherness has become both intense and unstable.

In the end, to equate postcommunism with postmodernism or to subsume the former in the latter is to perpetuate the practice whereby Western pre-occupations and views of the social world get extended to everywhere else. Whether coming from the modernist or postmodernist camp sociologists should be sensitive to the economic and cultural preconditions of particular developmental paths. Discussing what they see as the distinctive social structure and trajectory of the Ottoman Empire, Tosun Aricanli and Maria Thomas (1994) claim that the

> historical trajectory of western Europe can neither define the course of a non-European historical transformation nor is it suitable for constructing a comparative model encompassing both the European experience and the rest of the world.

If this principle is extended to the parts of Europe and Asia that for four or seven decades remained apart from Western capitalism, then there is no reason to assume either that Western organizational forms will necessarily emerge or that a single model will come to characterize the postcommunist settlement. Moreover, the grounds for proposing an elective affinity between postcommunism and postmodernism are less valid than they may initially appear. For one thing, Bauman's nightmare vision of modernity as carceral power emphasizes "discipline" at the expense of the contrary tendency toward "liberty," or inalienable rights and freedoms (Wagner 1994). Promethean modernism is in some ways (such as Goethe's *Faust*) a literary construction, which many critics of modernity have mistaken for a real social formation. The nightmare vision of disciplinary power and administrative control built into the fabric of everyday life is based on an over-deterministic view of social order. Not only is the implementation of these systems more haphazard, partial, and fragmented than Bauman and others suggest, but they are also blunted by the countervailing power, which those subject to them are able to develop. Similarly, the model for the concept of surveillance, Bentham's Panopticon, was never actually built – it was an idea of a carceral institution that could not be fully realized. Indeed, there is considerable evidence of the chaotic disorganization of Soviet systems and their extensive dependence on informal methods of integration, beneath the official appearance of planning and discipline (e.g. Filtzer 1992; Ray 1996: 100–33; Hoffman 2002). Thus the Soviet crisis may have origins quite different from that of capitalist corporatism – a possibility that is addressed in chapter 6.

Further, sociological postmodernism constructs a typology of characteristics defined by opposition to modernity. Modernity, on the one hand, is characterized by vertical and horizontal differentiation; high and low culture; organized capitalism; and separate institutional, normative, and aesthetic spheres. Postmodernity by contrast involves de-differentiation, cultural transgression, disorganized capitalism, and an implosion of distinct value spheres (Crook et al. 1994: 34; Lash and Urry 1994: 272). Such typologies leave open the question of what social processes may be driving these changes, and many postmodernist writers claim to eschew causal explanation (e.g. Lyotard 1979). Others, however, suggest that postmodernist culture is grounded in structural transformations of capital (e.g. Harvey 1994; Lash and Urry 1994; Smart 1992). If this is the case, then such transformations are unlikely to be globally uniform, but will vary with different institutional settings – an important insight from world systems theory was that increasing global integration does not result in greater uniformity but on the contrary in increasing inequalities and combinations of difference and diversity.

The "postcommunism is postmodernism" argument overlooks the specificity of the Soviet system. The bases of social solidarity are complex and the Soviet systems deployed a range of traditionalist as well as modernist forms of control. As well as aggressive modernization, the Soviet system cultivated a cult of the sacred – the Lenin Mausoleum, the Books of Heroes, the hagiography of leaders instilled through the education system and public festivals. Indeed, after Stalin's "dizziness with success" speech in March, 1930, in which former advocates of radical change were condemned as

Trotskyites, wreckers, and opportunists, there was extensive re-traditionalization of Soviet culture (Hough 1978: 251; Filtzer 1992: 117; Ray 1996: 53–4).[12] Soviet exhortations invoked an ideal of revolutionary heroism that is rather at odds with the idea of modernity as a process of disenchantment, rationalization, organizational impersonality, and formal legality. From the standpoint of the latter, the claim that Soviet systems were "modern" would be hard to defend. In terms of a sober "Weberian" vision of modernity, the charismatic ideal of selfless revolutionary heroism, of shock workers and Stakhanovites, the amalgam of bureaucratic discipline and charismatic correctness (Jowitt 1983) had more in common with the *pre*modern cult of warriors upholding "honor" as a prime virtue than the modern ethos of disenchanted skepticism.[13] Janos (1991) argues that the Soviet Union was a garrison state ruled by a political class whose self-justification derived from the external orientation of a militaristic ideology, which in turn justified a barracks economy and society. Soviet societies were in some ways similar to Weber's (1978, I: 232–3) description of patrimonial status structures (*ständische Herrschaft*) where administrative staff accumulated assets and preserved privileges through the nomenklatura system (Voslensky 1984). Rather than develop an ethic of formal bureaucratic impersonality and a separation between public office and private appropriation, by the 1960s the Soviet system had created a clientelistic power structure in which state officials treated public property as benefices that gradually acquired the status of customary property rights (Naishul 1993).

Again, Fehér, Heller, and Márkus (1983: 210) argue that "the ethics of Bolshevism are in themselves a manifestation of . . . the de-enlightenment process. Loyalty and obedience to the sovereign as supreme values belong to a world prior to enlightenment." These would include the ethic of vigilance (*bditelnost*), military preparation (*voennaya podgotorka*), and struggle (*borba*) that successive mobilization campaigns during the 1920s and 1930s attempted to inculcate (Slepyan 1993). Arnason (1993) claims that Russia's peripheral position in Europe, combined with its internal "Asiatic" influences, fashioned an alternative modernizing paradigm that both challenged Western modernity and offered a prototype that claimed to prefigure its future (Arnason 1993: 22ff.). The continuity of Russian traditionalism within Soviet Marxism was ensured partly through the incorporation of the elitist-populist revolutionary tradition of Chernyshevsky and Tkachev within Leninism (Arnason 1993: 64–8), and the absorption of the Tsarist bureaucracy into the Soviet apparatus after 1917 (Fainsod 1963: 250).

If the drift of this analysis is correct then postcommunism may not represent the exhaustion of modernity, but rather a fresh beginning. It also raises the prospect of understanding the collapse of authoritarian systems as a vindication of a kind for modernization theory – if the process of adaptive upgrading reached a tipping point where centralized and authoritarian structures were no longer viable. Lipset and Bence (1994) argue that

Sovietologists failed to predict the failure of communism because they did not address the larger theoretical issues of societal transformation that are found in modernization theorists and theories of large-scale social change. This is a view shared by a number of recent commentators who are discussed in the following section.

Modernity/modernization revisited?

The decline of postmodern theory has been accompanied by a revival of theories of modernity and modernization in order to make sense of the problems and trajectory of postcommunism. Eisenstadt (1992), for example, suggests that the anticommunist revolutions took place within already modernized societies, and that the rebellions did not overthrow traditionalistic *ancien régimes*. On the contrary, regime changes occurred within existing political institutions and were ratified by the legal frameworks of the outgoing states. Postcommunist societies now confront problems of modernity that were "previously latent," such as tensions between general and discrete interests, the continuity and boundaries of the state, confrontation between different modes of legitimacy, and different aspects of the modern political process. Likewise, Habermas depicted the Eastern European revolutions of 1989 as "revolutions of recuperation" (*die nachholende Revolution*) "overcoming distance" with Western Europe. By contrast with the classical revolutions of modernity (the English, American, French and Russian), which were oriented toward the future, the anticommunist revolutions expressed a desire to connect up with the inheritance of bourgeois revolutions, taking their methods and standards entirely from the repertoire of the modern age. The democratic spirit of the West, he says, is catching up with the East (Habermas 1990, 1994: 62), where antistatist and democratic ideas of civil society, anti-political politics, and the self-limiting revolution, created the opportunity for a new communicative civil society in Europe East and West (1994: 72). Again Holmes (1993: 310–29) argues that the anticommunist revolutions were only marginally related to a general crisis of modernity and actually recreate conditions of early modernity such as imperfect democracies and markets with high levels of conflict. This renewed attention to theories of modernity has taken two forms. First, there is a revival of modernization theory by sociologists such as Lipset (1994), Rostow (1991), and Huntington (1999), who were writing in the 1960s and 1970s, or by those who have revisited their concerns. Second, theorists such as Bauman have largely abandoned postmodernism and differentiate between successive stages within modernity – in Bauman's case, "heavy" and "liquid" modernity, for Beck and Giddens "simple" and "reflexive" modernization.

Modernization theory is invoked both as an explanation of the collapse and as a way of framing future developments. For example Vassilev (1999) argues that modernization theory provides an explanation of the collapse of communism in Bulgaria. Under communism a middle class grew within a differentiated social structure and "adaptive upgrading" of the social and technological infrastructure. A combination of factors encouraged values of individual liberty and created a "revolution of rising expectations." These included: urbanization of a previously largely rural population and better levels of education – with the proportion of intellectuals in the party increasing from 8 to 39 percent between 1944 and 1986. This came to a head with the rejection of authoritarianism and the movement of many intellectuals from the Party into the Union of Democratic Forces in 1990. Thus the democratic revolution of 1989–90 was "the natural outgrowth (as well as the unintended consequence) of the regime's success in fostering economic and social progress."

A similar point could be made about the effects of perestroika in the Soviet Union in the later 1980s, which was driven by the "modernizing elite" around Gorbachev. Four of the central objectives of perestroika emphasized the need to modernize and upgrade Soviet economy and society. First, it aimed to seriously restructure the system of welfare benefits and entitlements that were reinterpreted as a state paternalist system of *garantirvannost,* sapping initiative and efficiency (Cook 1992; Zaslavskaya 1984). Rising real incomes would be set against fewer entitlements and reduced subsidies, meritocratic distribution, and increases in inequality, the effects of which would nonetheless be mitigated by social welfare, unemployment benefit, and retraining opportunities (Gorbachev 1986; Hauslohner 1989). Second, decentralization and horizontal integration of enterprises would replace command structures and end the "petty tutelage of enterprises by ministries and departments" (Gorbachev 1986). Cooperatives and joint ventures would be encouraged, while prejudice concerning "commodity–money regulations" would be overcome within a "regulated market economy" (Agenbegyan 1988; Gorbachev 1986). Third, widening the base of participation, combined with political rights and personal liberties, was linked to an attack on unelected nomenklatura positions and privilege (Yakovlev 1993: 103; Gorbachev 1986; Whetten 1989: 39). The emphasis of this shifted after 1989 toward more radical democratization and the formal rational legal state (Gooding 1990; Goldman 1991). Fourth, according to Yakovlev's reflections on the process in which he was a key player, perestroika furthered the routinization of organizational charisma by instituting a thorough disenchantment with what was left of the CPSU's mythological aura (Yakovlev 1993: 114).

Some neomodernization approaches show sensitivity to the nuances of the postcommunist transformation, the uncertainty of the process, and therefore are less committed than earlier versions to ideas of convergence or universal processes. Muller (1992) argues that the "upheavals in Eastern European countries have demonstrated to the social sciences in a painful manner" that they do not "have any adequate theory suited to grasp [these] dynamics." Further, he places his arguments within the "revival of modernization theory" that has followed the failure of "late capitalism" and "dependencia" theories. But his conclusion is pessimistic. The absence of capital, the strength of ties to the old system, and risks of ethnic conflict mean that the most likely outcome is "modernization without modernity" – reforms without clear or stable outcomes. Similarly, Kurtz and Barnes (2002) point to the "wide range of regime outcomes in the region" and argue that "economic liberalization . . . appears to have no connection with democratization." They explore the causes of different postcommunist regime transitions in Eastern Europe and the former Soviet Union, emphasizing the increasingly prominent thesis that economic liberalization promotes political democratization. Their results are based on a multilevel design strategy, first analyzing data on 26 postcommunist countries over a seven-to nine-year period using time-series/cross-sectional methods and then turning to a comparative analysis of four purposively selected cases to explore the causal mechanisms implied but not tested in the quantitative analysis. However, they do find support for the claim that large agrarian sectors are unfavorable to democratic development, whereas positive influence from outside agents can play an important role in transition dynamics. More critically, Blaney and Inayutallah (2002) point out that modernization theory has assumed that the culture of the West is the framework for understanding other societies. On the contrary, the idea of a world culture is difficult to sustain and should be replaced with that of "multiple modernities," a view that Eisenstadt (2001) had also embraced. They argue that there is a "recessive theme" within modernization approaches that understands and nurtures difference. This is to be encouraged through "dialogue" between relatively traditional and relatively modern cultures, though quite how this is to happen they do not say.

What is driving these changes? Much of this literature invokes a technologically driven and linear view of temporal development. Rostow claims that "One cannot look about in Warsaw or Moscow, Budapest or Zagreb, Krakow or Sarajevo without knowing that this part of the world is caught in a technological time warp" (Rostow 1991: 61). Eisenstadt (2001) offers a more nuanced view – identifying six factors: technology, political struggles, shifting hegemonies of international systems, confrontations between centers and elites, cultural conflicts, and confrontation between Western and Asian civilizations. His account emphasizes conflict (rather than evolution) and eschews ideas of necessary logics of development – some of the distinct ways in which democracies such as India or Japan developed were greatly influenced by their respective cultural traditions. Even so, in such an open, uncertain, and multidimensional analysis it is unclear what differentiates this from more general sociological approaches. It makes no specific claims (because all outcomes are uncertain) and is unclear about even what is meant by "modernization" at all, since "modernity" accommodates diverse forms. While some elements of modernization theory have been salvaged – such as the import-ance of functional differentiation and the role of a liberal middle class – the universalism and teleology have been left out. In this form the theory may generate some valid questions about the divergent patterns of change in dif-ferent parts of the postcommunist region but does not provide any sense of overarching process.

Other theorists seek to replace the modernity–postmodernity distinction with the claim that there are (at least) two modernities – again arranged in (implicitly) in temporal sequence. However, the tendency in classical mod-ernization theory to over-generalize social change and to invest it with tele-ology is evident here too. Bauman, for example, appears to renounce his earlier postmodernism when he claims that "the society which enters the twenty-first century is no less 'modern' than the society which entered the twentieth" (Bauman 2001: 28). The contrast between "heavy" and "liquid" modernity is essentially a contrast between Fordist, bureaucratic, centralized societies of nation states and military-territorial competition on the one hand, and post-Fordist, globalized, fluid, post-bureaucratic societies on the other. The former was the world of the *Konzlager* in which the limits of human malleability were tested under laboratory conditions (Bauman 2001: 25), as he argued previously in *Modernity and the Holocaust*. Communism was situated within "heavy," and postcommunism within "liquid" modern-ity in which there has been a "dissipation of politburos" and individuality has replaced the collective. A possible difficulty with this is that while Bau-man established some well-known contrasts between industrial and postin-dustrial society the distinctions are painted very broadly and are too general to give much purchase on the explanation of change in particular locales. Is the most one can conclude from this theory that when certain sorts of changes occur (for example, dismantling the welfare and industrial institu-tions of former communist societies), these are part and parcel of a wider trend, which they both exemplify and intensify?

Nonetheless, Bauman offers a broad framework through which to under-stand the complex social changes of which postcommunism is a part. From this perspective we can comment on the last theory to be considered in this context – reflexive modernization, which is associated particularly with Beck, Giddens, and Lash. This is hung loosely around the end of commun-ism in that the discussion opens by noting the significance of 1989 as evi-dence of profound social changes currently in progress. But there is no detailed analysis of the nuances of these changes. Moreover, Beck and Gid-dens mean rather different things by "reflexive modernization." Central to Beck's theory is the idea of the "risk society" – a state in which (principally ecological) risks generated by industrial society rebound as a defensive at-tempt to transform hazards into calculable risks. The hazards of pre-industrial society (famines, plagues, natural disasters) were experienced as pre-given, whereas risk awareness and monitoring aim to render calculable what was incalculable, and this in turn brings into play new forms of agency, choice, calculation, and responsibility. Industrial societies were organized within national territorial spaces within which risks were managed in part collectively (for example, through welfare systems) and in part through public and private insurance. But risks today threaten irreparable global damage (such as a nuclear accident) that cannot be limited either individually or collectively and against which financial compensation is obsolete. Elliott (2003: 36) summarizes the thesis as: the "key problem of reflexive modernization is one of living with a high degree of risk in a world where traditional safety nets (the welfare state, nuclear family etc.) are being eroded or dismantled."

For Beck, reflexive modernization denotes a new form of society that is contrasted with the "simple modernization" of industrialism. Reflexive modernization opens "the possibility of a creative (self-)destruction for an entire epoch: that of industrial society." This undercuts "its formations of class, stratum occupation, sex roles, nuclear family, plant, business sectors and of course also the prerequisites and continuing forms of natural techno-economic progress" (Beck 1994: 2). Beck's concept (like some neomodernization approaches) pulls together in a fairly undifferentiated way most contemporary developments under the banner of "reflexive modernization," which encompasses "nationalism, mass poverty, religious fundamentalism . . . economic crises, ecological crises, possibly wars and revolutions, not forgetting the states of emergency produced by great catastrophic accidents" (Beck 1994: 4). Indeed, ecological risks are central in his account and to his view that risks arise globally from unforeseen consequences of modernity's attempts to control nature. This is not to be approached only pessimistically, though, but seen as a "providential gift for the universal self-reformation of a previously fatalistic industrial modernity" that can gain from them the impetus to assure viability in the future (Beck 1994: 51–2). Beck offers a vision of a new modernity of novel personal experimentation and cultural innovation, not least because new technologies themselves create new risks and ethical dilemmas – such as those that surround genetic engineering. Beck claims that reflexive modernization involves individualization and the possibility of a new politics based on demonopolization of expertise, open participation and decision-making, public dialogue between agents and public, and norms of self-legislation and self-obligation. The old nature-like structures and boundaries are seen to be fluid and insubstantial.

Beck et al. (2003) develop a more systematic model of transition from "*a first modernity* that was largely synonymous with the nation-state to a *second modernity*, the shape of which is still being negotiated, [in which] modernization ends up stripping away the nation- and welfare state, which at one time supported it but later restrained it." Table 5.1 summarizes the main contrasts between "first modern societies" and the "second modernity." This also broadly captures some of the features of the transition to postcommunism. Previously autarkic nations, based on scientific-industrial logics and paternalistic notions of protection of citizens, are increasingly integrated into the global system. Collectivism has given way in part to increased indivdualization, the goal of full employment is abandoned along with an ideology of scientific rational planning, and ecological awareness increases. Some of the earliest manifestations of recent anticommunist mobilization were around ecological issues – such as protests at the proposed Gabcikovo-Nagymaros dam in Hungary and Ecoglasnost in Bulgaria. *The Risk Society* was published soon after the 1986 Chernobyl disaster in the Soviet Union that had underlined the potential for catastrophic ecological damage from industrial society. The end of communism illustrates the process of the automatic operation of modernization processes blind to their consequences and dangers. Crises in communism were driven by a confluence of mounting system problems and the unintended consequences of efforts to correct them. But for the anticommunist movements like Solidarity, too, the eventual outcome – transition to "mafya capitalism" was far from what they had desired or expected. Likewise, the restructuring of welfare and social benefits is part of a project of individualizing responsibility for risks arising from a privatized and marketized society.

But on a more detailed level it is less clear that Beck's claims about a "second modernity" generalize so well. Beck et al. (2003) concede that the model is Eurocentric and that the paths of non-European societies still have to be described. The same problem applies to postcommunist societies, some of which may approximate "second modernity" more than others do, as we have suggested in chapter 4. What Beck does say about "Eastern Europe" is grossly overstated. He claims that "there [in Eastern Europe] the citizens' groups – contrary to the entire social science intelligentsia – started from zero with no organization, in a system of surveilled [*sic*] conformity, and yet with no copying machines or telephones, were able to force the ruling group to retreat and collapse just by assembling in a square" (Beck 1994: 19). This might conceivably apply to the Leipzig marches that probably did not have much in the way of resources, and to the Romanian demonstrations that sparked the revolution, but as a summary of the process it is simplistic.

Further, several of the claims made in table 5.1 are problematic in various ways, some of which we will proceed to explore. Nation states continue to exist within a context of globalization (see chapter 6) and individualization is still structured by collective identities, albeit of a postcommunist nature – especially nationalist and underpinned by collective memories (see chapter 8). The transformation of gender roles has involved sustained mobilization of women as collective actors (rather than the product of some quasi-evolutionary movement of reflexive modernization) and in postcommunism feminist agendas have so far made little headway, as noted in chapter 3. Beck's thesis does not deal well with the social structuring of risk (Elliott 2003: 24ff.) and individualization is part and parcel of the global and local

Table 5.1   *First modern societies and second modernity*

First modern societies	Second modernity
Nation states defined by territorial boundaries	Globalization undermines the nation state
Individualization bounded by collective life still rooted in premodern structures such as the sexual division of labor	Erosion of collective life and more intense individualization. Transformation of gender roles and sexuality as part of a "denaturalization" of social divisions
Work societies (for adult men) in which unemployment is so low it can be considered fictional	Flexible employment and consumption "progressively independent of income"
Nature is conceived of as outside society and an object of exploitation for endless growth	Global ecological crisis and incorporation of "nature" in "society"
Belief in progress through rationality and instrumental control	Recognition of extra-scientific justification, debate through *ad hoc* institutional means of reaching a decision
Functional differentiation into subsystems	Dissolving fundamental distinctions and fluidity of boundaries

Source: Summarized from Beck et al. (2003).

restructuring of capital, which the postcommunist transformation illustrates well. Rising poverty and inequality in postcommunist countries has followed rising unemployment and declining state benefits (see pp. 47–59). Further, we may be able to find examples of de-differentiation (the increasingly cultural inflection of economic action, for example) but modern societies remain dependent on complex systems of differentiation and specialization. The emergence of postcommunist social systems illustrate this – as new boundaries have appeared between polity and economy, civil society and the state, public and private realms, along with increased articulation of gender, ethnic, and social class differences (see chapter 7). It is difficult to sustain the view that a "second modernity" has "dissolved" fundamental divisions. This is not to say that none of these changes are occurring but that their mode of appearance differs in the postcommunist world, from which standpoint the argument looks rather parochially located within the confines of Western Europe. More fundamentally for Beck's thesis, though, is the possibility (invoked by Bauman, above) that the shift from "first" to "second" modernity is part of a broader crisis in which global reconfigurations of capital are shattering modernist culture and breaking down earlier notions of progress – transformations within which risk forms only a part.

For Giddens reflexive modernization is more about overcoming and defining a relationship with "tradition." Reflexive modernization is a "radicalizing of modernity – an evacuation, disinterring, and problematizing of tradition" which entails a new concept of the self. Tradition was to do with the control of time, which involved organizing the medium of collective memory (Giddens 1994: 63–4). This was accomplished through ritual that enmeshed tradition in practices that had, however, to be interpreted by guardians, who possessed "formulaic truth" (1994: 65). Guardians are not like modern "experts," though, since their truths are not communicable to others and their authority derives from status in the traditional order rather than the possession of expertise. Although the advent of modernity involved a clash with tradition, this confrontation was only partial. The capitalist spirit of accumulation was a new form of motivation but became an "endless treadmill," an end in itself and drive to repetition. It was "tradition without traditionalism" (1994: 70).

The new era of "reflexive modernization" overcomes earlier partial modernization and brings into being a new self and relationship with tradition. Reflexive modernization entails the excavation of most traditional contexts of action, a process that is closely linked to both risk and globalization. As Giddens argues: "Few people anywhere in the world can any longer be unaware of the fact that their local activities are influenced, and sometimes even determined, by remote events or agencies" (1994: 57). Similarly, individual actions – such as purchasing a particular item of clothing – affect the livelihood of someone living on the other side of the world and may contribute to ecological decay. Life becomes increasingly experimental and the global experiment of modernity intersects with the penetration of modern institutions into the tissue of day-to-day life. We are all caught in everyday experiments whose outcomes are open. This awareness and the institutional changes associated with it entail a process of "detraditionalization" in which the reflexive project of the self depends upon a significant measure of emotional autonomy and new forms of intimacy. Freed from the constraints of collective habit, we have no choice but to choose, and many areas of life are governed by *decisions,* although who takes these and how are matters of *power* (1994: 76). Globalization necessarily involves the disembedding of tradition because in a world where no one is "outside," pre-existing traditions cannot avoid contact with others. Traditions may be discursively articulated and defended *only* through dialogue with others. In modern societies tradition is called into dialogue with alternatives – for example, gender divisions were once segmented, but now gendering of identities is placed in question. Giddens suggests that the alternative is fundamentalism, which he calls "tradition in its traditional sense" (1994: 100) which protects tradition against radical doubt through the assertion of formulaic truth without regard to consequences.

We will make only a few brief comments on this. While Giddens is right to make central the relationship between modernity and tradition, it is not clear why he (and Beck) regard this as surpassing classical sociological theory, for which it was also a prime concern. The claim that post-traditional subjects make lifestyle choices is hardly new (see, for example, Simmel's essay on Fashion) and the idea of the reflexive feedback of unintended consequences was central to both Marx's theory of the crisis of capitalism and Weber's theory of its origin. Further, as one of us has argued already (Ray 1999b) Giddens's account of "fundamentalism" is insufficient since this movement is itself detraditionalizing in many respects, and indeed emulates aspects of the modernist Jacobin revolutionary mode of organization (a point noted too by Eisenstadt 1996). A crucial question here is what factors structure the "choices" between civilizational dialogue on the one hand and that assertion of moral and cultural absolutism on the other. But reflexive modernization is vague about the drivers of the changes identified and provides next to nothing by way of empirical support for the claims that they are occurring at all. It is also (as its exponents latterly acknowledge) Eurocentric – recreating the sense of necessary temporal change that, like earlier versions of modernization theory, is insensitive to the possibility that actors in the global system undermine "traditional" relations and cultures in some places while preserving them in others. In relation to postcommunism this would essentially be a theory of convergence (on a reflexive future) but the evidence for this is sparse. In particular, Soviet societies waged war on tradition in some respects while in their search for legitimation they harnessed national symbols and cultural memories (see chapter 8) along with invented traditions associated with the Revolution. Since the end of communism, the past, tradition, and identities bound up with these have been subject to fierce contestation and a search for an authentic past purified from communist "falsification." This process gets occluded in theories of modernization, where the non-Western subject is caught within homogenizing images that, as Hörschelmann (2002) argues, "leave unaffected many conceptions about 'them' and the Western self." The Other can then evade the globalizing effect of reflexive modernization only through disingenuous and coercive practices that are probably bound in the end to fail. Like earlier versions of modernization theory, these theories actually assume a hierarchy of modernist constructions of time, place, and change. The diversity of the emerging postcommunist world eludes simple theoretical schemas and its understanding requires more historically grounded approaches.

Diversity, Conflict, and the Failed Socialist Civilization

The implosion of Soviet communism marked the failure of a state socialist civilization, and what has followed has been the outcome of combinations of local traditions and practices with new developments. There is growing evidence to suggest that the idea that the postcommunist countries are approaching optimal or universal states of development is wrong. The nature of the changes since the late 1980s, in particular the pace and scope of marketization and democratization has varied, sometimes dramatically both between and within countries (Dawisha and Parrott 1997). There are at least two issues to consider here. First, there is the possibility that rather than necessarily sweep away premodern or simple modern forms, the global system erodes traditional systems in some places but supports them in others. Second, there is the possibility that decisions of local actors might result in what appear to Western analysis suboptimal outcomes but which may be rational and part of abiding sets of arrangements when viewed in context. On the one hand, parts of the postcommunist region, especially those lined up for accession, are integrating into European Union economies, reorienting trade toward the EU and developing social and political systems similar to those of the West. It should be noted, though, that this applies mostly to the relatively small areas of Central Europe and the Baltic States. In other places the patterns are more paradoxical and reflect the combination of postcommunist strategies, global influences, and underlying cultural and structural conditions. One example is the unprecedented reliance on non-monetary exchange (NME) in transactions among enterprises in the post-Soviet economic transformation – these include practices such as bilateral exchanges of goods, clearing schemes, shipping of output to perhaps six partners in a network of mutual obligation, and inter-enterprise debts. Tomson (1999) argues that firms engage in NME in order to discount nominal prices that remain well above market-clearing levels. These "distortions" effectively operate to sustain a subsidy regime that has hitherto shielded much of Russian industry from the pressures of market forces. Systems of NME are rational (and optimal) from the point of view of the actors involved and arguably have wider social benefits, although they are evidence of apparently premodern and non-(market)rational forms of behavior. Again, in parts of the former Soviet Union oil revenues are being used to rebuild a Soviet-style economy with heavily centralized bureaucratic systems organized around industrial output (McCann 2004). While modernization models predict a shift away from industrial to information- and service-based activities, in the Ukraine during the 1990s employment in coal and gas extraction and metallurgy was actually increasing, against the background of a steep overall rise in unemployment (Lazarenko and Sobolev 2001). Finally, the trend in postcommunist countries is for public sector employment to decrease as a share of total employment, with the processes of privatization and decommissioning in the military-industrial sector. However, in some Russian federal republics, where unemployment is growing, public employment is growing quickly. Most of this growth has occurred in the 89 regions and especially in ethnically defined territorial units that have received large federal transfers and loans. Gimpelson et al. (2000) argue that this occurs because regional governors use public employment as a protection against unemployment, a means of patronage, and of redistribution. These are only a few examples and have been presented in passing. Nonetheless, they serve to exemplify the claim that particular configurations of economy and society reflect particular combinations of history, culture, global position, and decisions by actors. While theory may attempt to identify general trends it also needs to identify in what conditions these trends should continue to operate and what kinds of conditions might offset them.

Classical modernization theory and theories of postmodernity have attempted to insert the Soviet system into a frame of reference derived largely from Western experience. Postmodernist triumphalism parallels neoliberal triumphalism in that they both celebrate the hegemony of the West. Reflexive modernization aims to escape from the modern–postmodern polarity but recycles some well-known and over-generalized changes in sociocultural organization. A different way of approaching this is to suggest that in the first place, the Soviet system was not a "variant" of modernity – it was "something else." This something else was defined by the particularity of Russian history, its position within the emergent capitalist order during the eighteenth and nineteenth centuries, the configuration of post-Revolutionary political forces, and the diverse cultural resources on which they could draw for legitimation. The again diverse experiences of communist Eastern Europe reflected the consequences of establishing a Soviet system largely through military occupation and the ways in which this interacted with local social figurations. Likewise, the trajectories of postcommunist development have again reflected the combinations of these paths with the circumstances of disengagement with the system, which have been contested and resisted. Grabher and Stark (1997: 55) argue that "institutional friction preserves diversity; it sustains organizational routines that might later be recombined in new organizational forms." The lesson for sociology here is that the concepts of neither modernity nor postmodernism are adequate for postcommunism because neither do justice either to the specificity of the object or to the ways in which global processes become embedded in locales. In some cases these will lead toward organizational forms similar to Western Europe and in some cases along a "road to elsewhere." There is no temporal sequence, and part of our departure from the assumptions of classical modernity is to recognize those configurations of local and global culture, economy, and politics generate uneven and divergent social forms. The most important lesson from these debates is that linear and bifurcated stage theories are no longer viable and we need to understand the complex organization of globalized postcommunism.

6

Globalization and Convergence

I woke up with a start, sensing a change in the atmosphere around me. Glancing out the window I could see a cluster of lights glowing in the distance. After seventeen hours of continual travel we were approaching the internal German border. . . . After some delay the train moved on, passing through an area of heavy forest before emerging a few minutes later at the border itself. There I saw it in all its ugliness. A huge fluorescent snake stretching as far as the eye could see, floodlit and deadly, all the way from the Baltic Sea to Czechoslovakia, slicing Germany in half. A couple of minutes and we were through, pulling into Marienborn station, the East German half of the checkpoint. It was almost a cliché. Drab and old fashioned, the station was dimly lit and dirty. . . . Barely moments later I heard heavy footsteps in the corridor, which came crashing into the compartment. Without warning all the lights went on and a systematic search of the compartment and its passengers got underway. This was followed by more heavy footsteps, this time belonging to a guard who appeared to be carrying a portable immigration desk around his neck. It consisted of a large box . . . [from which] he analyzed passports, issued visas, and carried out other indeterminate exercises. The most disturbing thing about his appearance, however, was the machine gun that was casually slung over his shoulder . . . a reminder of what sort of country I was entering.

Cliff Docherty, *Berlin 1983*.

The Berlin Wall, constructed in August 1961, in the face of growing migration from the eastern to the western sector of Berlin, became an emblem of the Cold War and the division of Europe into opposed blocs. As well as being a physical presence and threat to life for those attempting to cross it illegally[1] the Wall entered the imagination as a focus of intrigue and espionage, epitomizing the division of territories and people by borders. Its fall in November 1989 was equally emblematic – of the end of the division of Europe and the wider collapse of communism. It had wider significance, too, for sociological theory in that the end of the Cold War was the prelude to the maturity of the concept of globalization, which then became one of the central concepts in sociology. After 1989, it was possible to imagine a "borderless" world in which people, goods, ideas, and images would flow, in the sense that *the* major border dividing East and West had gone and had collapsed dramatically. Moreover, the world after November 1989 was one of increasing speed and unpredictability, and despite other significant changes in the Soviet bloc during 1989, the fall of the Wall took most people by surprise. The "semi-free" Polish elections in July, the increasing turmoil in the USSR, and the emerging multiparty system in Hungary were evidence of the accelerating changes in communist regimes. Yet, few people at this point imagined that the whole system (in Europe and Western Asia) was on the edge of collapse. Indeed, the suddenness of the collapse was not initially welcomed by all Western leaders, and some commentators feared that the end of the Cold War would replace a stable world with one that was much more fluid and unpredictable (e.g. Kaplan 1994). The stable order that had been provided by the ritualized confrontation between the US and USSR was relatively slow-changing and predictable – it had its rules, technologies, ideas, and organizational forms. By contrast, the postcommunist order was not only less certain but was changing at an accelerating pace. In the process many certainties and boundaries of social life too were undermined. However, as new divisions and exclusions arose, the fall of the Wall turned out to shift the borders rather than to remove them.

Global Neoliberalism

One important aspect of this was the impetus given to theories of globalization by the collapse of borders separating Eastern and Western Europe. This was enhanced by the fact that the revolutions of 1989 furthered the emerging global hegemony of neoliberal thinking among Western governments, international development and financial organizations and, increasingly, policy makers in the new Europe. These were found both in the "communist" administrations, for example of Wojciech Jaruzelski (Polish Head of State 1981–9) and, in the new governments, people such as Yegor Gaidar (Russian economics minister in 1991–2) and Leszek Balcerowicz (Polish finance minister 1989–91). The move toward neoliberal policies in the postcommunist countries occurred with differing degrees of commitment in different countries. But the framework of policy was structured around the three "izations" – marketization, privatization, and liberalization – which were required by the World Bank as conditions for loan programs. In Poland the program of "shock therapy" introduced by Balcerowicz pursued reforms aimed at liberalization and deregulation, which involved freeing prices, withdrawing state subsidies from state-owned enterprises, wage controls, allowing the establishment of firms at will, and deregulating domestic and foreign trade (Say 2000). The initial effects of these reforms included an unemployment rate of 14.3 percent by 1992, increases in poverty, especially among pensioners and children (Danecki 1993), and a 17 percent decline in growth (Say 2000).[2] In addition, shock therapy reflected the growing global consensus around neoliberal thinking, which crossed the traditional political spectrum of left and right and suggested that the world was, potentially at least, converging around a shared set of socio-economic principles. Broadly speaking these were:[3]

- Economic growth required minimal state interference in the economy, which should be extensively privatized, leaving the state a "facilitative" role, especially of guaranteeing fiscal discipline (Falk 1999).
- Entrepreneurial behavior is (potentially) innate and needed freedom from the state to flourish (Seldon 1991). Comprehensive welfare systems created a culture of dependency and hampered self-reliance and enterprise, so welfare should be "rolled back."
- Free trade was essential to economic prosperity. Economies should be opened to global competition and wage and price levels allowed to reach market equilibrium.
- Health, welfare, and subsistence are individual, not collective responsibilities; therefore, people should be encouraged to plan for the future through private insurance and guaranteeing they have employable skills (this has been discussed in chapter 3, pp. 47–51).
- Neoliberal agendas were often (not always) socially conservative, as part of the ethic of individual responsibility was an emphasis on familial privatism partly aimed at strengthening the family as a unit of "welfare," thereby reducing the cost to the state.[4]
- The neoliberal prescription for former socialist societies was to introduce "shock therapy" to dismantle state institutions as quickly as possible and soon after the transfer of power to the postcommunist government. Because of the huge political and social costs of shock therapy, there was a view that this needed to be done quickly while there was widespread expectation of rapid change. This would diminish to "normal" levels as people lapsed into their former habits and expectations (Balcerowicz 1993).

After the end of communism the world appeared to be converging on a new model of competitive capitalism; socialism was discredited in both its Western, social democratic and Eastern, statist varieties. "What happened in 1989," says Giddens,

> was not just a crisis for Marxism. It was also, and continues to be, a crisis for Western socialism too. . . . If you look back to the writings of the sixties, even early seventies, among Western socialists, they mostly thought the welfare state would continue to expand. They mostly thought that Western societies were on the right track. They mostly thought that socialism could be achieved in the West, although socialism for them was reformist socialism, rather than revolutionary Marxist style socialism. (Giddens 1999a).

The contrast between Western social democracy and Soviet socialism could be elaborated into more fundamental differences than those of *method* – reform as opposed to revolution. In the postwar period Western socialist parties regarded a mixed economy of state and private sectors as desirable, and by and large supported the Western military alliance. But Giddens wants to show that the crisis of 1989 affected not only the Eastern European region but was global in both its causes and effects. Similarly, Thomas Friedman says: "The world is 10 years old. It was born when the Wall fell in 1989. . . . And technology, properly harnessed and liberally distributed, has the power to erase not just geographical borders but also human ones" (Friedman 2000: 1). This initial optimism was widely shared. Habermas, for example, wrote of 1989 offering Europe a "second chance" to realize the idea of a communicative civil society in both East and West – but this time free from "Eurocentric narcissistic self-absorption" (1994: 72). Stephen Holmes (2001) talks about the end of "the long postcommunist 'decade' " which had been the "heyday of happy globalization." This optimism was undermined by the deepening recession in the late 1990s, by the failure of many postcommunist countries to implement neoliberal policies, and especially by September 11. Even so, the fall of communism was a major impetus for theories of globalization that rapidly became a core concept in sociology after 1989.

The Globalization Debate

Globalization is difficult to define since it refers to multiple processes and trends. One comprehensive, if general, definition claims that "[g]lobalization may be thought of . . . as the widening, deepening and speeding up of worldwide interconnectedness in all aspects of contemporary social life, from the cultural to the criminal, the financial to the spiritual" (Held et al. 2000: 2). Globalization is one of the dominant, though highly contested, concepts of contemporary sociology and is fraught with ambiguities. It is unclear, for example, whether globalization is a process or outcome. It is not a unitary phenomenon but a complex overdetermined effect of multiple structures and their (often unintended) consequences. It refers to a loose agglomeration of processes, including the following disparate and incomplete list:

- the international division of labor and global or multinational production processes (Jessop 2000);
- the "weightless economy" (Quah 1996) based more on trading information than goods;[5]
- the emergence of a global culture (Robertson 1992);
- global finance and capital movements (Ohmae 1994);
- international organizations (Held et al. 1999);
- global flows of images, commodities, people as refugees, tourists, and travelers (e.g. Appadurai 1996; Urry 2000a, 2000b);
- global social movements (Keck and Sikkink 1998), global civil society, and citizenship (Urry 1998, 2000b);

- multiple and fluid identities (Maffesoli 1996; Poppi 1997);
- global risks, pandemics, and organized crime (Beck 1995).

This chapter will not attempt to address all of these, but will critically analyze the concept of globalization in relation to the postcommunist condition.

There is considerable disagreement as to the pace and significance of globalization. "A new eschatological narrative haunts the world," says Lloyd, of a "doom-laden, dystopic future or homogenized free-market utopia" in which the "Anglo-global-speaking consumer flits on an endless quest for ever greater material satisfaction" (Lloyd 2000). "Hyper-globalization" (or "radical") theses predict a "borderless world" and other utopias (or dystopias) of global homogeneity. Here globalization leads toward an end state in which the whole earth will be criss-crossed by global processes to the extent that individual places lose significance and there is a single global society. Disembedded production and consumption chains, placeless capital, homeless subjects, fluid global networks bypass and reconfigure locales. For the strong globalization thesis, all socialities are formed within a context of global flows, including resistance to globalization itself (Robertson 1992).

Critics of globalization differ in their approaches. Some argue that such processes are occurring but regard them as undesirable, perhaps representing contemporary forms of imperialism, which are open to resistance (e.g. Petras and Veltmeyer 2001). Others are skeptical that the process is occurring at all and regard the core claims of globalization theory as unfounded. For example, Hirst and Thompson (1996) argue that in the late twentieth century the economy returned to an international mode that it attained between 1870 and 1914 but which remained grounded in national and regional economic and political economic functions. Weiss (1996) argues that although there was internationalization in the later twentieth century there is little evidence of genuinely *global* integration, while the nation state remains the main institution through which economies are organized. Others regard globalization as conceptual imperialism that projects American concerns and viewpoints worldwide, thereby facilitating the very process of globalization (Bourdieu and Wacquant 1999).[6]

This chapter is an assessment of the validity and limits of some types of globalization theory – it avoids identifying with the so-called radicals or skeptics in order to address new patterns of social solidarity and inequality of mobility.[7] Aspects of this debate have become a bit tired and the meaning of globalization needs to be understood in more nuanced ways than just increasing global interconnections. Urry's (2002) attempt to develop new thinking on globalization through the metaphor of complexity will be referred to in this discussion. However, our argument is that globalization does depict profound social changes in contemporary social organization. These include the shift from industrialism to what Castells (1998) calls "informationalism" – the emergence of information rather than production-led capitalism that is flexible with networking, distant communication, and decentralization. This is bound up with unprecedented levels of spatial differentiation between core and peripheral economic activities, the retrenchment of welfare, and a postcommunist world in which systemic alternatives have become hard to imagine.

One point worth noting is that the very complexity of this process makes it senseless to attribute causality to globalization or to subsume everything under it so that whatever happens can be its result. Moreover, the complexity of globalization is such that it cannot be judged, as a whole, either beneficial or nefarious, and such perceptions will change with current events. It is further widely recognized that integration of the whole world is a prediction – and as such should be viewed cautiously. Many areas of the world are excluded from global flows, including much of the postcommunist world, most of Africa and Latin America, and the Chinese hinterland (Waltz 1999).

Giddens (1990) proposes a model of global integration on four dimensions: the nation state system, the world capitalist economy, the world military order and the international division of labor. Underlying these dimensions, he suggests, is cultural globalization, within which he includes communication technologies that exert influence through mass media. However, the four dimensions are not separate – the capitalist economy constitutes the global division of labor, and is facilitated by, but also transforms, the nation state system which is crucial to the world military order. It is not obvious that culture underlies these processes since the information and communication technologies are developed and sustained by commercial forces such as MTV, Xerox, Microsoft, etc., which are key parts of the global capitalist economy. A crucial question here is: how pervasive is this system and what are its effects?

A debate with considerable relevance to the end of communism is the question of the role and future of the nation state. World War II was followed by the establishment of institutions of international governance – the United Nations Organization, the General Agreement on Tariffs and Trade, the World Bank, the International Monetary Fund – and the creation of structures of regional integration. In the West the latter included the Common Market, the European Free Trade Area, and the North Atlantic Treaty Organization. In the East there were parallel structures such as the Warsaw Pact and the Council for Mutual Economic Assistance (Comecon).[8] However, these international institutions were premised on the national state as key actors in a period in which transnational empires (notably the British and French empires) were breaking up in the face of anticolonial nationalist movements and the number of nation states in the world was increasing. Nations were agents that made treaties, managed their economies, and pursued national interests through international bodies. The two decades or so following 1945, as many commentators note, was the heyday of economic nationalism combined with Fordist production and consumption (e.g. Brown and Lauder 2001). The Keynesian welfare state was extensively involved in social and economic management, there were often large state-owned sectors in capitalist economies, and national firms were protected by trade tariffs and exchange controls. Western Fordism was matched in the East by "Soviet Fordism" – an application (and exaggeration) of the organizational forms of capitalist Fordism, such as the synchronization of production flows, gigantic scale, and product standardization (e.g. Murray 1992; Voskamp and Wittke 1991).[9]

By the 1970s economic nationalism was being undermined by the emergence of flexible transnational production systems, trade liberalization, and oil price increases, and by the 1980s the autarky of the communist countries appeared similarly threatened. This leads some theorists to suggest that the global economy is undermining national economic systems in general. This argument suggests that the nation state is dysfunctional in a borderless world in which primary linkages are between regions and the global economy rather than through the state (e.g. Ohmae 1993). According to this view, national sovereignty is transferred upwards to interstate institutions and downwards to regions, which become increasingly autonomous and viable units. Daniel Bell has famously said that the nation state is now "too small for the big problems of life and too big for small problems" (Bell 1987), which leads to a process of subnational fragmentation. Global flows of finance, media images, risks, consumption patterns, populations, and power destabilize traditional notions of national spatial boundaries, which become increasingly "hollowed out" (Jessop 1992).[10] The extent to which these are happening, along with its possible implications, are matters of extensive debate. Two points are worth noting. First, the end of the Keynesian welfare state (KWS), loss of territorial control of flows of finance, deregulation, and privatization may not mean the end of the state as a capacity-generating agent, located in territorially based institutions. Second, the debate has been couched in terms of the conflict between the KWS and neoliberalism but this may already have become passé since both modes of state formation and economic regulation might have been transcended by global complexities.

There are those who take the alleged decline of the nation state as a basis for making wider claims about the redundancy of traditional sociological theories. Urry, for example argues that "sociological discourse has . . . been premised upon 'society' as its object of study" (2000b: 6), that with the demise of the nation state has now been surpassed. Urry acknowledges that there are various senses of "society" in different sociological perspectives but claims that these formulations neglect "how the notion of society connects to the system of nations and nation-states" (2000b: 7). Societies come to be understood as sovereign entities organizing the rights and duties of each

societal member, while the spheres of economy, politics, culture, etc., constitute territorially bounded "social structure." As an alternative, Urry suggests
that postnational and postsocietal analysis should develop metaphors of
complexity and chaos.

How far does post–Cold War globalization undermine the established
conceptual systems in sociology? It is difficult to summarize the wide-ran-
ging debate about globalization, but a useful distinction can be made between convergence and divergence theories. The former, such as Ohmae
(1994), is often influenced by neoliberalism, and suggests that economic
integration will generate an increasingly homogeneous system of market
economies, liberal democracy, free trade, and regional regulatory governance. Divergence theories, such as Urry's, emphasize the unevenness of globalization processes that create inequalities, excluded regions and groups,
along with resistance by "rebellious multitudes" (Hardt and Negri 2000).
The latter approach is the one that is presented here.

Sociology and Globalization

Global integration was anticipated in much early social theory, which is not
to deny that features of the present transformation might be qualitatively
distinct from what has gone before. Confronted by the dramatic transformation of European society in the nineteenth century, classical social theorists
focused in different ways on the dislocation of community and the disembedding of social relations in the modern world (Ray 1999c). Classical
conceptions of "society" offer multidimensional and fluid conceptions of
social relations that acknowledge the internationalization of world connections. There is not the space to do any more than allude to examples of this.
There was Saint-Simon's vision of a politically and socially integrated Europe and a system of international governance (his journal was entitled *The
Globe*) based on common practices and shared values (Ray 1999c). Likewise, Comte's concept of the future was one in which national identifications would be superseded by commitment to Humanity guided by
transnational universal values (Comte 1976: 168). Marx, of course had a
grasp of global process unrivaled by other classical theorists, to the extent
that he tended to overlook the ways in which national capitals and interests
would counteract internationalization of both capital and the revolutionary
proletariat. The historical mission of capitalism was to "demolish Chinese
walls" and bring the world within a single system of production. Hence,
"national differences and antagonism between peoples are daily more and
more vanishing, owing to the development of the bourgeoisie, to freedom of
commerce, to the world market, to uniformity in the mode of production
and in the conditions of life corresponding thereto" (Marx and Engels
1969). Weber's grasp of social development was historical and global in the

sense that he was concerned with world-shaping events – the rise of capitalism, the growth of bureaucratic organizations, rationalization as a world-historical fate, the rise of world religions. Further, his conceptual focus was on social action rather than "societies" and the ways in which action was structured through multiple configurations of economic, cultural, institutional, and value systems (Weber 1978: 4).

It is true that the organic tradition of social thought has tended to regard societies as territorially defined spaces, although here too there are subtleties. These include Durkheim's view that social integration in highly differentiated organic societies was possible only through commitment to abstract and formal principles of human rights, and his own pioneering involvement in the human rights movement pointed to the possibility of transnational forms of sociality (e.g. Durkheim 1969). Durkheim was aware that the simple and spatially contiguous settings of social integration were undermined by industrialization and increasingly abstract solidarities. For Talcott Parsons common forms of adaptation, goal attainment, integration, and latency bind societies together, although these interact collectively and separately on multiple levels. Parsons (1970: 23) defines "society" as follows. "It is not essential to the concept of society that it should not be in any way empirically interdependent with other societies, but only that it should contain all the structural and functional fundamentals of an independently subsisting system." He did not say that these systems equated to nation states, but in practice they would tend to do so.

A central theme in some accounts of globalization is that the conventional sociological notion of the social and in particular the concept of "society" as a bounded, self-functionally integrated entity is redundant. Let us be clear, though, that this is not a debate about a word, "society." The issue concerns the conceptual structure of the sociological endeavor and the nature of our explanations of social phenomena. There is a claim, made more explicit in some writers than in others, that the structural mode of explanation, in which outcomes are the effects of underlying processes, has also had its day. Instead, we deal with chaotic turbulence in which entities that were once seen as "empty" or dependent on social processes, such as things, spaces, and time become in themselves constitutive of forms of sociality. The globalized world of diverse mobilities of peoples, objects, images, information, and wastes points toward a "sociology beyond societies" (Urry 2000a). Whereas past sociology regarded society as a uniform space, the world of mobile subjects, information networks, technohybrids, imaginative and virtual travel is "post-societal." Urry even suggests that Thatcher might have been right to claim "there is no such thing as society," or at least that "the riposte to [her] from the sociological community was not fully justified" (Urry 2000a). The networked subject is an exchanger and consumer embedded in complex social relations with things in the ways indicated above.

According to this view, the exceptional challenge to classical and more recent sociology is to develop models of sociality that are fluid and complex. The post-societal agenda requires "new rules of method" (Urry 2000b: 18–19) the gist of which are that sociology has given insufficient attention to multiple hybrid mobilities of people and objects and the ways these generate novel spaces and temporalities. Sociology needs to mobilize theory and research to address these in the context of a "post-societal epoch" that will draw on concepts of chaotic systems and decentered networks rather than on structure and social order. The core concepts of the new socialities are space (social topologies), regions (interregional competition), networks (new social morphology), and fluids (global enterprises). Mobility is central to this thesis – the globalization process is constituted by the complex movement of people, images, goods, finances, etc., across regions in faster and unpredictable shapes, all with no clear point of arrival or departure (Urry 2000b: 49). We are being asked to abandon methodological nationalism and methodological territorialism and conceive of social spaces, such as cyberspace, as non-territorial and "distance-less" (Scholte 1996). These kinds of arguments imply that exchange, flows, and ephemeral movement across surfaces and fiber-optic cables now constitute the extent of the social.

This is a challenging thesis, although some of the steps in this argument may not be sustainable. Urry says that (for much sociology) "to be human has meant that one is unambiguously a member of a particular society. . . . Society involves an ordering through a nation-state, clear territorial and citizenship boundaries and a system of governance. . . . Societies involved the concept of the citizen who owed duties to and received rights from their society" (Urry 1998). The concept of society has always been wider than that of the state or citizenship, which is a juridical relation to a state, not to the abstraction of "society." Further, the premise of this argument is the much disputed demise of national societies, yet Urry does not counter claims to the contrary, to the effect that globalization is actually associated with the *rise* of the nation state (e.g. Fulcher 2000; Weiss 1998).

"Society" has meant many different things in sociological theory. It *might* imply a territorially bounded entity with an internally self-closed structure and interrelationships of subsystems, such as economy, culture, polity, and community. The concept can refer to the "property" of a specific group of people but just as easily admit the notion of social relations beyond the nation. Critiques of reified understandings of society are so well established as not to need repeating here, but this is not what really seems to be at issue. The core issues seem to be whether national boundaries remain relevant for determining global flows and whether there are coherent, underlying structural processes that might account for these patterns.

To regard flows, scapes, networks, etc., as constitutive of sociality in a broad sense risks "desocietalizing" the social. Sociology has an important role to demonstrate that what may appear to be spontaneous flows are actually embedded in constituting and constraining cultural and economic structures. Classical sociology was resistant to the idea that exchanges, such as economic life, could be abstracted from the broader framework of institutions and social relations. Thus Comte thought economics was too abstract; Durkheim wrote of the non-contractual bases of contract; Marx regarded the apparent autonomy of the market as a fetishistic illusion; Simmel regarded money as an expression of the stylization of culture. Weber shared this broad and historical view of the integration of economic and social analysis, reflecting the influential German Historical School. He described as "societalization" (*Vergesellschaftung*), the constant formation and dissolution of social relationships, in ways that presuppose conflict and cooperation. A similar theme runs through Parsons and Polanyi. So, even abstract systems and exchanges (like markets) are culturally embedded and supportive but constraining social, organizational, institutional and normative frameworks, as we saw in chapter 3.

Urry (2002) makes the important point that mobilities such as air travel require "multiple stabilities" or moorings, such as airport cities like Chicago's O'Hare. Thus there is no increase in fluidity without extensive corresponding systems of immobilities. This dialectic of mobility/moorings gives rise to complexity in the global system. This principle allows us to look at the persistent and embedded forms of sociality that underpin a mobile and fluid world. They may also, however, lead us to appreciate the impact of local and culturally specific forms of life on global processes. This can be explored in relation to the limits of globalization in the postcommunist world.

Did Globalization Cause the Fall of Communism?

There is a widely held view that the end of communism was caused by the very process of globalization to which it helped give rise. One version of this thesis is that changes in global economy and society placed ultimately irresistible pressure on the system to change. The Soviet system described by Chirot (1991: 5) as the "most advanced nineteenth century economy in the world" had epitomized the dominance of society and economy by industrial production. By the 1980s the capitalist world had undergone the post-Fordist transformation to a system of "informationalism" in which the dominance of industry is replaced by that of information. Soviet systems were terminally weak in the areas of most importance to globalization – high-technology communications and information, openness of economies, risk taking, and flexible labor markets (McCann 2004). Detailed accounts of the emerging crisis in state socialism (e.g. Castells 1998: 4–69) point out that the system was increasingly unable to manage an overextended military–industrial complex. It could no longer cope with the irrationalities of the

Plan, which was locked into the old industrial base while the political-bureaucratic control of information blocked innovation and prevented the successful deployment of IT (see also Shane 1995). This was not a purely economic and administrative crisis but also a crisis of legitimation and motivation in which there was a profound loss of confidence among the political elite in their ability to govern (Ray 1996). Lockwood (2000) similarly argues that the emergence of a global division of labor during the 1980s weakened the state as an economic actor, while the more involved it was in economic development (as in Soviet societies) the more dramatic were the effects of globalization (Lockwood 2000: 47). The Soviet growth model had pursued the autarkic development of heavy industry, but attempts to introduce new imported technologies in the 1970s had opened the system up to global pressures and increased dependence on the West (Lockwood 2000: 78). This was particularly acute in countries with high levels of debt to Western lenders, particularly Hungary and Poland (Zloch-Christy 1987; Ray 1966).[11]

These arguments are consistent with sociological theories of crisis and political change, and focus on the dynamic interaction of crisis tendencies from within these systems and exogenous pressures, such as rising indebtedness and dependence on global trade. But the role of external pressures should not be exaggerated. Urry (2000b: 41–2), Waters (1995), and Bauman (1992) emphasize the growth of mobilities and consumer cultures in Eastern Europe in the formation of crisis, as the frustration experienced by unsatisfied demand provoked mass disaffection. Gradually, fluid-like movements transgressed the regional frontiers of each state socialist society. The Berlin Wall had been the most dramatic example of an attempt to insulate "society"; thus its fall showed the bankruptcy of the model of autarkic productivism. Waters (1995: 139) similarly describes the collapse of communism as "a mass assertion of the right to privatized consumption."

Along with the lure of Western consumption styles there is the argument that global television both allowed the mass transmission of an alternative culture to Eastern Europe and accelerated the process of collapse itself. The consequence of being able to watch worldwide the mass demonstrations in one East European city created a kind of "domino effect" in which events were swiftly emulated elsewhere – after Warsaw, Budapest, then Leipzig, Berlin, Prague, Bucharest, Sofia, and so on. Time and space were thus compressed as imagery and methods were transmitted from one city to another. As news of the breach of the Berlin wall spread, people from all over Germany and neighboring countries drove to watch and participate in the making of "history." Giddens, who was present at the fall of the Wall says this:

> People were putting these ladders up against the wall and we all started to try to climb up [them]. But we were actually stopped by the TV crews . . . [who] said, "please don't climb these ladders until we get up first, and we'll film you

coming up to make history." . . . And interestingly enough, they even took more than one shoot. Some people had to climb up twice while they were being filmed, so they got good footage. I don't think you would have had the East European revolutions, the 1989 revolutions, without the influence of globalization of television as a kind of dialogic communication. (Giddens 1999b)

This is a good story that tells us something about the management of "news" and the making of "history," but the conclusion does not follow, any more than the fall of communism can simply be explained in terms of the lure of Western consumerism. The transmission of Western news and lifestyles via satellite communications was probably an additional factor undermining the legitimacy of the ruling parties in the 1980s, especially in Central European countries (Czechoslovakia, DDR, Poland, Hungary, and Estonia). But we should not underestimate the extent to which even in the later 1980s the region as a whole and especially the Soviet Union remained isolated from the rest of the world and preoccupied with largely internal issues. These included political reform and its consequences, economic liberalization, shortages, planning failures, rising inflation, corruption, and the general frustrations of everyday life. The gradual and cumulative process whereby these systems went into crisis had complex origins. There were long-term systemic problems such as the imbalance between capital goods production and the availability of consumer goods, the irrationalities and failures of the planning process, authoritarianism, and fossilization of the system that had no effective learning mechanisms. The inappropriateness of industrial technologies to the needs of a rapidly changing economy had been internally acknowledged by reformist economists from the 1960s (see, for example, Aganbegyan 1988). The global pressure from the arms race was certainly an exacerbating factor, since the burden of defense spending was made worse by the low productivity of capital (Easterly and Fischer 1994). The problem, however, lay in the inability of the system to create the conditions for implementation of new technologies, which would have required decentralization, breaking down bureaucratic constraints, allowing local and private initiatives, and, crucially, relaxing the control of the Party over everyday life.

These problems interacted with crises of social integration, where the ruling ideology was widely held in contempt and cynicism was widespread. The official mechanisms of integration – employment, welfare, mass organizations, and privileges – were increasingly supplanted (especially in Central Europe) by informal networks, unofficial and semi-legal economic activity, and everyday coping strategies. Reform programs such as perestroika and glasnost that were intended to release new energies and overcome stagnation while reinvigorating the socialist project had hugely unintended consequences. Gorbachev's memoirs, for example, detail the disintegration of the reform process as economic, political, and social forces spiral out of control in 1989–91 (Gorbachev 1997). When the crisis became acute in the second half of 1989, this was often as a result of internal events and revelations undermining the legitimacy of communist rulers. For example, prior to his rehabilitation and reburial in June 1989, the Hungarian government released tapes from the secret trial of Imre Nagy, the (communist) leader of the anti-Soviet revolutionary government in 1956, who was executed in 1958. This rehabilitation, intended to add legitimacy to the reformist Hungarian Socialist Workers Party government (by claiming to be Nagy's heirs), had the reverse effect of delegitimating a system that had been premised on suppression of the truth of 1956 and its brutal aftermath.

Global integration through trade, debt, and televisual communications exacerbated the effects of long-term systemic and social problems, but they were not the primary causes of the collapse. In fact, even at the end of the 1980s the Soviet Union was still relatively disconnected from global processes, other than the arms race which, it is true, had significant impact on the thinking of those seeking détente with the West. The Americans played to Soviet anxiety about the relative weakness of their military technology when announcing the Strategic Defence Initiative (SDI) in the 1980s.[12] In terms of international trade, however, "the Soviet Union was less dependent on trade than would be expected for a market economy of equivalent size and development" (Smith 1993: 163). Between 1985 and 1989 debt to Western financial institutions grew from $10.2 billion to $37.3 billion, and although modest by international standards the consequences were exacerbated by a rising balance of payments deficit (around $5.1 billlion in 1990) and growing loss of Western bank confidence in the Soviet Union's ability to service its debts (Smith 1993: 161). Underlying this was a structural problem that the reforms of the 1980s had attempted to address, namely that the centrally planned system was incapable of generating domestic innovation or the volume of exports required to sustain the required level of imports of technology (Smith 1993: 176). This remained a problem for the Russian economy through the 1990s. In other words, increasing pressure from the global system was *part* of the reason for perestroika, as it is for postcommunist economic strategies, but does not in itself explain why the system spiraled into crisis and collapse.

Further, the fall of communism and its differential national patterns illustrated the importance of local and regional forms of social solidarity and traditions. The fall of the Berlin Wall and the rapid reunification of Germany within a reconstituted nation state attested to the strength of national solidarity and identity rather than its demise. Again, only in Poland was there sustained mass opposition to the communist system. Polish Solidarity, which was crucial in the delegitimation of the Soviet system, was a Catholic syndicalist workers' movement in alliance with dissident (often Jewish) intellectuals. This uneasy coalition is understandable in the context of Polish syndicalist and Bundist history in the nineteenth and twentieth centuries. Solidarity was deeply suspicious of, if not hostile to, the capitalist system and Western values. The legacy of this was apparent, despite considerable erosion since the 1990s, in a considerably higher number of enterprises organized by worker-management collectives than in any capitalist society (EBRD 1995). It is difficult to explain this, and the particular trajectory of postcommunist development in Poland, without reference to "Polish society" – its culture, collective identity, and history. Similarly, in the former Soviet Union there was little opening to Western flows of goods, capital, and culture prior to 1991 and the system collapsed largely as a result of unintended consequences of reforms, the intention of which had been to stabilize the regime. This can again be understood only with reference to Russian society and history. That the collapse of communism was global in its effects (which are highly variegated) does not mean it was caused by globalization or fluid mobilities. Without understanding the embedding and "placing" of these processes, we will not grasp the nature of contemporary social change.

However, we do not wish to substitute one partial theory (that globalization caused the end of communism) with an equally one-sided claim that globalization had nothing to do with it. Integration into the global (Western) system through telecommunications, and economic and military competition exacerbated multiple internal dysfunctions within the Soviet systems. It is also true that the collapse of communism was global in its *consequences* (this is discussed below). However, we should not conclude from this that globalization is creating a homogeneous world. On the contrary, the prime effect of globalization has been to constitute uneven modes of integration and distance from global networks. This will be illustrated further by examining the nature of postcommunism.

Fluids and Solids: Markets and Embedded Capital

There is an assumption in some globalization literature that technological changes drive, and indeed meld with patterns of social interaction. Urry suggests, for example, that interaction with machines, especially networked computers, creates cyborgs (techno–human hybrids) opening up new dimensions of agency (Urry 1999). People leave traces of themselves in informational space and can be mobile through space – they can "do" things without being present. We could note, though, that the externalization of persons through labor and technology is essential to human self-reproduction and is not specific to the age of the Internet. Moreover, we need to ask how complex social and object relations become inscribed into process of social and cultural reproduction in such a way that social life is possible. Giddens might be right that if one instantaneously communicates with someone across the world sociality has been "stretched," but this mode of communication *facilitates* and does not constitute the interaction. The mode will structure what is possible, depending on its speed, ease of use, specifications, and so on, and social conventions might influence its content. Emails and, even more, text messages tend to be brief or even curt and avoid conventions of spelling, grammar, etc. The underlying processes and social bonds are a more significant topic for analysis than modes of communication, which is being acknowledged in management and organization literature. Zack and Mckenney (1995), for example, argue that "communication is a social process. . . . Therefore, . . . we must understand how existing structures and social contexts influence patterns of organizational communication." It is the shared social solidarities among the communicators that will sustain the interactions; solidarities that are in turn embedded in contexts of institutional power and organization.

In chapter 3 we examined how it is it that, despite inequalities, actual and potential conflicts, rationality crises, and all the other threats to social integration, most societies remain cohesive most of the time, persist, and are able to reproduce themselves. The experience of Eastern Europe bears strongly on this question. During the communist period, informal networks were crucial to strategies to circumvent, subvert, and above all channel goods and services where the official systems were failing, inefficient, or mistrusted. At the same time these informal networks of labor exchange, non-monetary reciprocation, illegal dealing, moonlighting, and clientelism were symbiotic in complex ways with the official systems in which people also generally participated (Ray 1996). This "second economy" was often described as a new means of social integration, creating a "parallel society" through self-provisioning mutual reciprocity (Dallago 1990; Sik 1998). This second society displayed qualities of trust, reciprocity, and need satisfaction – the bases of social solidarity – as opposed to the cynicism, apathy, and shortages in official society (Bugajski and Pollack 1989: 187). These culturally embedded forms have had a huge impact on the forms of market organization that could emerge in postcommunism.

This suggests that we need to understand globalization in terms of a dialectic of the global and the local, that some writers, notably Giddens and Robertson, have termed "glocalization."[13] The consequence of this (like Urry's "mobility/moorings") is that the effects of globalization are uneven and heterogeneous across the world. The mobility of capital, for example, presupposes the relative immobility of labor in order for capital to flow and3 relocate to areas of comparative advantage. Globalization theories have been criticized as being Americo-or Eurocentric (Bourdieu and Wacquant 1999), but things are more complex than this. Take, for example, the notion of the market (see table 6.1 on p. 135). On the one hand, there is the market of neoliberal textbooks and policy discourse. These markets are characterized by fluidity, rapid entry and exit, and high impersonal trust, as smart capital flows seamlessly across borders driven by global consumption and regional advantages. This is a spontaneous order of auction market prices, high risk, and rapid entry and exit dependent on institutionalized and impersonal trust. These are the kinds of markets analyzed by advocates of globalization convergence as deterritorialized, transparent, flexible – governed by an "electronic herd" moving vast amounts of capital almost instantaneously (Friedman 2000: 375). On the other hand, there are markets that bear greater resemblance to postcommunist arrangements, are highly networked, clientelistic, localized, and stable. Impersonal trust will generally be low and trust will be dependent on face-to-face contacts and connections (see Ray 1996: 179–84, for a more detailed analysis). Both of these are exaggerations, of course, but unless one understands the complex solidaristic ties and processes that enable the daily world to occur, one will have great difficulty understanding how social life happens at all in many parts of the world. This is precisely the difficulty with convergence theories of globalization that assume that transnational and delocalized networks are "weightless fluids." Further, these bonds constitute and are constituted by inequalities and exclusions in ways discussed below.

Postcommunist Economies

The fall of communism in Europe and Western Asia was heralded by many Western social scientists as further evidence of a global economic and cultural convergence. However, in the core of the former Soviet system (Russia and its "near abroad") it is likely that global economic integration will be slow and the central state apparatus will attempt to regulate the terms on which commodities circulate with the West. Leo McCann (2004) demonstrates that the effects of economic globalization on Tatarstan have been very limited, while the old economy and social networks substantially remain in place, albeit in some state of decay. If it continues, this process of differentiation will create new economic and political blocs with internally differentiated regimes of regulation and organization. There is not yet, nor is there any immediate prospect of, a homogeneous global order, since particular states will pursue strategies of locational advantage with reference to their historically accumulated modes of sociocultural learning and resources of legitimation. This section will show how the combination of globalization and cultural differentiation facilitates new understanding of the interaction between global and local settings.

The cultivation of informal networks "makes sense" since it could act as a defense against global economic penetration. To understand how this might arise we need to note that the transition to capitalism in postcommunist countries encountered problems that are without historical precedent. In particular, there was an attempt to convert outdated and authoritarian industrial societies into democracies able to compete economically with postindustrial societies. The various solutions found to these problems render expectations of "reconvergence" inappropriate, especially in view of increasing diversity within the postcommunist region itself. These problems include:

- the historical pattern of industrial concentration in large plants, with whole regions dependent on a single enterprise for employment and welfare;
- a dearth of domestic capital or savings and highly selective foreign buyers, mainly interested in hiving off those parts of industries with growth potential;
- an obsolete industrial structure, which in Russia was heavily geared to military production, supported by powerful political blocs in the State Duma and Senate;
- the consequent political choice between asset liquidation, mass unemployment and social destabilization on the one hand, and continued subsidy and protection of state enterprises on the other;
- a diminishing revenue base which leaves few domestic resources to tackle problems of environmental destruction and crumbling infrastructure, which in turn impede economic internationalization.

This is not to say that these problems were and are insoluble, but that "solutions," understood as relatively durable if contested social arrangements, will differ from those in the West. Postcommunist societies have by and large not yet become extensively integrated into global circuits of capital, and levels of direct foreign investment have generally been lower than many expected in the early 1990s. Between 1990 and 1993 foreign direct investment (FDI) increased ten times globally, but China and Mexico received more than the postcommunist bloc as a whole. Some postcommunist countries were more successful at breaking the cycle than others, especially those in Central Europe – the Czech Republic, Hungary, and Slovakia received two-thirds of the postcommunist FDI total, but the rest, with 91 percent of the population, received only 32 percent of inflows (EBRD 2000).[14] For example, the level of FDI in postcommunism has been considerably lower than many expected a decade ago. Between 1990 and 1995 Central and Eastern Europe and the Former Soviet Union (FSU) received 15 percent of total capital flows to developing economies and there was a differential pattern of investment, with Hungary receiving the largest per capita share, Poland 22 percent, the Czech Republic 16 percent, Bulgaria 2 percent and the FSU negligible. Cumulative FDI in the Russian Federation had reached only $20 billion by 2000 (McCann 2004) and only $100 million was exchanged per day on the stock market in 1997 (Gustafson 1999: 75).[15] In determining the direction of investment flows simple factors such as low-cost labor and natural resources are less important to competitive

Table 6.1 *Idealized and embedded markets*

Idealized global markets	Embedded local markets
"Fluids"	"Solids"
Weightless	Heavy
Finance/service-driven	Sunken capital and high exit costs
Auction market prices	Customer market prices
Spontaneous order	Visible construction of relationships
High risk	Personal networks and obligations reduce risk
Abstract rules	Situationally specific rules
Institutionalized (systemic) trust	Low impersonal trust and high informal regulation
Expansion of credit	Credit limited and tied to obligations

advantage than skilled scientific and technical personnel and advanced infrastructure. The crux of the issue is that flows and mobilities of capital and labor reflect the embeddedness of capital in localities in the global economy while national boundaries remain relevant to its decision making and global organization (Yeung 1998). Thus the effects of globalization are embedded in particular locations within national territories.

Capital flows globally in fast and sophisticated ways. However, as Jessop (2000) argues, it flows into concrete moments where it is materialized in specific types of spatiotemporal locations, which "justifies the analysis of comparative capitalisms and of their embedding in specific institutional and spatio-temporal complexes" (Jessop 2000). Capital remains dependent on fixed, place-bound ensembles and configurations of technology, means of production, industrial organization, and labor process combined. Post-Fordist economic restructuring in Western societies has created new dynamics of inclusion and exclusion. These arise in part from Veltz's (1996: 12) paradox: that capital depends upon increasing interdependence between the economic and extra-economic factors making for structural competitiveness. This generates new contradictions that affect the spatial and temporal organization of accumulation. Temporally, there is a contradiction between short-term economic calculation (especially in financial flows) and the long-term dynamic of "real competition" rooted in resources such as skills, trust, collective mastery of techniques, economies of agglomeration, and size. The latter take years to create, stabilize, and reproduce. Spatially there is a contradiction between the economy considered as a pure space of flows and the economy as a territorially and socially embedded system of extra-economic as well as economic resources and competencies (Jessop 2000).

The EBRD *Transition Report* in 1999, one decade after the fall of communism, conceded that "talk of graduating from the transition in the mid-90s was premature. It is now clear that the institutional and behavioural underpinnings of the transition are weak, which creates difficult long-term challenges." Postcommunist societies, it argues, lack social capital, voluntary compliance with laws, trust, cooperative behavior, and basic codes of conduct. It refers to bureaucratic interference, undermining of the judiciary, corruption, dubious business practices, and poor governance. At the same time, as we have seen (pp. 80–5), a culture of informality and illegality creates conditions for Mafia-type organizations that feed on generalized lack of trust and consequentially high demand for protection following the break-up of state ownership of the economy. Inequalities have risen since the beginning of the transition. According to the World Bank (2002) the countries of Europe and Central Asia started the transition with some of the lowest levels of inequality in the world, but since then, inequality has increased steadily in all transition economies and dramatically in some of them. Countries such as Armenia, the Kyrgyz Republic, Moldova, and Russia are now among the most unequal in the world, with Gini coefficients (a standard measure of inequality) nearly twice their pre-transition levels. In Russia the Gini coefficient has risen from 0.28 (1989–90) to 0.48 (1995–7) (for a definition of the Gini coefficient see p. 205, n.8).

Customer market prices involve tight social relationships between buyers and sellers that influence prices, in which customers avoid shopping costs by sticking with a single supplier. Since 1992 there has been an increase in barter in the Russian economy, which has been estimated to account for around 50 percent of trade. In this virtual economy no one pays in money, no one executes settlements in reasonable time, mutual debts are formed, which remain unpaid, and wages are declared but not paid (Tomson 1999). In this economy of networks, obligations, and knowledge built on informal contacts and mutual complicity, people from the former Communist Party enjoy extensive cultural capital. The state has acted as rule maker and party to asset transfers, usually without clear laws of governance, and much private enterprise remains, as in the past, dependent on favors, patronage, and influence from state officials. Ganev (2001) argues that the former state sector is the same resource base from which postcommunist politicians and non-state actors derive revenue. There is therefore competition between governments and non-state agents for access to resources through the privatization process. He concludes that this explains one of the "puzzling and troubling developments in the ex-Soviet world: the 'weakening of the state' " (Ganev 2001). Many analysts see corruption as a cause of poor economic performance, but this is also a way of protecting local enterprises against global competition. Corruption ensures that market entry is dependent on local knowledge – one has to know who to bribe, how and when to give a bribe, and be part of the relevant networks of influence. Thus local enterprises may go to considerable lengths to preserve their position (Krastev 1998). Readers may wish to recap on the example of Bulgaria (pp. 80–5, *passim*), which is an example of these processes.

The Postcommunist World: Bi, Multi, or Mono?

So far we have stressed how globalization is instantiated in different ways in different places, creating divergence and difference within the global system. This section will examine this process with reference to global polarization and conflicts. The Cold War world was a bipolar one divided territorially into two blocs plus the non-aligned countries (mostly in the "Third World") left as a ground of contestation and proxy wars. The Cold War was dominated by technologies of weight and size – the numbers and force of nuclear weapons, industrial competition measured in volume output and productive capacity, transportation costs, and the space race. The postcommunist condition, by contrast, is governed by speed – of commerce, travel, communication, and the microchip, which doubles in power every eighteen to twenty-four months. These information technologies facilitate the postindustrial economy and the mode of "informationalism" (Castells 1998). The Cold War was a system with implicit rules of engagement – the division of the world into spheres of influence and the formation of territorial blocs. Confrontation between states, especially the superpowers, took place through the arms race and the principle of mutually assured destruction (MAD) that also created a common interest in reaching détente through treaties and summit meetings. With postcommunism the rules are those dictating that global free trade maximizes prosperity and growth, along with privatization and the opening of borders to the global economy. The Deal, as Friedman (2000: 146) comments, is more significant than the Treaty in structuring global integration. But what kinds of global fractures are now emerging, especially in view of the "war on terrorism" and claims that conflicts between "the West" and "Islam" point toward a new, postcommunist bipolarity? How do these questions relate to debates about globalization?

The first thing we should note is that globalized postcommunism is a world of increasing diversity and inequality. Convergence theories of globalization claimed that "[t]he end of the Cold War and the collapse of communism discredited all models other than liberal democracy" (Friedman 2000: 145). But the postcommunist condition is actually one of increasing divergence and conflict in which the uneven moorings of global processes in different locales will undermine such linear predictions. For example, there is growing divergence between developed and less developed countries and growth in trade within the developed world largely excluded the postcommunist countries. Indeed Boyer (1996: 35) argues that "technological change is endogenous, that is, the equilibrium growth path depends on past efforts in research and development, education, and product differentiation. Thus rates of productivity growth are likely to vary from one country to another, without unilinear global convergence." There is no compelling evidence of across-the-board convergence, and national governments have considerable latitude in macro-economic policy making (Garrett 2000). Despite the crisis of socialisms in East and West, available statistical evidence does not conform to any general trend toward economic convergence in productivity levels and standards of living (Boyer 1996). National boundaries demarcate the nationally specific systems of education, finance, corporate management, government, and social conventions (norms, laws, innovation, and entrepreneurship). Where global economic and social integration occurs it is dependent on political processes (Boyer 1996) and therefore on the internal configurations of particular countries. The World Bank (2002: 11–13) argues that characteristics of postcommunist countries at the start of transition affected their economic performance and can be aggregated into structure, distortions, and institutions. *Structure* refers to things like the share of industry, degree of urbanization, share of trade with the socialist bloc, the richness of natural resources, and initial income. *Distortions* refers to factors like hidden inflation, black market exchange rates, terms of trade within the Council for Mutual Economic Assistance (CMEA) (which affected the impact of its collapse), the extent of reforms already undertaken and the pretransition growth rate. *Institutions* refers to variables such as experience of markets ("market memory"), location in relation to Western markets, and previous experience as an independent state. Although policy choices in the transition period will have an impact on these factors, the report acknowledges that these will themselves be formed under endogenous influences such as the possibility of consensus, the nature of the political system, and the pattern of previous policy decisions. In general these factors favored the Central European and Baltic States while the former Soviet Union and Balkan States have fared less well on most socio-economic indicators, thereby giving rise to increased diversity within the postcommunist region.

In this world of increasing difference there is a bifurcation between the *relatively* safe zones within the West, and the "wild zones" of failed states, barely functioning economies, criminality, trafficking of people and illicit goods, and civil wars. The postcommunist countries are poised between the two zones. Central European countries (Poland, Hungary, Czech Republic, Baltic States, Slovakia, and Slovenia) joined the EU in 2004 and two further countries (Bulgaria and Romania) hope for accession in 2007. But the rest of the postcommunist world (containing nearly 90 percent of its population) is unlikely to gain entry into global networks or imperial sovereignties in the foreseeable future. However, it is worth keeping in mind that the example of Multigroup in Bulgaria (see chapter 4) illustrated how there are multiple modes of integration into the world system. One should not then regard "wild zones" of illegal materials, drugs, trafficking of people, and organized crime simply as the "other" of global capitalism. They are also its underside – a stage of primitive accumulation and positioning within the global order that to some extent, as in the case of trafficking of people, presupposes the existence of global networks that link together "wild" and "safe" zones. Difference and inequality then are concomitant with the intensification of globalization.

More generally there has been a reconfiguration of global power and organization since the end of the Cold War. Is this evidence for a quickening and deepening of globalization, understood as the widening, deepening, and speeding up of worldwide interconnectedness in all aspects of contemporary social life? In some ways, yes. The fall of the Wall increased mobility of people, objects, and images across the planet but did so in ways that demonstrates the persistence of other kinds of barriers. The relationship between globalization and migration, for example, is complex since deregulation in one area does not automatically imply loosening of restrictions in another. Various kinds of forced migration has resulted in at least 140 million migrants and refugees worldwide, and this differential arose *along with* the process of globalization in the twentieth century, which has been increasingly uneven with differential abilities to stretch, compress, and shape capital and resistance. Contrary to claims that the significance of borders is eroding, some states are working to endow them with meaning in innovative ways and immigration policy is crucial to the maintenance of the national community (Goff 2000). Flows of global movement are proliferating while the fortification of national boundaries is becoming more vigilant – a trend intensified since September 11, 2001, and by the rise of anti-migrant politics in Europe. Capital increasingly defines labor costs in terms of lowest global costs and through subcontracting in home and overseas markets is able to achieve lowest costs in some sectors, such as textiles. Low-cost and often forced labor migrations are crucial facets of global mobilities (Papastergiadis 2000: 40). The presence of undocumented workers (especially from postcommunist countries) in advanced capitalist economies has the effect of reducing costs in sectors that are structurally dependent upon them, such as textiles, minicabs, cleaners, food service, and agriculture (Rivera-Batiz 1999). Migration and ethnic divisions epitomize the differential way in which global elements are localized, labor markets are constituted, and culture de-and reterritorialized (Sassen 1998). There are indeed decentered, flexible, and knowledge-rich networks continually restructuring themselves according to the signals of a fast, fluid nexus of global scapes and flows. But borderlands are taking on increased significance as resources and means of exploitation since human beings have considerably less freedom to move across international borders than does capital (Donnan and Wilson 1999). Every state is seeking to maximize investment opportunities for transnational corporations while closing its doors to the forms of migration that these economic shifts stimulate (Papastergiadis 2000: 2–3). The 1998 Schengen Agreement institutes extensive systems of control on and surveillance of migration into the EU from further east, especially the former Soviet Union and the Middle East. These controls include expansion of the Eurodac computerized fingerprint database to refugees and asylum seekers, harmonization of sanctions on carriers of illegal migrants, and a raft of policing measures and requirements for controls on external borders.

It is in this context that we should look at the issue of international conflict, which raises questions about new forms of global polarization. It is fairly clear that the old pattern of territorially based blocs in actual or potential conflict has gone, at least for the present. Giddens says: "although this is a contentious point I would say that following the dissolving of the Cold War most nations no longer have enemies. Who are the enemies of Britain, or France, or Brazil? The war in Kosovo didn't pit nation against nation. It was a conflict between old-style territorial nationalism and a new, ethically driven interventionism. Nations today face risks and dangers rather than enemies, a massive shift in their very nature" (Giddens 2001). Of course, this does not mean that military conflict has diminished in the postcommunist world but that its fractures fall less clearly along the borders of nation states. Indeed, Shannon (2002) suggests that a world dominated by non-state entities may be a more historically relevant condition of global power relations as we enter a "post-Westphalian" age in which familiar distinctions between soldier, civilian, and state break down.

However, there have recently, and especially since September 11 and the "war on terrorism," been suggestions that the world has already entered a new bipolar phase in which "the West" confronts "Islam" as two opposed blocs. One of the best-known advocates of this view is Samuel Huntington (1999) whose "clash of civilizations" thesis reflects thinking among the neoconservative group of Republicans close to President Bush.[16] Huntington's thesis is that the fundamental source of global conflict after the end of the Cold War will be cultural and between "civilizations." This is because the end of the Cold War released cultural and civilizational forces that had been developing in non-Western societies for centuries (1999: 39). The basis of these conflicts appears to be primal: "Civilizations are the ultimate human tribes, and the clash of civilizations is tribal conflict on a global scale. In the emerging world, states and groups from two different civilizations may form limited, ad hoc, tactical . . . coalitions to advance their interests against entities from a third civilization. . . . Relations between groups from different civilizations however will almost never be close, usually cool and often hostile" (1999: 207). There will be various phases in these relations – cold war, trade war, quasi-war, uneasy peace, troubled relations, intense rivalry, coexistence, and arms races – but "trust and friendship will be rare" (1999: 207). He initially sets out a multipolar model of potential conflict between several civilizations – "Western," Latin American, African, Islamic, Sinic, Hindu, Orthodox, Buddhist, and Japanese – but it is the potential conflict between Islam and the West that has occupied most attention. Indeed, Huntington says himself: "some Westerners . . . have argued that the West does not have problems with Islam but only with violent extremists. Fourteen hundred years of history demonstrate otherwise," and this conflict will make that between democracy and Marxism-Leninism appear "superficial and fleeting" (1999: 209). Thus his thesis focuses on a new, apparently bipolar conflict in which the language and matériel of the Cold War can be redeployed.[17]

While not wishing to ignore the significance of this thinking for the imaginary play of world politics (see below), the suggestion that the Cold War has already been replaced by a new bipolarity is mistaken. The "clash" thesis assumes the existence of timeless and intractable historical conflicts, but the post–Cold War world is one in which collective identities can be radically altered and in which "memories" are elastic and changing. There are serious problems with the personification of enormous entities of the "West" and "Islam" in a way that overlooks the internal dynamics and plurality of both (Said 2001). Islamist movements struggle for hegemony *within* Islamic societies as much as with the "West" and are the focus of bitter conflicts with local states. A less bipolar focus would make connections between the violent activities of Islamist groups and various kinds of religious and political violence elsewhere, such as the Branch Davidians, Japanese Aum Shinrikyo, the Oklahoma bombers, neo-Nazis and the Ku Klux Klan and fundamentalist Christians who bomb abortion clinics. The appearance of such hate groups with access to resources and the capacity to commit mass murder is a global phenomenon but does not support a bipolar view of the world. Further, the polarity of the West and Islam activates what Said and others have described as deep antipathies toward Islam in the Western imagination, which ignore the extent to which Islam was *within* the west from the start – there is a long history of cultural exchange, and the Renaissance drew on Arab humanism, science, philosophy, and historiography (Said 2001). In addition, there patently is no bipolarity comparable to the Cold War and there will not be, unless Al-Qaeda come to power in (say) Saudi Arabia and half a dozen other major states.

Hardt and Negri (2000) argue that "empire" or "imperial sovereignty" is replacing nation states – the emergence of dynamic and flexible systemic structures articulated horizontally across the globe. This new form of sovereignty is deterritorialized and decentered. Empire, however, generates its opposite – rebellious multitudes, the other of empire – "the resistances, struggles and desires of the multitude" (Hardt and Negri 2000: xvi, 398). Similarly, Johnson (2000) argues that violence that appears to arise from outside the West – from "terrorists" or "rogue states" – "often turn[s] out to be a blowback from earlier American operations," such as support for the Afghan mujahedeen (2000: 8). This may not be a very nuanced explanation of why and how opposition arises within the global system, but it does capture the sense of the postcommunist world as experiencing conflicts based on the unintended consequences of actions on a global scale. An antisystemic challenge to the global American "empire" comes from Islamist movements that occupy postcommunist space and mobilize energies of fanatical devotion and unquestioning loyalty, and a Jacobin ethic of violence purging the old society to usher in a new purified utopia (Ray 1999b). Multiple identities and movements have replaced the ideological divide between capitalism and communism, along with the formation of transnational identity politics, antiglobalization protest movements, and ecology movements.

Indeed, in Ray (1993: 128–50, 1999b) one of us argues that, contrary to the claim that there is a conflict between politicized Islam and modernity, the Islamist revolutionary movement in Iran was cast in the mode of a modernist, Jacobin-style movement centered around a state project of modernization and rationalization. There was then no essential conflict between Islamist movements and cultural modernity; rather a process of cultural interpenetration and hybridity between various strands of global ideology and organization. Ray (1999b) further predicted that as an authoritarian etatist project, the Iranian Revolution would begin to decompose in much the way that the state socialist regimes had done. This process is still slowly working itself through the conflicts between Iranian supporters of the reformist President Mohammad Khatami and the "traditionalist" chief of state, Ayatollah Ali Hoseini-Khamenei. However, the focus of the global Islamist movements has shifted from the Iranian statist project to the postnational, post-territorially organized Al-Qaeda.

Huntington's thesis, though, is rooted within the Cold War mapping of the world into territorial and strategic divisions in which there are mutual game plans and wars of position and attrition. However, the nature of post–Cold War terrorism is different from early forms and more consistent with the notion of post-territorial global processes (Hudson 1999).[18] This is so in at least six senses, following analysis by Bergesen (2003). First, there has been an organizational shift to international networks that form loosely coupled organizations (Al-Qaeda, after all, is "the network") rather than professionally trained and hierarchical organizations. Second, contemporary groups less often explicitly claim responsibility for violent acts where in the past these would have been occasions for issuing a political statement. Third, demands are often vague and hazy – not only did Al-Qaeda not explicitly claim responsibility for September 11, but this atrocity was not accompanied by any set of demands. Groups engaging in political violence in the past pursued specific objectives such as removal of British rule in Northern Ireland for the IRA, or ethnic–national separatism, such as with Basque political violence. Fourth, there has been a shift from largely political to religious motives – among Islamist groups, Christian fundamentalists, and Aum Shinrikyo. Fifth, there has been a global dispersion of targets and victims beyond the immediate site of grievance. Targets may have global symbolic significance, as with the World Trade Center, or local significance as with the Jewish social center in Casablanca, bombed in May 2003. Finally, the violence is more indiscriminate and makes no distinction between combatants and civilians, and often specifically targets the latter. It does not suggest a replaying of conflicts between territorially based blocs. We might add to these the increasing importance of symbolic targets. The Japanese attack on Pearl Harbor, with which September 11 was initially compared, had a strategic, pre-emptive purpose of devastating the American navy. But September 11 had little strategic purpose in this sense; it was an attack on symbols of American (and Western) global power (the Pentagon) and finance (the Twin Towers). Overall, then, in the postcommunist era globalization facilitates global–local networks that are bound together by identity and digital communications rather than closely linked and spatially fixed solidarities. The era of territorial bipolarity has given way to one of multiple, often non-state forms of violent conflict in which the politics of the spectacle may be more significant than clearly defined strategic objectives.

Nonetheless, the idea that there is a new postcommunist global bipolarity between the West and Islam is significant for the social imaginary[19] of international relations that has increasingly informed US policy since September 11. Indeed, although Huntington's thesis was superficial and implausible, there is a risk that it will become a self-fulfilling prophecy since it (or a version of it) is believed by Washington and is fed by the dual fantasy ideologies of al-Qaeda and Washington, for both of whom the world is viewed in terms of Manichean divisions between irreconcilable Good and Evil. Belief in the particularities of the "Arab mind," asserted for example in Patai's (1976) influential book, entered US strategic thinking, which is illustrated by De Atkine's (1999) linking of Huntington's thesis with US global strategic considerations. Moreover, the use of sexual humiliation in the torture of Iraqi prisoners in 2003–4 was apparently rooted in the belief, derived from Patai (1976: 216), that "Arabs only understand force and . . . the biggest weakness of Arabs is shame and humiliation," especially around sexuality. The use of pseudo-social science combined with ideological fantasies of a global war on terrorism threatens to bring to fruition a "clash of civilizations."

The imaginary nature of this construction of the global is evident in the way in which US policy has been pursued unfettered by the real constraints of the Cold War. *Budapest Analytica* (March 16, 2003) points out that the period that followed World War II saw the emergence of an international legal order which the Western powers gradually built up on the basis of the UN, OSCE, NATO, Council of Europe, and EU treaties and conventions. It was generally accepted that if international crises had to be resolved by intervention, the states intending to intervene were expected to obtain international legitimacy for action through the UN Security Council. The presence of two superpowers created a degree of constraint on the capacity of each for unilateral action (at least outside each "sphere of influence"). However, in launching its attack on Iraq in 2003, for the first time since the bipolar world ceased to exist, the US chose to ignore the framework of international legality (the UN Security Council) and extensive international reservations and criticism. By relying solely on its military and economic might, the leaders of the US made it clear that their country does not consider itself bound by the international system of conventions built up after World War II, which will therefore lose their credibility and value. This could be viewed as an attempt to establish US hegemony in what would then become a monopolar world – a project that originated prior to September 11, and possibly before the end of the Cold War itself (Johnson 2000, 2003). But the actual consequences of this action could paradoxically create new forms of bipolarity and undermine the concept of "the West" itself. Although the US was always a dominant partner in NATO, prior to 2003 its members took resolutions by consensus in accordance with generally accepted rules. But NATO developed a rift over the war on Iraq and the American government sought approval from as many member and applicant states as possible, rather than from the alliance as a whole. The long-term consequence of this could be to undermine the Euro-Atlantic security system as a pillar of the postwar world order and to open a new bipolarity between the US and Europe. As a result, world politics could be deprived of the point of reference of "Western democracy" and in its stead we would have a global area in which geopolitical interests were pursued with ruthless egoism and without regard to international institutions. Or, alternatively, the "Western alliance" may fudge deep differences and maintain an uneasy unity. But although the US and its allies may use the language and imagery of the Cold War, its mode of operation enacts a post–Cold War world in which the bipolar spatial boundaries of the past have dissolved.

Globalization and Postcommunism

In conclusion, then, globalization is a product of many forces – technology, transnational corporations (TNCs), neoliberal competition, the global market and interlinked economy. We do not dispute that globalization stands apart from earlier theories of modernization, colonialism, world systems, and Marxism. Nor do we dispute that globalization attempts to liberate itself from territorial assumptions and avoid state-centered approaches that equate "society" and "nation." However, globalization is a complex process and specific organizational features of contemporary society drive it, which does not render previous notions of society redundant. The flows of people, capital, and culture are crucially shaped by, indeed are embedded forms of, the material relations of wage/skill levels and market protection. Migrations are not autonomous movements but are structured by specific forces such as TNCs (effects on small-scale producers), military action (displacement and refugees), the IMF (mobilizing the poor into survival strategies), and neoliberal state strategies (Sassen 2000). This has intensified since the 1980s but does not represent a fundamentally novel departure in human affairs.

Globalization is an overdetermined process in which social relations are reconfigured along various dimensions. This should not require the abandonment of existing sociological frameworks but rather points to the centrality of embedding global movements within contexts of cultural reproduction, power, and capital. For example, there is an implicit technological determinism in many accounts of post-societal sociology but the case for this is weak. States remain key drivers of the process of globalization such that while media, cultural images, electronic money, and so forth can be moved with relative ease across national borders, physical objects and people can be monitored and controlled with increasing intensity. At the same time, though, states' actions are experienced globally in a complex web of unintended consequences in which new conflicts and forms of violence take shape around non-state networks and actors, creating new levels of volatility and complexity in the postcommunist world. Part of what makes the "war on terrorism" both unwinnable and potentially unlimited is that it is framed by a discourse of state-based conflicts in an era of global postnational conflict.

This chapter is not, then, a critique of globalization. It is a call for caution in relation to a concept of which Bauman says: "All vogue words tend to share a similar fate: the more experiences they pretend to make transparent, the more they themselves become opaque" (1998: 1). Despite its current vogue, the concept will no doubt in due course go the way of other vague and overextended concepts. However, the processes to which it refers are real, although the concepts of globalization and mobilities need to be situated within processes structured by economic, political, and cultural embedding. In this analysis the notion of "society," with all the qualifications noted here, is not redundant. Nor, actually, is the notion of the nation state. The concept of a territory bounded by systems of welfare, language, taxation, currency, institutions, and histories is relevant to the twenty-first century. But it is not, of course, *exhaustive* of modes of sociality, which sociologists have generally recognized as being complex and multidimensional. The flow of people and objects across borders, the very experience of transnationalism, is itself dependent on, and in some ways reconstitute, borders. Flows cross borders and in the process enable the innovation of identities, whose configurations will, in turn, depend on the embedding of national and transnational relations within locales.

Urry is right to point to the crucial importance of mobilities in the contemporary world, and the symbiosis between mobility and immobility. Just as we need a sociology of mobility we also need a sociology of immobility that addresses the social embeddedness of global processes while showing how unevenness, not convergence, is their necessary outcome. The happy, long decade of globalization is over – the belief that the end of communism heralded the resolution of global conflicts and contradictions proved to be an illusion. Growing disparities between and within countries might be taken as evidence of the limits of globalization only if one naively expects this to result in increasing homogeneity and convergence. Globalization is uneven in its effects and is thus creating a world of increasing inequalities and difference. To grasp the challenges facing sociology in the twenty-first century we need a theory of the interrelations of states, borders, nations, and societies in the context of global transformations.

7

Civil Society East and West

Many theories of democracy, from Locke through Hegel and Tocqueville, claim that in complex societies relations between individuals and the state are mediated through a sphere of civic activity and values. In this literature, civil society constitutes a defense against both excessive state power and atomized individualism, while the rise of authoritarianism and totalitarianism is attributed to its absence or destruction. Democratization and social activism are therefore associated with its revival or, for some postcommunist countries, its emergence for the first time. During the 1980s a ferment of new ideas arose from new social movements and the communications between them, which included and were influenced by the growing anticommunist movements in the East, especially Polish Solidarity. Speaking about the role of social movements in the fall of communism, Adam Michnik (1999) referred to the importance of links between Polish Solidarity and anticommunist movements in Hungary and Czechoslovakia on the one hand and peace and leftist movements in the West on the other. He saw these networks as part of a "rebirth of civil society," that also included ideas of "anti-political politics" and "détente from below." In conjunction with the "new social movements" debate, these developments re-posed questions for Western social theory that had not for some time been central, in particular concerning the foundations of democracy and plurality. This neglect in Western social theory had been compounded by a decade or more during which (to some extent under the influence of Marxism) the state had predominantly been theorized with reference to debates about the logic of capital. What had been neglected, though with some exceptions (notably Habermas's work) was understanding the liberal state as institutionally embedded in democratic processes within which a degree of consensus was necessary to achieve strategic goals. The rediscovery of the concept of civil society during the 1980s fed into debates about trust and social solidarity, exemplifying a reciprocal influence of theory, East–West and West–East. Habermas (1990, 1994) argued that the revolutions of 1989 gave Europe a second chance to create a communicative civil society, but this time free from "narcissistic self-absorption." The democratic spirit of the West, he said, was "catching up with the East," where the guiding ideas were anti-statist and democratic, of civil society, anti-political politics, and the self-limiting revolution (Habermas 1994: 72). The democratic spirit of the Eastern European opposition was indeed seized upon by Western intellectuals already seeking a way out of the impasse of social theory dissatisfied with the dilemmas of post-Marxism, but unable to conceptualize new forms of theoretical and political engagement (e.g. Cohen and Arato 1992; Keane 1988).

Civil society became a central concept through which many participants in the anticommunist revolutions theorized these diverse movements and offered outlines of the shape of postcommunist societies. However, the question of the appropriateness of civil society for understanding postcommunism goes to the heart of understanding twentieth-century history and problems of governance and social solidarity. The concept originated in pre-industrial societies and had largely passed out of currency in sociology. Its resuscitation in the anticommunist movements was an attempt to place the communist experience in a wider, indeed universal, context and the antipathy of "state vs. society" replayed a central antagonism of classical political theory. Clearly, there is a question as to the wider applicability of a concept that arose in the particular circumstances of the collapse of communism, but the limits of state power and the appropriate organization of non-state relationships are issues of broader concern. During the formation of anti-communist movements, the idea of civil society became closely tied up with the concept of the public sphere, with both concepts pointing toward a deep democratization of society that departed from conventional models of representative democracy. Both these concepts are fluid, problematic, and open to various, sometimes-conflicting interpretations, and while in some postcommunist formulations these take on similar connotations, they actually have different origins (Seligman 1995). The notion of an active public sphere in which citizens engage in reasoned argument over affairs of state and morality derives from (idealized) notions of the ancient Greek *polis* in a political tradition running through Machiavelli and Rousseau to twentieth-century theorists such as Arendt and Habermas. Central concepts here are *virtue*, the moral requirement to be a good citizen, and rational debate. Ideas of public disputation, activity, and ideally (if not necessarily) face-to-face contact imply a small-scale relatively homogeneous society. This was the kind of city-state republic, participatory rather than procedural, envisaged by Rousseau (Patomáki and Pursianen 1999). Civil society, by contrast, refers to more complex, organic, and differentiated orders, emphasizing privacy and the separation from the state, while the public sphere required engagement with the state. Civil society, like the public sphere, originates in Greek and Roman political philosophy (Aristotle's *politike koinonia* and Cicero's *ius civile*), but is more closely identified with eighteenth-century political philosophy. The emphasis here was on the importance of a realm of privacy, economic exchange and association, and consequently the limitation of the state. The importance of contract and economic relations to many (though not all) theories of civil society invites association with the growth of the political power of the bourgeoisie in Europe. Despite these different emphases, though, many theorists understand civil society as a public realm of voluntary association essential for the stability of democracy. The concept is surrounded by controversy – for some opening up the space for radical politics against global political and corporate power, while for others it is a vacuous term unable to deal with the novelties of global postcommunism.

Civil Society and Social Differentiation

In the context of its deployment in the anticommunist social movements and elsewhere in contemporary politics, it is worth keeping in mind that the concept of civil society originated in the processes of social differentiation associated with the early modern European societies. With the depersonalization of political power, separated from the familial rights of monarchs, barons, and landlords, the idea of the state as the personal property of the sovereign and benefice of officials slowly gave way to the idea of impersonal rule bound by rules. In the process, sovereignty was transferred from the figure of the monarch to the state, which also underwent a process of differentiation, into administrative, judicial, and representative, functions. Further, the development of trade, commerce, and markets increased the complexity of economic organization while establishing the dual notion of social activity, divided into political and civil roles. "Civil society" described the new commercial social order, the rise of public opinion, representative government, civic freedoms, plurality, and "civility." Thus civil society depicted a realm of contractual and voluntary relationships independent of the state, which thereby became merely one area of social activity among others. At the same time, political economy and philosophy began to address the question of the social context for the existence of the state (political society) the nature of which was no longer taken for granted. In particular, Enlightenment social theory (e.g. Condorcet 1976; Montesquieu 1949; Rousseau 1968) regarded the despotic state as an enemy of human progress and well-being and began to examine the social conditions for democratic or constitutional forms of government. This set the scene for the idea of a fundamental antipathy between state and society in which the former had to be restrained by the civil institutions of the latter – on which the anticommunist theorists drew.

Even so, some of the precursors of contemporary usage had set out to justify the existence of the state through exploration of the basis of its sovereignty. In the seventeenth century, Thomas Hobbes's theory of the sovereign state (Leviathan) was premised on the existence of two branches of society – political and civil – tied by a "social contract" between subjects and the state. Hobbes constructed a hypothetical "state of nature" in which essential human tendencies posed an ever-present threat to social peace, where "the life of man was solitary, poor, nasty, brutish and short" (Hobbes 1994: 71). However, rationality and mutual self-interest persuade people to combine in Agreement, to surrender sovereignty to a Common Power, the state, established by covenant to constrain those who would otherwise violate the social peace. With the social contract comes a separation between political and civil society – two systems in which "men [are] joyned in one Interest" as parts of the body (1994: 131). The political system is constituted by the Sovereign Power and civil society by subjects "among themselves." Although the political system was the dominant part, this expressed the idea of differentiated civil and political life as mutually sustaining systems, in which the realm of private activity, while governed by sovereign laws, was otherwise bound only by conscience (*in foro interno*) and the rules of civic association.

Disputing Hobbes's negative views of human nature, John Locke's concept of the social contract further enhanced the status of civil society, as a space of association, contract and property regulated by the law. "Those who are united into one body, and have a common established law and judicature to appeal to, with authority to decide controversies between them and punish offenders, are in civil society one with another; but those who have no such common appeal . . . are still in the state of Nature" (Locke 1980: para. 87). Leaving the state of nature for Locke involved entering a commonwealth of men of property who contract authority to the state for their self-protection, but they do not do so unconditionally. Law is derived from God-ordained natural rights, which inhere in civil society, to which the state is ultimately answerable. Unlike Hobbes's Leviathan, which was the *product* of a covenant but not a *party* to it (and hence not bound by it), Locke's constitutional state was constrained by the law, violation of which rendered it non-legitimate.

In Hobbes and Locke, though, despite differences between them, civil society was an aspect of government (Locke used "political" and "civil" society interchangeably) while in subsequent theorists it became an autonomous sphere separate from and possibly opposed to the state. Based on limited networks of aristocratic men, and an emerging public/private dichotomy, the model of free association and debate was often that of the coffee house, in which public activity actually took place in small and exclusive social circles. Civil society theories were concerned to defend the idea of a space for public debate and private association at a time when such liberal principles were not widely shared. David Hume's *Inquiry Concerning Human Understanding* (1758), for example, found it necessary to argue at some length that, as a result of the "frailty and corruption of human nature . . . no man can safely be trusted with unlimited authority." This applies in particular to matters of conscience, thus the idea that even "a wise magistrate" may justly adjudicate on matters of philosophy is "pernicious to the peace of civil society." For Hume's contemporary, Adam Ferguson, the development of civil society reflected the progress of humanity from a simple, clan-based militaristic societies to complex commercial ones. However, this process of social differentiation and loss of community threatened increased conflict and weakened the social fabric. Civil society, with a strong connotation of "civility," has the potential to establish a new order requiring dispersal of power and office, the rule of law, and liberal (i.e. tolerant) sentiments, which secure people and property "without requiring obligation to friends and cabals" (Ferguson 1966: 223). Again, civil society is inseparable from good government, but moreover, the reference to friends and cabals indicates an important point that is sometimes missed in subsequent debates. Civil society does not refer to just *any* kind of informal or private social relations, which exist in all societies, but to morally guided, rule-following relations that make possible anonymous social exchanges. It thereby facilitates social integration in impersonal and potentially conflictual situations.

The implicit tension here between the new conflicts of commercial society and the moral demands of social peace appeared explicitly in Hegel, for whom civil society was divided between ethical life (*Sittlichkeit*) and egotistical self-interest. Civil society appears here as a *process* rather than in the frozen architecture of Hobbes's *Leviathan*. Objective Spirit achieves self-knowledge through differentiation into discrete spheres, which nonetheless form a totality. In the family, socialization toward moral autonomy transformed biological and psychological needs into individual desires. But in complex societies private life is transcended though association in civil society, the sphere of production, distribution, and consumption, which meets a system of needs that are modified and multiplied in the process. It has its own regulatory institutions (Justice, Public Authority, Corporations) guided by morality, although they remain instruments for achieving personal, egotistical ends. To some extent Hegel's view of civil society anticipated Marx's critique of class polarization and dehumanization, as "the conflict between vast wealth and vast poverty steps forth, a poverty unable to improve its condition . . . [which] turns into the utmost dismemberment of will, inner rebellion and hatred (Hegel 1967: 149–51). However, this will be overcome if the constitutional-legal state (*Rechtsstaat*) synthesizes ethical life with the public domain of civil society while transcending them. Differences of class, rank, and religion dissolve in universal law and formal rights.

Whereas eighteenth-century civil society theorists looked toward a future society that was increasingly differentiated and commercially driven, Marx's critique of civil society suggested a very different commitment. By regarding civil society simply as the equivalent of bourgeois society, an arena of conflict, class oppression, and illusory emancipation, Marx only partially echoed Hegel's view and disregarded the latter's concept of civil society as

Sittlichkeit. Marx's critique of civil society was in part a critique of the limitations of Hegel's *Rechtsstaat,* in which formal legal equality is merely an illusory dissolution of differences of class, rank, and religion, which masks their perpetuation within civil society. In part too, though, it involved a fundamental rejection of the very process of social differentiation into institutional orders (such as private life, the economy, and civil and political association) that Hegel and most eighteenth-century theory had taken for granted. For Marx, the proletarian victory would substitute for the old civil society a classless association in which there would be neither political power nor the antagonisms of civil society (Marx 1978: 169). Marx's vision of communism was radically de-differentiated, in which boundaries between the civil and political, like those of class, nation, and religious difference wither away. Marx's critique drew on Rousseauist and radical Jacobin concepts of a public sphere of equals, combined, as Gellner (1994) noted, with antimodernist nostalgia for a lost unity of humanity, rather than an organic concept of socially differentiated networks.

It is significant too that Marx's critique was developed most explicitly in his essays on the "Jewish Question." Ostensibly entering the debate about Jewish emancipation, Marx sought to show that even if the state could stand above the particular interests of civil society (birth, rank, and occupation), this would not emancipate society from their influence, but on the contrary would allow each free rein. "Genuine human emancipation" required a radical challenge to the very differentiation between the civil and political society central to Hegelian theory. Marx's *On the Jewish Question* and *The Capacity for Present-Day Jews and Christians to Become Free* (1844) distinguished political from human emancipation, arguing that real human emancipation would require the democratic control of society over production and the abolition of private property. Not only is legal emancipation an illusion, however, but it is not really a question of the emancipation of the *Jews,* but rather of society *from Judaism.* In these essays, Marx (like his fellow "left Hegelians" Bauer and Feuerbach) regarded Judaism both as a religion and as a metaphor for modern commercial society, and his argument deploys a crude racial stereotype of Jewishness as "huckstering" and the embodiment of commercial degeneracy (Greenfeld 1992: 384).[1]

The implication here is that "emancipation" would require the elimination of the kinds of social difference (religious, cultural, ethnic, etc.) central to complex and pluralistic civil society. This analysis was open to the claim that when actual communist governments systematically abolished civil society and forged an atomized population into an outwardly conformist and undifferentiated mass, they were merely putting Marx's theory into practice. Ignatieff (1995), for example, regards Marx's critique of civil society as "catastrophic," leading to the Leninist contempt for legality. We should caution against this view since there was no necessary progression from

Marx's theory to Leninism, and by the end of the nineteenth century there were various Marxist positions on legality and revolution.[2] Lenin's thinking was strongly influenced by Russian populism and the exigencies of the post-Revolutionary situation, as well as by Marxism (Szamuely 1988). The problem was not so much that Marx was against legality *per se*, so much that his view of a future society was informed by romantic images of a highly de-differentiated order in which divisions of public and private, state and society would disappear. But whatever the logical connections between Marx and Leninism, underlying the celebration of the concept of civil society in anticommunist movements was the reclaiming of a concept rejected by Marxism.

The classical tradition of civil society theory formulated a concept closely associated with liberal market values and community involvement. This idea runs from the Scottish moralists (such as Ferguson) through Tocqueville (1946) and Durkheim (1969) to contemporary writers such as Robert Putnam (1993, 2000). Observing the US in the 1830s, Tocqueville (1969: 65) noted that "Americans of all ages, all stations in life, and all types of disposition, are forever forming associations. There are not only commercial and industrial associations in which all take part, but others of a thousand different types – religious, moral, serious, [and] futile," which was the key to their ability to make democracy work. Putnam has similarly argued that norms and networks of civic engagement indeed powerfully influence the quality of public life and the performance of social institutions. The relationship between a strong and active civil society and the consolidation of democracy has become central in debates about the postcommunist transformation. This classical notion of civil society (that Foley and Edwards, 1996, call "Civil Society I") claims that a democratic polity is secured by being embedded in dense networks of civil associations, such as clubs, trade associations, voluntary societies, churches, parent–teacher associations, sports clubs, and the like, that generate "social capital."[3] The denser the networks the more secure are the bridges between civic life and political associations along with institutions of the state. Active, voluntary, and informal groups and networks make for more stable democracy and protect against incursion by the state. The bridges envisaged here are based on institutional links along with shared moral and civic values of reciprocity (e.g. Bryant 1995). Civil society in this sense has a recursive property; it protects against state incursion yet strengthens the (liberal democratic) state. Conversely, the absence of civil society is both an explanation and reinforcement of authoritarian yet ineffective government.

Underlying this view is a theory of social solidarity in complexly differentiated societies. Gellner (1994: 99–100) writes of the modern "man" as "modular," that is, having the capacity to combine associations and institutions without these being total and underwritten by ritual. Civil society creates a social "structure . . . not atomized, helpless and supine, and yet the structure is readily adjustable and responds to rational criteria of improvement" (Gellner 1995: 42). Civil society as a network of institutional and moral links is not monolithic but accommodates a plurality of "groups within groups, their sense of identity . . . always multi-layered" with many possible "we-images" along with corresponding images of the other (Mennell 1995). Here, civil society is not so much a definable social space as a complex web of processes and connections.

Civil society further carries the connotations of civility, *civilianization* and pacification of society entailing a profound change in public sensibilities. Norbert Elias (e.g. 1994) noted how the growth of increasingly mannered social interaction, roughly from the end of the Middle Ages, was accompanied by increased public intolerance of violence. Repugnance toward physical violence increased with advancing thresholds of shame and embarrassment surrounding the body – acts once performed publicly, such as defecation and sexual intercourse, become intensely private. The development of modern societies entails a long but uncertain process of pacification in everyday life in which the realm of private, civil interactions increases. The more people are caught up in longer and denser networks of interdependence, the more people attune their actions to those of others and learn to restrain violent emotions (Mennell 1995). The emergence of civil society accompanies the demilitarization of societies, as a declining proportion of the population have experience of the armed forces and the cult of the warrior and military discipline give way to civilian, non-hierarchical, and voluntary forms of association. However, pacification requires the taming of warriors, which is a universal problem in establishing social order, since the cult of violence and military heroism continually threaten to reappear for example in terrorist movements (e.g. Elias 1996: 403ff; Mennell 1995). This analysis is relevant to post-Soviet societies in which the official ideology emphasized the cult of the heroic (revolutionary) warrior and mobilization in the Great Patriotic War and where the industrial-military sector accounted for 60 percent of GDP. The formation of civil society is bound up with the extension of civilian democratic control over the armed forces and military policy (Bruner 1996; Cottey et al. 1999) along with a wider building of informal networks, trust, and tolerance. Hobbes emphasized the role of the state in securing social peace; Locke the role of civil society in restraining the state. Sociologists could learn from postcommunism (and other democratic transitions) that the legal state and social solidarity are necessary conditions for each other, though in fragile symbiosis.

Core Debates

However, this analysis is complicated by the fact that civil society is an elusive, indeed fuzzy, concept and has been subject to a variety of criticisms.

Five of these in particular are relevant to the use of "civil society" in Eastern European theory:

- The concept is exclusive, since civil society is not really universal but always constrained by particularistic criteria of membership.
- Despite its attempt to grasp social complexity, it does not do so successfully.
- This is because it is grounded in an image of active citizenship that is untenable in contemporary societies.
- Civil society anyway fragments society into potentially warring factions. This problem is similar to that of social solidarity (see chapter 3) that can unite collectivities but also fracture them into warring camps.
- Its reference is to national configurations of state and society, but in an age of globalization we need to understand the emergence of a global civil society (this will be considered in the final section of this chapter).

The concept is exclusive. In many ways echoing the Marxist critique, feminist critics have argued that the gender-neutral language of civil society and the public sphere conceal how the role of citizen has been linked to the capacity to bear arms, which has been predominantly a masculine role (Fraser 1989; Walby 1994). This fusion of citizenship, militarism, and masculinity reinforces the male occupation of the public sphere that is inscribed into the public/private dichotomy, resulting in a civil contract among brothers combined with the feminization of the private sphere (Okin 1991; Pateman 1988). Habermasian distinctions between public and private roles treat the family as a black box in which patriarchal power remains invisible. The male citizen-speaker role links the state and the public sphere to the family and the official economy while the worker-breadwinner role integrates the family with the economy and the state, confirming women's dependent status in each. It is not clear, though, that these criticisms negate the very ideas of civil society and the public sphere, nor do they show that inclusive, non-gendered institutional forms are impossible. Nonetheless, there *will* always be boundaries to any concept of civil society, a problem that arises with notions of "global" civil society, which is discussed below.

Civil society does not address social complexity. It is claimed that civil society assumes the existence of a homogeneous community and takes too little account of functional differentiation and the interpenetration of state and society in complex societies (Seligman 1993). It is often unclear whether civil society refers to societies, groups within them, or individual citizens (Gibson 1998). Citizens confront different authorities via a series of roles – taxpayers, proponents of resolutions, voters, writers of letters to editors, supporters of interest groups, etc. – that are divided according to the requirements of the political system (Luhmann 1982: 153). The binary opposition of civil society and the state could be described in terms of what

Luhmann calls a political code, which simplifies and steers otherwise highly complex communications. As such it operates as a rhetorical counter to the sovereignty of the state, which invokes the myth of the collective sovereign "people." But any attempt to make this a reality, such as the unconstrained communication (supposedly) envisaged by Habermas, or the permanently open democracy of civil societarians, would be chaos (Luhmann 1982: 287–8). The breadth of the meaning of civil society is a source of ambiguity, giving it a nebulous and undifferentiated character (Ely 1992). This may be particularly so with Habermasian accounts, (e.g. Cohen and Arato 1992) that insert the concept of the public sphere into the domain of potential communicative ethics, thus merging civil society with routine linguistic practices. Again, Kumar (1993) regards the concept as meaningless since the very existence of civil society presupposes the state, that is, a state bound by legality that will not trample over civil rights. He argues that other, more familiar concepts (such as state–individual, democracy, liberalism) may more adequately cover the theoretical ground covered by civil society. [4] One could counter this with the point that civil society entails the idea of embedding public and economic relations in civic culture and associations, and its relationship with the state is symbiotic rather than disengaged. That is, one presupposes the other – rather than standing in opposition. However, critics of the concept are right to warn against its high elasticity – it can be pulled and stretched to include almost any non-state activities.

Civil society is grounded in an untenable concept of active citizenship. Is a public sphere of active citizens in the Arendtian or Habermasian sense consistent with development of complex and multi-layered societies? For example Habermas's (1989b) well-known critique of the erosion of the public sphere in late capitalism claims that the commercialization of mass media replaced rational and unconstrained debate by public opinion research, through which political parties "extract" loyalty from publics in instrumental fashion. At the same time, increasing state intervention and the growing interdependence of research and technology resulted in a process of "technicization" whereby questions of moral value and political controversy were converted into managerial technical or planning processes (see Ray 1993: 51–3). But, especially since Habermas regards social steering by both the market and state as unavoidable (1989a: 339), it is not entirely clear whether he is describing a pathological and reversible process or essentially depicting the condition of modernity. If it is the latter, then ideas of a reconstructed public sphere of active citizens may be utopian and nostalgic. However, Putnam's point may still be valid that the more vibrant the civic culture, the better the quality of governance, "determined by longstanding traditions of civic engagement (or its absence). Voter turnout, newspaper readership, membership in choral societies and football clubs – these were the hallmarks of a successful region" (Putnam 1993).

Civil society is as likely to fragment as to integrate society. There is the danger, as a number of commentators have noted (e.g. Mennell 1995; Foley and Edwards 1996), that strong internal bonds within groups may lead to the fragmentation of civic groups into warring factions that actually increases the risk of public violence. Putnam similarly points out that "the external effects of social capital are by no means always positive . . . urban gangs, NIMBY ("not in my backyard") movements, and power elites often exploit social capital to achieve ends that are antisocial from a wider perspective" (Putnam 2000: ch. 1). Ethnic and religious solidarities that undermine multinational and secular states are often cited in this context (e.g. Kaldor 1993 and Sivan 1989, respectively). However, civil society theorists would generally counter this by stressing what Cohen and Arato (1992: 421) regard as essential to civil society, namely reflection on the core of collective identities and their articulation within democratic politics. In particular, following Habermas, the crucial factor here is that we inhabit a world of morally mature post-traditional ethics, in which public debate is constrained by procedural rules. Social integration requires that we agree not over substantive matters of identity and opinion but on the rules through which public debate and conflict will be conducted. Indeed, according to Misztal (1996: 197) it is the *disengagement* of political and juridical institutions from the lived bonds of solidarity, that is, a failure of civil society, that promotes new exclusive communities of trust, such as ethnic nationalism. In other words, vibrant civic associations, complex networks of trust, and high social capital facilitate active public spheres and political participation. However, weak and undeveloped civil society allows the collapse of public engagement and threatens to allow a return to authoritarianism, which erodes civil society further.

These arguments raise serious issues for the evaluation of anticommunist social movements and theories. Whereas the relationship between state and civil society in classical theories was complex, postcommunist conceptions often involved a one-dimensional polarization of authoritarian state power against the resistance of civil society. In so doing they sometimes implied that the latter was based on personal trust and mutual obligations. On the other hand contemporary societies are highly complex and social identities perhaps too multifaceted to be subsumed within the loose concept of civil society. So, what did the return to "civil society" achieve?

Renewal and Revival

There is some irony in the fact that despite Marx's pejorative treatment of the concept of civil society, its revival in the later twentieth century was a result, first, of the attempts by Eurocommunist parties to devise new strategies in the 1970s and, second, of its popularity among the anticommunist movements in Eastern Europe. Eurocommunists (especially the Italian Communist Party), theoretically informed by writers like Gramsci, Bobbio, Althusser, and Poulantzas, sought to avoid more traditional Marxist economistic reductionism and simplistic polarization of social and political conflicts. Gramsci had conceived of civil society as the sphere of noncorporeal forms of class rule, a cultural space between state and economy. Here the proletarian party could wage a cultural and ideological war to undermine the hegemony of the ruling class, creating a counter-hegemony of workers' clubs, social and educational organizations, assisted by the activity of "organic intellectuals." This restated the centrality of processes of social differentiation and situated civil society within a cultural and institutional realm rather than the economy. The Eurocommunist concept of civil society allowed for a broad articulation of movements and subject positions, moving away from a rigid adherence to the proletariat as the agent of emancipation. Despite the effectiveness of this strategy in bringing various social movements and parties into loose coalition and debate, it already pointed toward a post-Marxist politics in its abandonment of both materialism and the centrality of proletarian class struggle.

However, the major revival of civil society theory in anticommunist movements was popularized by writers such as Bernhard (1996), Fehér and Heller (1986), Geremek (1992), Havel (1988), Konrád (1984), Ost (1990), and Vajda (1988). Theorists such as Rödel, Frankenberg and Dubiel (1989), Arato (1981), and Cohen and Arato (1992) further excavated the concept, combining ideas of radical civic republicanism with Habermas's procedural discourse ethics. The central idea of these theories was to identify a social space for public discussion, of voluntary citizens' associations, that was neither narrowly merged with the market, nor an adjunct to the state. Again with Eastern Europe in mind, Sztompka (1993: 73) argued that civil society was the key to closing the chasm between public and private realms. It involved pluralism of voluntary associations, interest groups, political organizations and local communities, markets, and representative democracy as institutional arrangements linking the public and personal choices of active and informed citizens.

These critiques addressed the consequences of communism for a wide range of civil and interpersonal relations. The totalitarian system left a "deficit of civility and degeneration of intimacy" (Misztal 2000: 207) in which the state systematically invaded and undermined relations of trust, privacy, and intimacy. In the 1930s, for example, Stalin made a hero of Parlik Morozov, a 14-year-old boy who had denounced his father, who was subsequently executed, to the NKVD (Holmes 1997: 267–8). The intrusion of the security services and other state agencies into everyday life meant that anyone, including friends and relatives, could be an informer, which undermined relations of informal authority and trust. The post-Stalin period, after 1953, saw a gradual diminution of terror and surveillance, and although public speech and association remained tightly regulated, in some cases up until 1989, private life took on renewed intensity. Increasingly a gap appeared between official and private realms, the latter based on informal conduct, while the former had only limited relations of trust.

Václav Havel described the cynicism that resulted from the bifurcation between public acquiescence to the system (for example, joining parades and displaying Party posters) and private rejection. People were implicated in the system's crimes through their public affirmation of Party ideology. Moreover, the destruction of civil relations in communism represented something more pernicious, the triumph of impersonal rationality, in which communism was a complex mirror of all modern civilization. Communism, he said, was "the inevitable consequence of rationalism," of the break with *Naturwelt*, of an immediate prerational empathy with nature. Further, scientific civilization "fails to connect with the most intrinsic nature of reality and with natural human experience. It is now more of a source of disintegration and doubt than a source of integration and meaning. . . . The abyss between the rational and the spiritual, the external and the internal, the objective and the subjective, the technical and the moral, the universal and the unique, constantly grows deeper" (Havel 1994). Drawing on Weber, Heidegger, and the Czech philosopher Jan Patocka, Havel offered a vision of a future, of "living in truth," in which against the anonymous impersonal power of industrial civilization civil society reaffirmed the validity of nature and values – of democracy, rights, and spirituality.

The revolutions of 1989 were described as "self-limiting" in that they eschewed central control of power or any *pouvoir constituant*, and opposed radical revolution (Arato 1991). Their organization was diffuse, they offered no utopian vision of the future, and at times claimed to develop an "antipolitical politics" (Konrád 1984). In this postcommunist form, civil society was understood as a realm of values and activity that would not directly challenge the state so much as bypass, and thereby undermine it. For Adam Michnik communist power would be rolled back by civil society in a convergence of self-management and society independent from the state. He says, "we invented something like alternative society, which would fulfil a substantial part of its needs independently from a totalitarian state (Michnik 2001). In the writings of Agnes Heller during this period, civil society was seen as the nucleus of self-government by all members of society and invoked ideas of a permanently open democracy. So civil society became the site of an incipient public sphere, indeed, which reflected some accounts of Polish developments. According to Pelczynski, Solidarity achieved hegemony over Polish society during 1981 and began to undermine state power, despite the military coup of December 1981. Underground activists increasingly developed forms of resistance that bypassed and ridiculed, rather than engaged with, the state. In the process a new concept ("Civil Society II") emerged, in which civil society is explicitly antithetical to the state. The two versions are contrasted in table 7.1. Rather than embedding political processes in supportive but constraining civic networks, the later conception regarded civil society as a harbinger of a new type of society – anti-political, authentic, and based on informal social solidarity. The spaces of civil society and the public sphere here were often fused in that the private realm of autonomous self-organizing groups was to become an authentic public sphere alternative to the state.

Civil society then took on the connotation of society reasserting itself as autonomous and semi-autonomous groupings in ways detached from, and parodying, the state, a good example of which was the Polish group "Orange Alternative" (see chapter 5 above, and Ray 1999a). Against the instrumental *Gesellschaft* of communism it invoked a kind of *Gemeinschaft* of authentic and personal networks and loyalties. This was a civil society of cooperatives, religious groups, *samizdat* publications,[5] illicit dealing, informal networks. These were to become the nucleus of a new society of informal and non-state relations, a vision that was in many ways specific to the social context of the decomposition of communism (Arato 1981; Fehér and Heller 1986). Social movements such as Solidarity aimed to limit the state, or bypass it altogether through alternative networks, but not to seize it as an instrument of coercion, and in this sense they were quite different from earlier and more traditional revolutionary movements (Pelczynski 1988). The early Solidarity program of *podmiotowość* (self-management) was a radical alternative to Western democracy as well as to Soviet-type socialism. The democratization of the economy was understood as part of a decentralized social order of autonomous subsystems, managed along the lines of professional self-government (Glasman 1994). These notions of self-government transcend the liberal dichotomy

Table 7.1   *Civil Society I and II*

	Economy	*Polity*
Civil society I		
Classical conception (Locke, Ferguson, Hegel)	Capitalist market economy	Procedural democracy embedded in and limited by civil society
	Free exchange and association	
	Moral governance	
	Civility	
Civil society II		
Postcommunist conception	Networks of face-to-face interaction	Participatory democracy "bypassing" the state
		Republican virtue
		Social movements
		Self-governing political society

of public–private by bringing rational democratic procedures into everyday life, through extrapolation of the networks and practices of intellectuals in the parallel polity. Cohen and Arato (1992) argue that the new public spheres in Eastern Europe could provide a model for a more general idea of civil society that is appropriate in the West too. However, they also warn against an overly polarized view of "civil society vs. the state" that was derived from a particular historical context. In contrast to the highly differentiated view outlined above, the "Eastern European" model over-unifies civil society in a false solidarity and risks blocking the emergence of societal and political pluralism (1992: 67).

Recovering civil life after decades of state repression encountered problems of cultural reproduction. Jacques Rupnik (1999) argued that under communism subjects lost all autonomy and experienced erosion of memory in a "regime of oblivion," and a similar issue is addressed in Watson (1994). Rupnik argued that the practice of self-criticism and "confession," particularly among the nomenklatura, created complicity with the system and the subjugation of individual biography and collective memory to the demands of the Party. In the process, the transmission of collective memories of events and cultural practices that would normally take place through civil society was interrupted by the imposition of official histories consistent with Marxism-Leninism. This in turn could have serious consequences since the suppression of public communication allowed the private realm to be inhabited by largely uncontested, if covert, "memories" that could subsequently be mobilized. In Yugoslavia, for example, official histories and curricula insisted that World War II had been a people's liberation war – a struggle of class rather than ethnic or national aspiration – which occluded what many people "really knew" (Hoepken 1999). The language of socialism had not permitted an open discourse nor subjected Yugoslav history to unrestricted discussion. With the collapse of the Federation the Party lost control of memory, and secret histories of trauma and ethnic hatred were opened up. The collapse of Federal and communist rule was accompanied by the uncovering of (semi-) hidden massacres followed by new commemorative funerals, which provided a "supreme moment for transforming ritual into political theatre" (Hayden 1994: 172). Each subsequent antagonist in the civil war could mobilize the unexpiated trauma of suppressed memories, as did Milosevic in the prelude to the civil war, in 1989. A free and open civil society, by contrast, would allow the expurgation of traumatic memories and a genuine coming to terms with the past in non-ritualized and discursive language (Ray 1999d, 2000). The inability to mourn and to expiate past trauma along with the unacknowledged shame of historical defeats returns to haunt the present in the form of potentially violent "unfinished business" with imagined enemies. This is discussed further in chapter 8.

The inability of communist systems to deal with the past is part of a wider phenomenon. To understand postcommunist civil society we need to acknowledge that the particular form it assumes reflects the way the communist system worked. The deficiencies in central allocation of resources were partially filled through informal networks, and by symbiotic exchanges between the informal sector and the state, based on patrimonial protection through mutual security and political corruption. This could take several forms, such as work and payment *na levo* (on the left, illegally); non-monetary reciprocity, such as private housing built through communal cooperation (Sik 1988); dealing on the informal economy. For example, legitimate private producers would exceed limitations on private accumulation and siphon off inputs such as fodder, fertilizer, or transport from the state sector (Grossman 1977). The concept of civil society as a private realm of informal networks is derived from precisely these kinds of relations, a point some writers made explicitly (e.g. Szalai 1989). The civil society of the anticommunist movements was located in the "de-bureaucratized social spaces" (Ray 1996: 125–8) that emerged parallel to the formal, state sector. This meant that while using the language of civil society to reconnect with Western political discourse, the concept tended to reflect the unique conditions of communism. In capitalist societies public spheres had been colonized by the mass media and technocratic decision making, which encouraged civil privatism. But in state socialism the artificial and stereotyped discourse of the public sphere, combined with the rule of a secretive and clientelistic Party, left private networks, horizontal links, and face-to-face trust relations as crucial avenues of resource distribution.

Hankiss (1991: 310) points out that the terms "official" and "second" societies do not refer to two groups of people, but to two dimensions of social existence governed by different organizational principles. These were, nonetheless, dependent upon one another, in that the second society provided a degree of flexibility not permitted by the rigidity of the planning mechanisms.[6] In this sense the civil society that was to be the harbinger of a new society was also the means by which the socialist systems were able to survive for as long as they did by providing safety valves for popular dissatisfaction and permitting channels of resource allocation that bypassed the moribund planning process.

So, on the one hand the concept of "civil society" seemed to lie at the center of concerns with self-government, activism, and privacy, separation from the state, human rights, free economic initiatives, and the definitions of the social itself (Keane 1988: 20). But on the other hand there are crucial questions about its appropriateness in communist and postcommunist Europe. Is a concept derived from the early modern history of Western Europe relevant to the complex conditions of postcommunism? If so, which version of civil society is most appropriate? Have the aspirations of civil society theorists in postcommunist societies been fulfilled? In particular, how well does the classical conception ("Civil Society I") stand up against the models deployed in anticommunist movements ("Civil Society II")?

"We the People"? Postcommunist Civil Society

Surveying postcommunist civil society, no particularly clear picture emerges. On the one hand, there is evidence of innovative forms of vibrant civil involvement and activity since 1989 – see, for example, the list of organizations across Central and Eastern Europe at <http://www.civilsoc.org/>. On the other hand, though, many writers express disappointment with the results of 1989. According to Barbara Misztal, "instead of being a period of learning how to cooperate and build consensus the first several postcommunist years have reinforced the culture of distrust, the habit of informal dealings and the strengthening of particularistic visions and elements" (Misztal 2000: 218). Even in Poland, which saw the largest and most established anticommunist movement, activist notions of the self-governing republic were relatively short-lived. Hausner and Nielsen (1992) write of the "protracted death agony" of state socialism leading to a vacuum, in which the *ancien régime* disintegrated in such a way that new social forces failed to emerge. They refer to the social disembedding of market reforms, shock therapy as a "revolution from above" combined with the disappearance of mass-based social movements. In Poland, activist notions of the self-governing republic were relatively short-lived. Ost (1990) notes that the concept of "citizen" in Poland underwent several transformations. The "revolutionary subject of the Gdansk soviet" became the parliamentary delegate of the Gdansk Accords of 1981, although during martial law the notion of permanently open democracy returned again for a while. However, during the 1980s there was a radical questioning of Solidarity's syndicalist past and the ideal citizen as entrepreneur came to replace the parliamentary delegate as Kuron apologized for his past "communist sympathies." Michnik (1999) comments that "after 1989, the ethos of solidarity was replaced by the ethos of competition." Solidarity membership, which was around 10 million at the time of its defeat in 1981, had fallen to 2 million when the PUWP lost power in 1989–9 (Walicki 1991). The patterns of civic involvement are too highly differentiated across the region to draw any general conclusions, but in sombre mood Michnik says: "We thought that our revolution . . . in the name of freedom and normalcy, will be not only velvet and bloodless but also free from the phenomenon that Hume calls superstition [persecutions and religious wars]. But the collapse of communism brought ethnic chauvinism, bloody wars and religious intolerance" particularly in former Yugoslavia (Michnik 2001). He continues that their legacy has been (in different measure) radicalism of revenge (seeking out "former communists"), nostalgia for the past in the face of corruption and uncertainty, and crass commercialism.[7]

Participation in postcommunist elections is one (and only one) indicator of general levels of civic involvement and social capital and there is some evidence of political demobilization and disengagement in postcommunist countries. However, the picture is different across the region and can vary within countries over time. Kostov (1993: 224) argued that Bulgaria had undergone deactivation and privatization typical of other postcommunist societies, evidenced by low levels of participation in elections, especially local ones. In Hungary the participation rate in local elections in 1990–1 was 10–15 percent, though in 1994 it rose to 43 percent (*Eastern European Constitutional Review* 4, 1 (1995): 13).[8] Poland has had relatively high levels of political participation, but in the 2001 elections this fell to 46 percent, the lowest in its democratic history amid reports of widespread alienation from politics in general. In Bulgaria the election in 2001 of the previously unknown National Movement Simeon II, led by the former king, has been taken to reflect disenchantment with the political system and the established parties such as the Union of Democratic Forces and the Bulgarian Socialist Party (*Eastern European Constitutional Review,* 10, 4 (2001).

Comparative research (Howard 2000) again points to the weakness of civil society in postcommunist Europe. Results summarized in table 7.2 compared membership of various organizations and activities across three broad regions – postcommunist, older democracies, and post-authoritarian states in South America, South Africa, and Asia. This is clearly a very broad-brush approach and differences within each region are significant and likely to change over time. But the results do point to low engagement in public activities in postcommunist countries – with the exception of trade union membership, which has carried over from the former system. Howard explains this pattern in terms of strong feelings of mistrust of voluntary organizations; private friendship networks that were crucial to survival in the former system, persisting into postcommunism; and disappointment

Table 7.2 *Organizational membership by region (percentage)*

	Older democracies[a]	Post-authoritarian[b]	Postcommunist[c]
Church or religious	52.1	48.3	16.6
Sports or recreational	43.7	27.9	13.3
Educational, cultural, or artistic	27.1	21.9	7.7
Trade union	34.9	13.6	19.6
Political party	18.1	15.8	4.6
Environmental	14.6	14.9	3.2
Professional	21.7	13.2	6.6
Charitable	26.1	18.1	4.8

[a] US, Australia, Sweden, Finland, Norway, Switzerland, West Germany
[b] South Africa, South Korea, Chile, Brazil, Venezuela, Spain, Uruguay, Argentina, Philippines
[c] East Germany, Romania, Slovakia, Czech Republic, Hungary, Latvia, Russia, Estonia, Ukraine, Lithuania, Bulgaria

with the new political system. It should be noted, though, that Gibson (1998) offers somewhat conflicting evidence from more limited samples and based on network analysis.

In so far as one can speak of demobilization and disengagement in post-communism, one underlying factor may lie in the "transition recession" (Bakos 1994; Kazimierz 1993; Kolodko 2002) that followed the end of communism and is illustrated by the data in figure 7.1.[9] This further combined with widespread disorder, criminality, and collapse in social welfare support to lead some to speak of the "market failure" in Eastern Europe (e.g. Andor and Summers 2000; Potuček 2000). Inequalities have increased in the postcommunist period, in some cases dramatically, provoking new conflicts. Hedlund and Sundström (1996) argue that in the former Soviet Union, it was anticipated at the outset of the transition that

> high inflation, growing unemployment and a deterioration in the ability to maintain the old state-run safety nets would all combine to hurt socially vulnerable groups. . . . [Indeed] the distributional consequences were dramatic. All those with minor savings in the bank saw their capital being wiped out, and all those who lived on fixed incomes – state wages, pensions, or other transfers – experienced a sharp reduction in their real incomes. . . . The final outcome of the redistribution of incomes and wealth that has taken place during systemic change is clearly reflected in official statistics . . . in 1993 the richest 20 percent of the Russian population had at their joint disposal 41.6 percent of total (registered) incomes, while the poorest fifth had to make do with merely 5.8 percent. By 1995 the top 20 percent had increased their share to 46.9 percent while the bottom 20 percent remained at 5.5 percent.

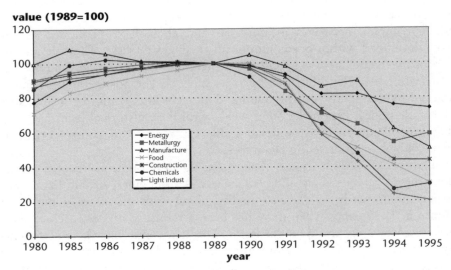

Figure 7.1   *Indices of production in major sectors of the Russian eonomy*
Source: Russian and Euro-Asian Economics Bulletin, 5, 1 (January 1996) (Melbourne).

Where people are preoccupied with economic insecurity, fearful of crime, and distrustful of political institutions, there is insufficient social capital to generate active civic life. Persistent economic crises exacerbated longer-term problems that further contributed to civic demobilization. Civil society is linked to trust in that it is dependent on the existence of norms of reciprocity and civic engagement. But the nature of communist rule meant that centralized power undermined norms of cooperation by eliminating negotiation from public life and undermining respect for anything other than official positions, which themselves came to be discredited (Misztal 1996: 197). Meanwhile the reconstitution of the former nomenklatura into new owners, entrepreneurs, and political elites reproduced former social networks and practices in the postcommunist context. This contributed to the formation of what Rose (1995) describes as "hour glass societies," with two largely disparate loops, elite and local informal networks, functioning relatively independently.

The postcommunist transformation, especially the creation of new impersonal market transactions has sensitized us to the importance of culturally embedded impersonal and personal trust networks. How these take shape will be affected by, and in turn influence, a wide range of cultural, political, and economic configurations. An important influence on the type of social system that develops is the way in which markets are embedded in cultural, institutional, and regulatory social relations. The development of trust is dependent on a number of conditions, including a legitimate and legal–rational state, relative (or perceived) absence of corruption in public life, active regulatory bodies, and embeddedness of economic and political institutions. If these conditions are weak, high levels of impersonal distrust are likely to be combined with trust based in personal commitments, client networks, and strong particularistic identities. This is particularly marked in the former Soviet Union (the center, after all, of the communist system) where complex networks of informal and clientelistic economic activity have developed within postcommunism (Ledeneva 1998). The role and nature of the "state" here is specific to postcommunist conditions and involves a fuzzy line between official and private spheres. The postcommunist state is marked by ambiguity, on the one hand actively interventionist in industrial and trade policy, yet on the other weak, with little historical legitimacy, and therefore ill-equipped to establish stable tax regimes or control organized crime, which is discussed in chapter 5.

Shlapentokh (2003) argues that in Russia developments revolve around the struggle between state and civil society. A brief emergence of liberal civil society in the early 1990s was quelled along with the siege of the White House in 1993, since when there has been a return to an "oligarchic" mode of civil society, especially under Putin. This is a condition where state legality is weak, genuine civic association almost wholly non-existent (but replaced by pseudo forms such as Civic Forum) and freedom enjoyed only by corrupt oligarchs. He concludes that in general, civil society, as forecast by many Russians, hardly existed in the country. The hostility of the Kremlin and local barons and the passivity of most Russians accounted for the low level of civil life . . . not long ago . . . society represented the epitome of collectivism. Today Russia is more atomistic and egoistic than many other countries in the world.

In this context, some of the enthusiasm for civil society dissipated in the wake of domestic inflation combined with recession and the weakening of social solidarity. Even in countries preparing for entry into the EU in 2004 this manifested itself in populist resistance to the EU and globalization. For example in Poland Andrzej Lepper's rural Self Defense movement, which organizes direct action to oppose integration with the EU, won 10.2 percent in the 2001 elections. The League of Polish Families, a party of ultraconservative and anti-EU Roman Catholics took 7.87 percent. For Tamás (1994) the revolutions of 1989 were made by the private sphere against the public with its "rational utopia" communism. However, the language of civil society was a myth, invoking a "tale of a non-coercive political order of mutual non-hierarchical contract." Indeed, for Lomax (1997) the early popular enthusiasm was betrayed by the postcommunist intellectual elite, who appropriated the term "civil society" but demobilized society and failed to develop civil initiatives and popular participation. Hann (1990, 1995) argues that the model of civil society vs. the state is derived from the pre-industrial history of the West and is too simplistic to examine the complex interpenetration of state and society in the communist period (see also Ray 1996: 200–28).

One interpretation of this situation is that in view of forty or so years of communist history in the region, the expectations invested in civil society were utopian. Problems of low trust and legitimacy arose from the communist experience. The communist states of Eastern Europe at least had weak legitimacy, which, combined with their routine surveillance of private activity, meant that there was heavy reliance on informal connections and mutual support. Decades of illicit dealing, falsification of records, informal arrangements between enterprises, complex maneuvers with state planners, and the extensive informal economy, created a culture of illegality shared by state officials and private entrepreneurs. Corruption was not confined to those engaged in activity on the side but extended, perhaps primarily, to those within the party machinery. Corruption and lack of trust in politicians has remained one reason for low participation in postcommunist elections and in civil life generally (*Eastern European Constitutional Review,* 10, 4 (2001).

However, a further interpretation of this situation is that civil society was anyway a culturally relative concept that was not appropriate to the region (or parts of it) and that the particular institutions that take shape are those most fitting to local needs and experience. In relation to Hungary, for example, Hann (1995) sees no evidence to support the notion that an effect-ive civil society has been able to develop in recent years. He suggests that the term was appropriated by urban intellectuals to bemoan the fact that (espe-cially rural) people were less willing than previously to display deference to cultural elites. It was noted in chapter 5 that corruption is a response to the poor competitiveness of local business, in global terms. Corrupt markets are clandestine and closed to outsiders since they place a high value on local knowledge – one has to know who to bribe, how and when to give a bribe, and to be part of the relevant networks of influence. Corruption protects local businesses from foreign competition, so local enterprises may go to considerable lengths to preserve their position (Krastev 1998).

These kinds of considerations lead some, such as McFaul (1993) to de-scribe as "uncivil societies" those in which there are activities outside the state but without a framework of legality which connects them to the state. This may, of course, be a transitory phenomenon not welcomed by those who have to live in them, who retain the hope for a more effective public sphere and active civil society. Perhaps the construction and consolidation of civil society should be viewed as a process rather than fixed presence or absence. This is an emergent process in which social movements and public activism in general will play a significant role. Part of the difficulty with some concepts of civil society is viewing it as a fixed quantity that is either present or not, weak or strong, etc. Such judgments need to be made with reference to the ensemble of social forces that shape civil society. In this context a wide range of factors are likely to affect the strength of civil society, including the relative strength of independent social movements, the extent of differentiation and pluralism within the political system, the inde-pendence of the judiciary and constitutional process, and the degree to which public institutions are embedded in supportive social and regulatory networks.

Further, we need to distinguish between societies (such as Hungary and Poland) in which the hopes invested in civil society by intellectuals have not been fulfilled and those in which there has been a return to repression. An example of the latter is Belarus, where President Aleksandr Lukashenka has reversed nearly all the advances in the field of human rights, freedoms, and democratization that had marked the perestroika era and the post-Soviet period. With state control reimposed on the media, public organizations harassed into closure, public protests suppressed, and political opponents silenced, "Belarus bears an eerie and increasing resemblance to Soviet soci-ety" (Drakokhurst 1997). The government is suppressing civil society by restricting freedom of expression, instituting a state monopoly over the media, and branding independent activists, NGOs, and their supporters as "spies" and "criminals." This has created a climate of intimidation that has weakened NGO morale and caused many NGO leaders to fear imminent closure.

In relation to the societies of Central Europe, though, there has been a cyclical process, in which demobilization has oscillated with mobilization but civil society remains (potentially at least) effective. This is summarized in figure 7.2 and draws on Bernhard (1996), who argues that the enfeeblement of civil society may itself be a transitional process. The period of mass opposition and citizen's activism corresponds to a strong civil society grounded in a sense of common purpose and unity in the face of a shared enemy. The phase of negotiation, in Poland the Round Table agreement between Solidarity and the PUWP, demobilized civil society because leaders are incorporated into the political process and people suspend activism pending the outcome of negotiations. The subsequent first free elections contested by independent political parties are the focus of a resurgence of public activism and civic consciousness as the elections engage popular energies. But entering the beginning of the postcommunist transition proper leads to demobilization and disaffection as new cleavages and inequalities arise, as the residual aspects of communism become apparent, the shock of marketization and privatization have the effects of encouraging individualism and privatism, and, for those with rising income, increased consumerism. Bernhard is optimistic that a resurgence of civic activism and strengthening of civil society will follow the early transitional phase.

Globalization and the Future of Civil Society

Civil society theory has been important in refocusing sociology on questions of democracy, civic participation, and the informal bases of social integration

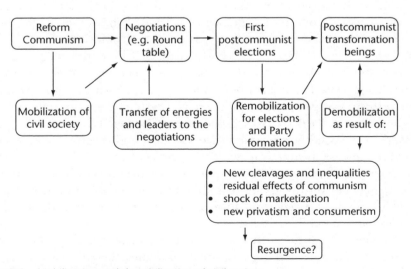

Figure 7.2 *Mobilization and demobilization of civil society*

(e.g. Putnam 1993). Civil society is a conceptual space that depicts a realm of sociality relatively autonomous from the institutions of government. Nonetheless, the complex intersections of global and local processes and the increasing functional differentiation of societies make problematic polarities (civil society/state) drawn from an earlier stage of social development. Civil society and public spheres are best viewed as multiple processes rather than as "sites" and as anonymously interlocked subjects and flows of communication, rather than homogeneous communities (Habermas 1992). A central theme in civil society theory, and indeed in sociology as a whole, has been the importance of embedding processes of money and power in supportive but constraining cultural and normative systems. Where civil society is positioned between the economy and polity, rather than being absorbed into either, it is possible to explore the mediating processes that connect institutional spheres to limit the extension of one into the other. Where (as is common in postcommunist societies) the boundary of the state and private activity is unclear, with few mediating institutions, the result is low trust, weak legitimacy, high crime, and corruption. As a counter to these, social organizations and NGOs often strive to generate a culture of civic regulation and public accountability, as with the umbrella of anticorruption organizations in Bulgaria, such as Coalition 2000 (see pp. 84–5 *passim*).

If civil society is viewed as mediating other institutional orders, then a crucial factor will be the way in which a system of needs is articulated within a framework of procedural rights that allow the articulation of substantive differences of interests, roles, values, and membership of voluntary associations (Rueschemeyer 1986: 151). Without juridical processes that offer defense against alleged violations, the "civil rights" enjoyed are very weak. So the existence of civil society requires not just the existence of nonstate organizations (which would apply to Lebanon in the 1980s and other "uncivil societies") but an acceptance of rules of behavior by both government authorities and citizens that self-limit their mutual claims (Heller 1988; White et al. 1993: 226–9). Further, the self-limitation of power does not arise spontaneously from the process of functional differentiation (as Luhmann suggests, 1982: 214) but implies a procedural threshold sustained by the diffusion of power through the social system. This can only occur, as Offe and Preuss (1991: 161) argue, when power is embedded (*vergesellschaftet*) in social norms and networks, local and diverse public spheres. Despite the diffuse meanings to which the concept of civil society is open, it captures crucial features of contemporary societies in which social integration is dependent on the fixing of public institutions in cultural and moral systems of regulation. These in turn presuppose the presence of social networks and active public citizens.

Civil society is a sufficiently broad term to pull potentially into its ambit all forms of non-state activities and networks, but thereby risks losing any specificity. Throughout Glasius et al. (2002), for example, "civil society" is extended to cover virtually any non-governmental activity but its meaning is hardly examined at all, nor is there any attempt to estimate the impact of the myriad transnational organizations listed. As with globalization, civil society cannot be an outcome of a process that it has itself initiated. And again like globalization, civil society is credited with manifesting in contrasting forms – social movements and NGOs restraining global capital ("good civil society") as against forces of social fragmentation and intolerance such as the Durban Conference Against Racism ("bad civil society") (Glasius and Kaldor 2002). Even Al-Qaeda is compared in some detail with civil society organizations – having communications, initiating new forms of action, providing training, and engaging in fund raising (2002: 24)![10] The conceptual difficulty with this is that if civil society can manifest in radically different ways then we need other concepts and frameworks to account for these differences and the circumstances that gave rise to them. Following Holmes (1997: 269) it may be useful to regard civil society proper (as opposed to networks and organizations in general) as having the following characteristics:

- Autonomous institutions distinguishable from family, clan, locality, and the state – thus civil society is public space that is neither governmental nor particularistic.
- Though separate from the state, civil society is demonstrably in interaction with it through networks of embedded social links that act in a way to constrain and regulate governmental power.
- Civil society proper is further a realm of ethical life – of Kantian respect, dialogue, and civility. It is a means through which identities and values can be reflexively examined without recourse to exclusions, threats of force, and dogmatism.

The disadvantage of the latter condition this is that it is an explicitly normative concept but it may at least enable some meaningful differentiation between what is civil society and what is not. Where does all this leave the idea of civil society?

The concept of civil society discussed so far exists within the boundaries of the nation state, which many argue has been undermined by the process of globalization, as we noted in chapter 6). In this context some writers suggest that a transnational or global civil society may be emerging. There are several possibilities here. One is a Hobbesian variant in which the title of sovereignty is transferred to a new Leviathan that brings order to the anarchy of local states. Another is a Lockean variant of a pluralistic global constitutionalism and transparent democracy able to counter the governmental and corporate powers yet providing support for a liberal supranational order. Much writing on global civil society inhabits the latter conception, although most developments in the direction of transnational governance, especially through the "war on terror," are closer to the former. Byers (2002), for example, argues that the US is the most powerful regime since the Roman Empire with twelve aircraft carriers, major stocks of precision guided missiles and bombs, a massive defense budget, that can defeat almost any opponent while suffering only minimal losses. Yet the US is in unilateralist mode and is dispensing with the framework of international cooperation and jurisdiction[11] with the acquiescence of its former rival Russia – which accepts military bases in Kyrgyzstan, Tajikistan, and Uzbekistan. In this sense the US could be seen as an emergent Sovereign in the Hobbesian sense. Unlike earlier imperialism, the US manages international justice not as a function of its own national motives, *but in the name of global right* (Hardt and Negri 2000: 180). Although they hint here at a potential for a kind of global Leviathan, we have noted already that the US is neither acting within a framework of international law nor acting as lawgiver, and anyway such a role would probably be impossible not least because of the degree of resistance this would engender.

On the other hand, in the Lockean variant the state/civil society couplet is projected and reproduced on the world stage along with shared norms, international social networks, multilevel democratic systems, and an equalization of human rights (e.g. Thomas 1998; Held 1995; Walker 1994). A post-state global civil society develops based on recognition of inalienable human rights no longer tied to specific states or national membership (e.g. Turner 1993; Frost 1998). Moving away from these traditional conceptions, perhaps novel forms of civic sociality could be facilitated by communication technologies (Bell 1980) along with decentralized, lateral organizational forms (Ahrne 1996). Thus global social movements establish new networks, resources, and social capital, providing the infrastructure for global democratization (Walker 1994; Smith 1998; Anheier et al. 2001). Again, Sassen (2002b) talks about the "space constituted by the worldwide grid of global cities, a space with new economic and political potentialities" which she sees as "one of the most strategic spaces for the formation of transnational identities and communities." Global telecommunications, flexible loyalties and identities, she argues, facilitate the formation of cross-border geographies for an increasing range of activities and communities of membership. She writes of new political subjects, transnational identities and transnational loyalties, for example in a Europe-wide concept of citizenship and cross-border affiliations, and deterritorialized global cultures, global solidarity and identification around issues such as ecological interdependence.[12] These foster the growth of ethical civil society and rights (cf. Sklair 2002: 299ff.). However, she does not distinguish theoretically between international networks and associations that expand rights and ethical civil society and those that consolidate particular and exclusive identities – such as racist organizations on the web (see Back 2002a, 2002b). Again, the technologies that facilitate global interconnections allow an explosion of informal activity but with both civil and uncivil consequences.

Further, in discussing global civil society there is the crucial issue of the quality of the outcomes and how these are to be achieved. In the postcommunist world one can point to the existence of an infrastructure of transnational organizations, associations, and networks. One example of this is the increasing juridification of international relations – for example, the prosecution of war crimes through the War Crimes Tribunals for former Yugoslavia (in 1993), Rwanda (in 1994), and the prospect of a permanent International Criminal Court (Held 2002). However, Held points out that "[t]he focus of the liberal international order is on the curtailment of the abuse of political power, not economic power. It has few, if any, systematic means to address sources of power other than the political" (Held 2002). There is an evident conflict between a deregulating neoliberal model and entrenchment of cosmopolitan values concerning the equal dignity and worth of all human beings. Global economic liberalization and the unregulated growth of capitalist markets across the world have resulted in heightened levels of social inequality which states have reduced will or capacity to address. Noreena Hertz (2001: 11) has described this as a "silent takeover" in which following the end of the Cold War "the balance of power between politics and commerce has shifted radically," so that "corporations are taking on the responsibilities of government." The global order will become increasingly conflictual and dangerous with the emergence of "wild zones" in the former USSR, sub-Saharan and central Africa, the Balkans, and Central America (Urry 2002).

Not all advocates of global civil society, however, share this pessimism. Glasius and Kaldor (2002) point to the accelerating numbers of and connections between International Non-governmental Organizations (INGOs) since 1990, and a further list of these is provided by Oliviero and Simmons (2002). The latter claim that INGOs have had considerable success in forcing global corporations to accept social responsibility such as the International Code of Marketing Breastmilk Substitutes that rose from the international Nestlé Boycott. (They do, however, point out that "no one has yet attempted to assess the overall effect of the CSR [Corporate Social Responsibility] movement.") Glasius and Kaldor (2002) cite as further evidence of global civil society the growth of "parallel summits" since 1990 such as the 2001 Porto Alegre meeting in Brazil attended by 11,000 people to protest against the Davos (Switzerland) World Economic Forum. These parallel summits, along with the extensive and interconnected anticapitalist, ecology, and peace movements, provide an alternative vision of a world order based on global norms of human rights, environmental protection, and social justice. One measure of their impact is the dramatic increase in their numbers and membership since 1990 and the increasing ratification of international treaties. They do, nonetheless, sound a note of caution when they observe that "September 11 was a moment when international law might have been taken seriously . . . [since] terrorists, human rights violators, and criminals are best defeated by scrupulously upholding the rule of law" (Glasius and Kaldor 2002: 27), but this is not what happened.

This caution is significant. Providing lists of INGOs and their networks does not amount to demonstrating the presence of an effective global civil society in which both corporate and state powers are embedded within normative frameworks. The aftermath of September 11 and the (unlosable yet unwinnable) war on terror casts doubt on these optimistic expectations for the development of global civil society. So too does the way in which the end of the Cold War has seen the global expansion of an Islamist ideology of resistance to the West that has filled the space previously inhabited by Third World socialism and communism (Dwyer 1991: 74). Though inimical to the idea of an ethically governed civil society, Islamist ideology is able to mobilize mass support across considerable areas of the world as a form of resistance to Sovereign power. None of this looks promising for the Lockean variant of a global civil society. At the level of the national state there is a shift from govern*ment* to govern*ance* (Jessop 1999) where the state becomes one agent among others operating in subnational, national, and international domains. The realm of the state, that was formerly "exterior" to civil society, becomes localized and hence "interior" to the realm of private interests (civil society) which becomes global, through transnational capital. Thus the local state may lose its cohesion and become a set of "disaggregated agencies" rather than the center of distributional politics (Miller 1993: 222). One consequence of this is that the nation state cannot sustain social welfare, and people's vulnerability to the effects of the market is increased. Meanwhile capital gains maximum mobility across national boundaries, taking command of *space* in a way that voluntary organizations rooted more in locality and *place* cannot do (Harvey 1994: 238). In this context a more likely outcome is a Hobbesian contract in which democracy is traded at the cost of weakening civil society in the sense defined here. Anticommunism re-posed questions about the analytical and political validity of civil society, but postcommunist practices have highlighted some of its limitations. We need to develop a more nuanced way of theorizing the relationship between institutions, political democratization, personal life, and public involvement. One issue here is the way in which institutions become embedded in cultural systems resources deployed to legitimate and pursue their objectives (a theoretical model along these lines was developed in Ray 1993).

Civil society was destroyed by communism and one indication of social and cultural renewal during the 1980s was its reappearance in new movements and identities – the "détente from below" that Michnik describes. But the promise of a new society founded on these informal civil networks was not fulfilled, even in Poland where it looked most promising. This was probably for a number of reasons, including generalized mistrust of public bodies and legacies of privatism that was functional under communism as an alternative channel of material and cultural reproduction but became more problematic in the context of democratic state building. The transition has been accompanied by recession, uncertainty, and dislocation which has demanded considerable readjustment to postcommunist realities – to a greater extent in some countries than others – but to some extent everywhere. These circumstances along with the institutional legacies of the *ancien régime* will inhibit the development of open civil societies. Part of the difficulty, though, lies in the civil society literature itself that does not adequately distinguish between the mere presence of networks and informal association on the one hand, and ethical civil public life on the other. This will be explored further in the next chapter. One of the crucial problems to be resolved by all complex societies is the management of infinitely possible connections between people who for the most part remain anonymous to one another. However, it should not be assumed that tight networks are evidence of "strong" civil life while loose networks indicate "weak" public engagement. On the contrary, more open, anonymous, and "weaker" networks may also be more receptive to cultural learning, respect for difference and democratic values. Tighter, closed, and exclusive networks (e.g. familial or ethnically based) may be more internally homogeneous and cohesive but generate factional and fragmentary conflicts. The circumstances that promote the development of the former as opposed to the latter will now be explored while introducing the further theme of modes of social remembering.

8

Modernity, Memory, and Postcommunism

People's cruelty and use of violence towards other people is central to the whole problem of civil society.

Mennell (1995)

The secret of redemption is remembrance.

Bal Shem Tov

A theme that has been pursued throughout this volume has been the place of communism within the social and cultural conditions of modernity and the implications of its collapse for the sociological understanding of these. We have examined the complex relationships between communism, postcommunism, modernization, globalization, and the formation of new social linkages. One of the central issues for the understanding of modernity is how collective and state-sponsored violence appears endemic and disrupts the fragile order of civil society. Conflict and violence frequently accompany social change, and this is true of postcommunism even if its extent has been less than that predicted by some. Mestrović (1994: 192), for example, regarded the crisis in former Yugoslavia as a microcosm of the fate of the postcommunist world, where conflagration threatened to engulf the region if not the whole world. There has been a much more differentiated contrast between many relatively peaceful postcommunist transitions and the civil wars in Yugoslavia, which requires differential explanation. This contrast raises further questions about the relationship between modernity, civil society, and violence in particular, the "civilizational paradigm." Norbert Elias argued that the central problem of the emergence of modern civil societies was the taming of warriors and internal conflict. The process of internal pacification within premodern societies associated with increased personal restraint and mannered conduct was facilitated by the growth of trade, towns, and a more complex division of labor, and the collection of taxes that allowed the emergence of civil society. The longer and denser are networks of interdependence, the more people are obliged to attune their actions to those of others and the less their interactions will be marked by overt violence. It is true that this paradigm has been criticized. Bauman in particular (e.g. 1999: 12–18) has argued that the "civilizing process" as a depiction of the emergence of modern societies is a myth and that violence, genocide, and the Holocaust were made possible precisely by the formal bureaucratic procedures of modern societies. However, the civilizational paradigm does not present a rosy view of a future without violence and Elias (1996) used his theory to shed light on Nazism and the Holocaust. He argues that a peculiar conjuncture of circumstances following World War I established a "decivilizing process" – a resurgence of warrior values, decay of the state's monopoly of force, middle-class resistance to the Weimar Republic, and an escalating double-bind of violence and counter-violence that ended in Hitler's rise (Dunning and Mennell 1998). More generally, as Mennell (1995) points out, the pacification of society is only one side of the coin since global interdependence and increasing proximity are also likely to produce more friction, tension, and violence as insecurity and fears release aggression and violence. One manifestation of this in the post-communist world is internecine strife and ethnic violence between groups with opposed narratives of memory and identity. Attempting to reconcile Bauman and Elias, De Swaan (2001) argues that state-organized violence involves a twofold movement of rationalization–bureaucratization *and* regression, break-down and barbarism. Following Elias he argues that this happens as a result of "disidentification" between ethnic groups along with a campaign to strengthen identifications among the rest of the population, thus creating increased polar-ization. He describes the result as a "dyscivilizing" process in which society is compartmentalized into areas where "peaceful" everyday life continues, and those such as the camps, where extreme violence is perpetrated against the targeted group.

How, then, should we approach the violence of some postcommunist transi-tions and what is the relationship between ethnic–national identities and vio-lence? King (2000) suggests that national heterogeneity is an impediment to democratization and peaceful development. Multiculturalism, King suggests, is a luxury in established democracies but an obstacle to the process of democra-tization. There are several counter-arguments to this claim. First, homogeneous "nation states" in the sense of territorially bounded areas that coincide with the single national and/or ethnic cultural populations are exceptional. Most states encompass multiple ethnicities as well as groups with differing national aspir-ations whose populations construct networks of belonging on multiple levels within and across borders (e.g. Walby 2003). This is true of most of the inde-pendent states that formed within the former Soviet Union. But in a globalized era multicultural states are the norm rather than the exception and the process of state formation or renewal has to find ways of dealing with this – such as establishing republican, juridical concepts of citizenship whose basis lies in ra-tional–legal formality rather than ethnic identity. Second, there is no single discourse of nationhood since national belonging is constructed in different ways – a notable distinction being that between membership by descent (*ius sanguinis*) as in Germany, as opposed to birth (*ius soli*) as in the US (Watson 2000). Thus the particular configuration of territory and cultural–national belonging is not something fixed but subject to historical and cultural processes. Third, we should be careful not to read back into history the tragic outcomes of the twentieth century and regard them as inevitable or endemic. Even in Eastern

Europe, a region of kaleidoscopic ethnic variety, ethnic conflicts do not loom large historically and "what might strike the unprejudiced student is the extraordinary stability, if not unqualified success, of ethnic relations in the area" (Kumar 2001: 12). This is not to deny, of course, that ethnic and *völkisch* states have been created on the basis of ethnic exclusivity and violence. But we noted in our discussion of the "clash of civilizations" (pp. 140–4) that it is not so much that there are timeless and intractable historical conflicts, but rather collective identities can be radically altered and "memories" are elastic and changing. Thus, finally, to understand the failure of this project and its spiral down into a process of dyscivilization, we need to examine the conditions in which it is possible to mobilize national, ethnic, or other identities in ways that promote violent exclusion of supposed enemies. In a context of dramatic social upheaval communities can externalize dangerous experiences onto "enemies" with whom they were previously intimate (Murer 2002). The collapse of Yugoslavia into genocidal war, for example, involved extricating and mobilizing national and ethnic identities that had in many cases been merged into a more diffuse, if always contested, "Yugoslavian" identity (Ramet 1991).[1] The civil war, reflecting a crisis in bonds of social solidarity and civil society, created an obsession with enemies within and what Kristeva calls "familiar foreigners." In this context we will examine the processes of memory, narrative, and cultural formation in an era of globalization.

Resurgence of Memory

There is presently a passion for the recovery and discovery of collective and individual "pasts," which are brought into the service of constructing and maintaining identities in a new memory politics. As Prager notes:

> Today the past has achieved a kind of iconic, even sacred status. Remembering the past is now widely understood as a valuable activity in and of itself; . . . We have become a society of "memory groups" where one's claim to group membership typically goes unchallenged because a common past . . . constitutes an area of discourse that cannot be contested. (Prager 1998: 1)

This reappraisal of the past has followed the end of communism in particular, partly because, as noted in chapter 7, the communist period was experienced as an erosion of memory in a "regime of oblivion." Collective memories (e.g. folk narratives, public rituals, architecture and landscape, education and culture) were placed under supervision and direction, so the "struggle to remember becomes a form of opposition" (K. E. Smith 1996: 11). The end of communism was also a disintegration of official collective memory and the articulation of multiple unofficial narratives of commemoration (Baron 1997). However, the ways in which the past is recalled and the mobilization of the trauma associated with these can have powerful and, as in the case of former Yugoslavia, destructive consequences.

This chapter explores the relationships between memory, commemoration, and postcommunism.

In this context, memory has recently become a major theme in cultural studies and sociology. This is not in itself a new topic in sociology, but whereas the older (Mannheimian) sociology of knowledge regarded ideologies as an expression of particular social locations, in a globalized information age such ideas seem reductionist. Globalization and the Internet create potential for multiple identities – cosmopolitan, local, and regional. Knowledge now inheres not in "consciousness" but (for example) in non-linear textuality, discourses and electronic archives, film and video. Gergen (1994) talks about the postmodern "multiphrenia" of memories that are exteriorized in print, film, photograph, cinema – not based on common experience but "parallel memory" (Lash 1999: 296). In web-based archives, the linearity of text and narrative memory gives way to non-linearity in virtual time, offering multiple levels and entrances, simultaneous presence, and virtual "experience." Thus between the sociology of memory of the 1920s (e.g. Halbwachs 1992) and the present lie the various postmodernist and cultural turns that frame our current understandings. As the idea of a subject that "possesses" memory has given way to one in which memory inheres in texts and archives, so has the politics of memory taken on increased significance.[2] There is a contrast here between the typical "modern" forms of commemoration – with clear lines between public and private symbols of commemoration – and more individualist post- or late-modern forms of private appropriation of public histories that resonate with more general themes of individualization addressed by Beck and others. Nonetheless, one insight from Halbwachs's work that we should keep in mind is that while monumental space draws people together and "exudes timelessness," its meanings will shift according to contemporary concerns.

Why has there been this recent resurgence? One stimulus has been the increase in disputed concepts of nationhood, which are crucial to many contemporary conflicts, in the context of state crisis. This resurgence of nationalism has occurred in the postcommunist world in which issues of memory, identity, and coming to terms with the past have been central. There has, further, been new confrontation with the Holocaust, which had entered ambiguously into official and popular memories of Eastern Europe (Misztal 2003). This has coincided with a resurgence of "memory" controversies in Western societies and has contributed to renewed theoretical debate within the social sciences. While for some, this revival of national and ethnic politics underlines the importance of shared culture and history in the creation of solidarity, for others, memory work is evidence of the simulated and depthless culture of postmodernity. According to the latter view, the heroic monumentalism of high modernity – the public encoding and enforcement of collective versions of the past – has given way to more privatized and pluralistic appropriation of memories and identities. These include the increased use of websites devoted to commemoration of genocide, and especially the Holocaust, in the twentieth century.[3] With this proliferation, "access" to memories that are defining for membership of an identity group is detached from place and community and becomes a form of private consumption.

But these virtual and imagined communities (as we noted in the previous chapter) do not necessarily enhance the expansion of ethical civil society. Anthony Elliott (2003: 178) argues: "The resurgence of nationalism throughout Europe . . . has been substantially based upon . . . an unleashing of primordial sentiments and attachments at the local, regional, national or continental levels, exposing the fractured and dispersed structure of the imaginary basis of intolerance . . . as well as the defensive rejection of ambivalence and uncertainty in the context of globalization." The nation is a mnemonic community whose *raison d'être* derives from both remembering and forgetting, especially where the past poses a threat to the unity of the nation. Thus memory and its appropriation have become central issues in societies emerging from the erasure of public memory and the survival of counter-memories. While these counter-memories acted as a focus of resistance to official rewriting of history, they could also have deadly consequences – as in the Yugoslavian wars.

Modernity and Commemoration

In modern societies the transmission of collective memory is not a continuous process but is subject to dislocation. One consequence of modernity was to erase traditional forms of cultural transmission while generating a sense of dependence on the past, especially through public memorials that engendered a distinctive form of memory and commemoration. Increasingly significant among these in the twentieth century were war memorials. No longer living within memory embedded in communities, where memory installs remembrance within the sacred, modern forms of memory are radically different to those experienced in archaic societies (Misztal 2003: 196). Merging personal and collective identity and memory, monuments replace the real site of memory, while shaping the past involved struggle for supremacy (2003: 204). The differentiation of a specialized religious field, the gradual pluralization of institutions, communities, and systems of religious thought correspond historically to the differentiation of total social memory into a plurality of specialized circles of memory. Two consequences follow from this. First, memory becomes subject to a homogenizing process – mass communication and media image production lead to saturation and focus on a perpetual present. Second, there is increasing fragmentation of memory for individuals, and different social groups attempt to construct their pasts in various ways.

A familiar sociological trope is that modernization creates "social amnesia," as a result of which the past becomes something to preserve and recover (Jacoby 1975; Koselleck 1985). Sociologists have often pointed to the transformation of time that occurs with industrialization, with reference in particular to the effects of mechanized work processes on the rhythms of life (Thompson 1967). Calendrical time in premodern societies was cyclical and punctuated with festivals that emphasized recurrence rather than linear time. These carried the risk of disorder and of inverting (albeit temporarily) the roles of the powerful and powerless, for example the Lords of Misrule and the Harlequinade. Popular festivals were often parodies of established customs and institutions (such as the mysteries of the Mass) which released social tensions and had the potential to threaten the powers that be. But this cyclical interruption of order with festive extravagance did not mark the movement of time, nor was it therefore invested with collective memory. Similarly, astrological time was heterogeneous, cyclical, and substantive, by contrast with the linear, empty, and disenchanted modern cosmos.

By the sixteenth century, though, European aristocracies were developing narratives of national memory – in England under the Tudors arose the idea of "God's Englishmen," which, like the Old Testament chosen people, claimed a unique future and distinctive past. This may have initially penetrated little into popular consciousness, but by the following century and especially after the Protestant ascendancy, this translated into a national consciousness marked by festivals linked to themes of time and deliverance. These included November 5, Armada Day, and, after the Restoration, Royal Oak Day, although these festivals of national commemoration were subject to reinterpretation by the reigning powers (Cressy 1994).

Industrialization, along with the rapid pace of technological and commercial change, brought about a rupture of collective memory – the intergenerational transmission of social knowledge and its relevance were dislocated by this social change. In this context the problem of social integration itself became a central topic of social and political reflection, and indeed a central theme in early sociology (Ray 1999b). Architecture, monuments, and public rituals played important roles in creating an external memory along with, for example, medals, postage stamps, statuary, and festivals (Olick and Robbins 1998). Ozouf (1988) argues that the first attempt to tie public festivals to a national calendar were the French revolutionary festivals, such as Bastille Day. These involved the transference of sacrality from religious to political objects – the tricolor cockades, liberty trees, red liberty caps, and the goddess of liberty (Hunt 1990). The rupture of cultures of transmission brought about by political revolutions and industrialism engendered a sense of detachment from the past. In the process, calendrical time was invested with progress and narrative, as a shell through which events moved. The theme of deliverance – having been saved from foreign invasion or internal subversion – was supplemented by public rituals and festivals around monuments and memorials, punctuating the movement of time as markers that looked back and forward. Nineteenth-century monumental architecture often harked back to classical antiquity, connoting a depth of time and distant origins. The Roman standard for a victory monument was the triumphal arch – evident in modernist triumphalism, such as the Arc de

Triomphe in Paris and Marble Arch in London. But these were not simply replicas of classical triumphal arches – within the Arc de Triomphe were inscribed the names of hundreds of Napoleon's generals, with the names of those who died in battle underlined; thus the status of the arch as a specifically war memorial was established. These were in part memorials to rulers, but also served to engender a sense of collective identity, while expressing aspirations of a self-confident bourgeois order. Memory processes have been imagined and communicated through a variety of spatial and visual metaphors that construct an architecture of internal memory places (Hallam and Hockey 2001: 77). Monumental solidity offered resistance to the possibility of everything melting into air, creating the appearance at least of timelessness and solidity.

The rise of nationalism was central to this process, since rapid social change and loss of cultural remembrance paved the way for new forms of imagined community (Anderson 1993). The anonymous collectivity of the nation was one way of creating a new sense of connectedness to the past and hence a rootedness in the present. Nationalism further had an advantage over liberal notions of market and rights-based individualism in that the former invoked more affective and transmissible solidarities. Nationalist concepts of loyalty invoke communities of memory, in which identity is rooted in notions of shared traits (ethnicity, culture, language) through which the remembrance of the past is protected and becomes a political instrument (Smith 1997). In this sense, as Gellner (1994: 107) noted, nationalism invokes both *Gemeinschaft* and *Gesellschaft* – the impersonal binding of anonymous people that is achieved by appeal to common community and history.

Landscape is central to nationalism, since territory becomes inscribed with history and temporality. Landscape is external – it is a visible and palpable synthesis of time and space, a fusion Bakhtin (1981) describes as a "chronotope," the intrinsic connectedness of temporal and spatial relationships. In this sense landscapes and monuments are chronotopes in which time has been condensed in space symbolically arranged and invested with myth and identity. This occurs in official commemorations, such as battlefields, monuments, and special days, but is also vibrant in unofficial practices. Yet these external memories require continuous mobilization and enforcement, since monuments can become invisible and fade into the background. Much reinforcement of national identities is "banal nationalism" (Billig 1997), that is, the routine ways of instilling a shared sense of the collective past inscribed into everyday events, such as saluting the flag. Even so, banal monuments are not innocent since they are often the sites of conflict between competing (often incompatible) histories and unstable in that they are subject to competing meanings.

Add to this, though, the role of globalized technologies in creating and sustaining "memory," and the process of their transmission identity is complex. Postmodernists tend to emphasize the fluidity of "memory" while others seek to identify real sites of cultural transmission. Anthony Smith in particular has argued that the ancestral land links memory to destiny (Smith 1997). By contrast to the ephemerality of "memoryless" global culture, Smith (1996) argues, the "obstinate fact is that national cultures, like all cultures before the modern epoch, are particular, time-bound and expressive and their eclecticism operates within strict cultural constraints." In particular, he says, national cultures display a sense of continuity across generations, shared memories of specific events, and common destiny on the part of the collectivity.

Smith implies that ethno-memories are the repository of a definable and stable group (similar to the older sociology of knowledge and ideology) but two issues are relevant to this. First, national identities are not stable and primordial, but unstable hybrids of conflicting passions, as "scraps, patches and rags of daily life must be repeatedly turned into the signs of a national culture" (Bhabha 1995: 297). Maintaining a personal narrative that instantiates and affirms a collective memory continually suppresses the irredeemably plural nature of modern identities. Second, an important issue here is how collective memories are transmitted, stored, mobilized, and made relevant to present concerns and projects. They are never just "there," and the sources of modern identity lie in multiple histories, media, and archives that are subject to revision, mobilization, and recombination according to contemporary cultural shifts and politics. It is true that commonly shared pasts create a necessary component of identity and history, providing an answer to the question, "who are we?" But this always seems to rely, as Kapralski (1997) notes, on the question of "who we were," and the existence of the group's collective identity also makes real a particular construction of the past. While Smith is right that the living transmission of cultural memory is an important component of national identity – it is also the case that the existence of national groups construct collective memories so that there is a self-sustaining process of remembering and collective identity. If this line of argument is correct, then Smith may be exaggerating the extent to which national–ethnic identities are primordially derived. Or at least, even if fragments of ethnic memories are primordial, their recombination may be mediated by electronic technologies, which impose their own structure on the content (Featherstone 2000). This suggests that collective memory has undergone a transformation in its mode of recall and representation.

The meaning and appropriation of public sites of memory is subject to contestation and struggle. "Memory is social because every memory exists through its relation with what has been shared with others: language, symbols, events and social and cultural contexts" (Misztal 2003: 19). Memories are organized around places and things that imprint effects on topography and space. However, in a period of increasingly postnational, diasporic identity, no single identity is given in definitely or in unchangeable form. A positive, if somewhat idealistic, view of this is that we witness both the privatization and democratization of sites of memory, in the sense that the perception of material objects (such as monuments) can be personal and liberated from the narratives embodied in them by the state. The old holidays and monuments have lost much of their power to commemorate and forge a single vision of the past, but they remain places where groups with different memories can communicate (Gillis 1994: 20).

Soviet Collective Memory and Counter-memory

The Soviet authorities were always sharply conscious of the need to control the transmission of collective historical consciousness (Baron 1997). Soviet modernism took much further than in the West the attempt to encode and embed its rule in monumental forms. Public commemoration was inscribed in public holidays, ubiquitous statues of revolutionary leaders, especially Lenin, war memorials and commemorations, mausoleums for dead leaders – a kind of necro-charisma in which death conferred quasi-sacred revolutionary legitimacy. Mausoleums, statues, ritual reliving of past and glorious struggles were ubiquitous features of the Soviet landscape. Especially following World War II (the Great Patriotic War) memorials were "indelibly inscribed into the Russian cultural landscape" (Bogorov 2002), although their construction was dogged by controversy, illustrating the contested nature of collectivised memory. "Who," asks Bogorov (2002), "was to receive the main credit for the ultimate, if bloody, triumph? A new 'socialist human being' forged by the trials of the Bolshevik revolution, alongside a new historic 'brotherhood of the Soviet peoples'? Or the unbending strength of the Russian national character, fortified by the ancient hatred of alien invaders? Then where was the place for the omnipotent Party's 'leading and guiding role?' Or the military genius of Comrade Stalin?" Critics and architects proposed monuments based on classical designs (a Soviet Pantheon) projecting an image of timelessness and the universal struggles of the Soviet people with Nazism, while others proposed commemoration of the centuries-old struggle of the Russian people against foreign invaders. The latter evoked Russia's pre-Bolshevik past and used cultural references to Russian Orthodoxy merged with images of Stalin, firmly situated within the Russian imperial tradition. One example of these monuments is the Komsomol'skaia-Kol'tsevaia metro station, which features an entrance crowned with a cupola and a spire, bearing a resemblance to a huge *shlem*, a Russian knight's helmet. The station's major hall is dominated by a huge arched ceiling bearing eight mosaic panels. These depict the most celebrated moments from Russian military history. Each panel is centered around a certain historical figure, starting from prince (and a Russian Orthodox saint) Aleksandr Nevskii, famous for his victories over the invaders of the German Teutonic Order, and ending with Stalin, reviewing the Soviet troops which had vanquished Hitler's Germany (Bogorov 2002). In this monumental architecture a crucial shift had occurred from a Bolshevik to national–imperial mode of legitimation. This was to have lasting effect – since 1991 the celebration of Victory Day in Russia on May 9 has remained one of the most popular holidays and its associated rituals remain a focus for the mythical narrative of nationhood.

Gorbachev's reforms hesitantly and ambiguously began to allow critical evaluation of Soviet history and, most important, a confrontation with Stalinist genocide. Though initially attempting to create a regulated space for remembrance and vacillating between promotion and restraint of debate, glasnost allowed the articulation of non-official popular counter-memories such as Tengiz Abuladze's film *Repentance* (1984).[4] These then rapidly took the form of revived or recreated national and ethnic memories and identities. The symbolic realm – public rituals and holidays, anthems and uniforms, monuments and street names – that had been crucial to Soviet legitimation became a battleground in post-Soviet politics. Post-Soviet Russian politics have seen recurrent battles over the content of Russia's state anthem and flag, over burying Lenin's corpse and closing his mausoleum on Red Square, and over the renaming of multiple locations still carrying the names of former Soviet leaders. Underlying these are fundamental questions of national identity – "what is Russia?" "who is Russian?" which in turn reflect the fragility of Russian statehood. The war in Chechnya, numerous challenges of ethnic and regional separatism within the Russian Federation, tense relations with neighboring Soviet successor states, and real or perceived threats from abroad all compounded to create a deep sense of national insecurity that permeates Russian society (Bogorov 2002). This in turn has led to an intense re-examination of Russian history, and each of the major competing forces on the political scene has offered its view of the historical canon. Competition among political elites for control over the sites guided their transformation from symbols of the Soviet Union into symbols of Russia. By co-opting certain monuments through transformation and commemorative maintenance political elites engaged in a symbolic dialogue with the public in an attempt to gain legitimacy (Forest and Johnson 2002).

This contestation has extended across postcommunist Europe. Kapralski (2001) points out that in the wake of the collapse of "official" commemorative activities the field has opened for often-bitter conflicts, illustrated by the conflicts over rhetorical ownership of Auschwitz. The connection between landscape, national identity, and remembrance is illustrated by these postcommunist conflicts over Auschwitz, which serves as a framework for competing national memories (Kapralski 2001). Kapralski argues that for Jews, Auschwitz symbolizes the Holocaust, the event that condensed a history of anti-Semitic persecutions, and therefore is a symbol of Jewish uniqueness in the face of annihilation. This is in a context in which the specifically Jewish significance of the site was largely denied during the communist period and the deaths of Jews de-emphasized in favor of the "Struggle against Fascism."[5] It has been suggested that for American and Western European Jews, going to Auschwitz involves passing through a secular ritual that confirms who they are as Jews (Kugelmass 1993: 419). For the Poles, Kapralski claims, Auschwitz symbolizes the Polish tragedy during World War II, which was a condensed history of German attempts to subordinate and eventually destroy the Polish nation. Polish nationalists, denied the chance to express national identity freely outside state-designed channels, redefine identity via the memory of Auschwitz – as a solely "Polish" place and a national–religious symbol. These conflicts came to a head in the early 1990s with the dispute over the Carmelite nuns at the site who had appropriated a camp building and erected more than 100 crosses (Misztal 2003: 121–2). This resulted in a fifteen-year conflict amid accusations of the Christianization of Auschwitz, which seemed doomed to remain unresolved. Although the convent was eventually moved outside the camp's boundary, a large wooden cross that had been erected at the height of the convent crisis in 1989 remained at the site. Both sides have now agreed that the cross will remain in perpetuity and some Jewish groups find this strangely appropriate. Rather than merely a memorial to the Polish victims of Auschwitz, they regard the cross as a symbol of divine abandonment – in accordance with Jesus's cry, "My God, my God, why hast Thou forsaken me?" Thus its presence at Auschwitz may be seen as a testimony to the absence of divine intervention which has so exercised theologians since the Holocaust (Klein 2001). As the collapse of communist official control on interpretation and commemoration of the past disappeared, such memorials have been subject to struggles for appropriation, especially by peoples in the past marginalized in a process that asserts claims to contemporary national formation.[6] Competing historical narratives and the commemoration of genocide are bitterly contested around landscape and monuments.

Nationalism and Death

Auschwitz is a powerful symbol, in many ways the ur-phenomenon not only of the Holocaust but of twentieth-century genocide. Sites commemorating mass death are especially potent since the rhetoric of national identity emerges particularly through the pathos of remembrance. But these meanings are never fixed and there is interplay between elite and popular uses of the monuments. Diverse social groups invoke the commemorative power of public objects and spaces such as war memorials, statues, and street names in different ways. Nationalism can be seen as a way of repairing the rupture in collective memory brought about by industrialization, but nationalism is linked to death in that the industrial age was *par excellence* the age of movement of weapons, troops, and populations through time and space. It was the age of mass "democratic" wars and armies, through which modernity's war machine heralded the depletion of time and space (Virilio and Lotringer 1983: 5). With the erection of war memorials national identity appealed to a putative community of the living and the dead. The commemoration ceremony of Remembrance "they shall not grow old as we who are left grow old" has the mnemonic effect of summoning the presence of the absent, and inviting participants to join with an imagined community including the living and the dead (Frijda 1997). The inscription of names on monuments speaks to a transcendence of forgetting that is poignant and disturbing and links individuals to the nation across generations. The externalization of memories of mass death occurred particularly after World War I, though these had precursors in war cemeteries such as Gettysburg National Cemetery.

The scale and scope of World War I had deprived survivors of the capacity for memory in the sense of relating encompassing narratives to account for their experiences. Walter Benjamin (1979) claimed that the War was a cataclysm that had left people without conditions for telling stories in that tactical and mechanical warfare, hyperinflation, the vast movements of population, and the scale of destruction wrested the events from the grasp of individual life histories. Lowenthal argues that memory's most serviceable reminder was landscape, and memorials and monuments locate the imagined or remembered past in the present landscape (Lowenthal 1979: 104). Winter (1999) believes that spatial memory (as distinguished from visual memory) transforms latent memory into active ("flash-bulbs lighting up") memory when an individual occupies a site associated with a ritual or event. He further claims that warfare, particularly in the twentieth century, is a time of dramatic and unique experiences, which leave dense memory traces, both social and individual. Witnesses of warfare, whether surviving soldiers, family members of those wounded or killed, surviving civilian victims, or their relatives, were all involved in memory work – that is, in a public rehearsal of memories. They acted in order to fill in silence, to struggle with grief, to offer something symbolically to the dead.

The effect was not *amnesia*, but a particularly modern form of public memory that became a sacred experience, the purpose of which was no longer to marvel but to mourn (Laqueur 1994). These war memorials further reflected the rise of mass culture and democratization. Earlier war memorials, where they existed at all, had commemorated only officers and royal leaders. Now each fallen soldier was commemorated by name, or at least regiment, in standardized format without personalized inscriptions (e.g. Schwartz 1982). This was a form of official, public memorialization that was no longer unambiguously progressive. One purpose of the war memorial was to serve as the center of rituals of mourning which bind together the putative national community in a sense of collective wrong. But the silent horror and pathos of World War I memorials, such as Vimy Ridge near Arras in northern France, is open to various meanings. War grave commemoration has elided the unambiguous meaning of national sacrifice to admit to the possibility that this was meaningless killing – emphasizing for example (as at Vimy Ridge) the closeness of the German and Commonwealth lines, separated year on year by a few meters. Over the years the landscape of the Western Front and the imagined landscape of sites that attracted travelers altered. The scenes of death and destruction to be found on the battlefields were, as Lloyd says, initially the centers of attraction for many travelers. When much of the devastation and most of the wartime aspect of the battlefields was removed by reconstruction, the travel objective shifted to the cemeteries and memorials built by the Allies, and the few remaining battlefield sites. Increasingly for travelers the imagined landscape was perceived within the context of the war's wider meaning, which shifted between, on the one hand, concern that the horrors of war needed to be remembered and avoided to, on the other, an appreciation of the heroism and the sacrifices made. Lloyd shows how this dichotomy between two approaches to the meaning of the landscape led to debate: did it sanitize, glorify even, war, or was it a lesson in peace? After the War, the first travelers to the Western Front were confronted by a landscape that denied not only order, but also civilization. Lloyd points out that an important theme of battlefield travel in the 1920s was sacrifice. In particular this was associated with the memorials and cemeteries that came to dominate both the actual and the imagined landscape during the 1920s and 1930s (Lloyd 1998: 100–1). It would be hard to argue that the war memorials and cemeteries are overtly patriotic structures that were designed to celebrate a major national triumph and mask the War's horrors. The sheer scale of the loss commemorated means that to lionize the dead and glorify war is both distasteful and inappropriate. The commemorative landscapes of World War I were invoked frequently by Britain's interwar peace movement, but these landscapes were not unequivocally antiwar statements consciously designed to indicate modern war's futility and waste (Heffernan 1995). A shift toward the demystification of heroic death in public commemoration has been accompanied by falling military participation rates in most Western societies along with the technologization of mass death, which is no longer labor-intensive.

Mourning or Melancholia?

We have suggested that memorials embed within landscape and ritual discourses of national collectivity complex processes of remembering and forgetting. But they are also ambiguous and open to diverse meanings. This very ambiguity enables the process of memory to be mobilized in the service of national formation, but it can also trigger the release of violence in the name of unexpiated historic wrongs. It may be useful to bear in mind Freud's distinction between mourning – memory work that enables reconciliation with loss – and melancholia, where the loss is continually revisited, is vital, intrusive, and persistent. The latter becomes a metaphor of modernity in which genocide cannot be presented within traditional historical perspectives (Freud 1984). This helps us understand the dynamics of civil conflict in the postcommunist world. Death and genocide evoke powerful responses and it is crucial whether these take the form of reconciliation with the past (mourning) or melancholic repression of grief followed by repetition of trauma that cannot be expurgated.

We have seen how the ways in which people remember their past are dependent on their relationship to their community, public discourses of legitimation, and the contestations between these. For Halbwachs, memory was social in that its content is intersubjective (we remember interactions with others), it is structured around social reference points (such as rituals and ceremonies), and it is shared (rehearsal of memories is associated with high levels of affect) (Paez et al. 1997: 153). These writers did not, however, address collective processes of *communication* (Connerton 1989: 10). Lury (1998) has further shown how self-identity and memory are redefined through the manipulation of personal and public photographic images. But (as Lury also notes, 1998: 12) it is not the remembered so much as the forgotten that provides the key to "rewriting the soul." Again, "remembering and forgetting are . . . locked together in a complicated web as one group's enfranchisement requires another's disenfranchisement" (Watson 1994: 18). In particular, the notion of trauma provided the point of entry into the "psychology of the soul" through which the forgotten could be therapeutically remembered (Hacking 1994).

Commenting on Freud's theory of aggression, Alford (1998: 71ff.) argues that "hatred is ego-structuring. It can define a self, connecting it to others, anchoring it in the world, which at the same time acting as a fortress. . . . Hatred creates history, a history that defines the self and provides it with structure and meaning." Moreover, "loving recitation of harms suffered and revenge inflicted, constitutes the single most important, most comprehensible and most stable sense of identity." If this argument is valid, then alongside the mannered interactions and civility, civilization also shifts powerful and disturbing emotions and experiences from the center of life to the periphery. In this process, public rituals and symbols of commemoration inscribe a collective narrative memory into individual life histories. Narrative emphasis on continuity and development leads to a unity of the self as a project with access to personal and collective memories. The connection is made clearly in Russian between *pamyat'* (memory) and *pamyatnik* (monument), thus linking individual and collective levels of commemoration. Being a member of a national community often involves taking ownership of a public, historical narrative that typically defines a degree of difference and sense of a nation beleaguered. In her interviews with survivors of the Latvian deportations of the 1940s, Vieda Skultans (1998) found that respondents often drew no temporal distinctions between the deaths of immediate family and historical events – such as the death of Namijs, a thirteenth-century Latvian chieftain who resisted a German invasion. Personal loss is shaped by and is located alongside textual memories adapted from school history and literature lessons (Skultans 1998: 18). Further, terror does not necessarily destroy civilizational values. Rather, witnesses to genocide say they cannot describe these experiences, and when they find their way into narratives they are no longer direct expressions of the past but draw on cultural resources to give the descriptions meaning (Skultans 1998: 22).[7]

An important contrast here lies in the way memories are communicated and the dispositions to which coming to terms with the past give rise – through mourning and memory-work or melancholia. One theme within the emergence of modern, post-traditional worldviews has been what Habermas (1989a: 335–7) calls the "linguistification of the sacred," in which the "spell-binding power of the sacred" is eroded by the collapse of binding worldviews and by the argumentative functions of language. On a more practical level, it is possible that open and reflexive discourse enables participants to confront the complexities and ambiguities of their identities and pasts in ways that diffuse violent emotions and effect reconciliation between antagonists. This at any rate is the idea behind practices of mediation and reparation and institutional processes such as the South African Truth and Reconciliation Commission. By contrast, many public commemorative ceremonies close off any open or reflexive reconciliation of past grievances. Durkheim pointed out the extent to which sacred public rituals reaffirmed collective solidarity through commemorative rites that relive the mythical history of ancestors and sustain the vitality of beliefs by rendering them present (Durkheim 1976: 371ff.). One might imagine that modern values deny credence to the idea of life as a structure of celebrated recurrence, but actually commemorative rituals are dependent on calendrical time that enables the juxtaposition of profane time with the sacred return marked by anniversaries (Connerton 1989: 64). Further, the sacredness of public commemoration (such as Remembrance parades) is dependent on a highly ritualized language in which stylized and stereotyped sequences of speech acts contrast with the linguistification of the sacred. Commemorative speech does not admit any interrogation of its discursive properties because its meanings are already coded in canonical monosemic forms (e.g. oaths, blessings, prayers, and liturgy) that bring into existence attitudes and emotions. For example, the words "they shall not grow old as we who are left grow old" do not admit discursive interrogation. Listeners are not invited to reflect on the benefits of immortality within a putative national community, set against the cost of premature death on the battlefield. The particular speech variant of commemorative and other public rituals is important because they therefore close off possibilities for the reflexive examination and juxtaposition of identities.

A special but crucial case of public commemoration is what Durkheim (1976: 404ff.) called "sad celebrations," that is, piacular (expiatory, atoning) rites which fuse mourning and melancholy with sacrifice and violence, justifying Alford's "loving recitation of harms suffered and revenge inflicted." Their effect is to generate anger and the need to avenge the dead and discharge collective pain, manifesting in real or ritual violence. Victims are sought outside the group, especially among resident minorities "not protected by sentiments of sympathy," and women serve more frequently than men as objects of the cruelest rites of mourning and as scapegoats. The context for piacular rites is often a social crisis and the pressure to bear witness to sorrow, perplexity, or anger. Participants imagine that outside are evil beings whose hostility can be appeased only by suffering. Thus piacular rites involve mourning, fasting, and weeping, with obligations to slash or tear clothing and flesh, thereby restoring the group to the state of unity preceding misfortune. The more collective sentiments are wounded, as Durkheim suggested, the greater is the violence of the response.

Memory of Kosovo Polje

We see something of this in the mobilization of Serbian national myths in the late 1980s. Despite the efforts in pre- and postwar Yugoslavia to fashion a unified federal state, national counter-memories kept alive old hatreds in the popular consciousness, that were intensified by the experiences of war and occupation. In her account of travels in prewar Yugoslavia, Rebecca West quotes her Serbian guide in "Old Serbia" (Kosovo) in the 1930s:

> We will stop at Grachanitsa, the church I told you of on the edge of Kosovo Plain, but I do not think you will understand it, because it is very personal to us Serbs, and that is something you foreigners can never grasp. It is too difficult for you, we are too rough and too deep for your smoothness and your shallowness. (West 1982: 835)

National identity is public (shared and reinforced through public affirmation and commemoration) yet private to the putative community of those who share the particular imagined historical memory. "Roughness" (Serbian *surovost*, with connotations also of rudeness and brutality) is contrasted with the cosmopolitan superficiality of those who can never participate in the ethnic–cultural community. In this case, where the traditional blessing for the newborn is "Hail, little avenger of Kosovo" (Kaplan 1993: 38), one is born with the weight of unexpiated desire for vengeance.

From 1987 for two years, Slobodan Milosevic had conducted a carefully orchestrated campaign of nationalist hysteria, focused on Kosovo but widening gradually to conjure up for Serb audiences an unholy alliance of Albanians, Slovenes, and Croats. Milosevic made the 600th anniversary of the Battle of Kosovo in June 1989 the focal point of this "anti-bureaucratic revolution" to displace political opponents within the Serbian ruling party – especially Ivan Stambolic (who was abducted and murdered in 2000). Milosevic's speech in June 1989 invoked the "heroism" of 1389 in a theme of betrayal and lack of unity, linking the historic defeat at Kosovo, the German occupation in World War II, and Serbia's weakness in the Yugoslav Federation. Now he claimed that Serbia was a victim of Albanian "fascists and secessionists" who threatened the Serbian nation with "genocide." The nature of this threat had been made clear in the 1986 Serbian Memorandum, signed by 212 academics and artists complaining that the Albanians of Kosovo were pursuing a policy of "genocide" against Serbs. The threat of "genocide" was demographic – it claimed that the proportion of Serbs to Albanians in Kosovo was rapidly declining – from 23 and 67 percent respectively in 1961 to 90 and 10 percent in 1991 (Serbian Academy of Arts and Sciences 1986). But this imagined threat of "genocide" tapped into and mobilized cultural memories of Serbian "sacrifice" and genocide in the past (Ramet 1991: 185).

A classically piacular ritual signaled the escalation of national mobilizations prior to the Yugoslavian civil war. This was the Serbian commemoration of the battle of *Kosovo Polje* (Field of Black Birds) in 1389, where the last Serbian prince, Lazar, was defeated by the Turkish Sultan Murat. That this defeat is celebrated in Serbian national narrative as a "holy and honorable sacrifice" illustrates an important point about national mythologies – defeats, because of their affective and sacrificial power, may be more central than the "faked up glories and imagined pasts" of standard national rhetoric (Anderson 1993). In Serbian legend the sacrifice of Lazar who (according to a Serbian poem) "chose a heavenly kingdom" was also a sacrifice for Christian Europe, allowing Italy and Germany to survive. This became the cornerstone of modern Serbia's national mythology. The uprisings at the beginning of the nineteenth century were represented as the revival of the Serbs' struggle against the Ottomans at the end of the fourteenth century. Through these poems and songs, modern Serbia claimed a vital continuity with a romanticized past as a means of underscoring its claims to disputed territory. Most of the songs contained stark moral messages (Glenny 1999: 11–12). Martyrdom became a theme in Serbian propaganda, and the Serbian Network (a website maintained by the Serbian government) claims that it would be wrong to claim that the defeat at Kosovo prevented Serbia becoming a great nation. On the contrary: "It was [defeat] that made us a great nation. It is our Golgotha; but it is at the same time our moral resurrection" (<http://www.srpska-mreza.com/>). As mentioned above, Milosevic made the 600th anniversary of the Battle of Kosovo in June 1989 the focal point of his "anti-bureaucratic revolution." Demonstrations were organized throughout Serbia, Kosovo, and Vojvodina, which were among the opening moves in the war. The "coffin" (with the alleged remains of Lazar) toured every village in Serbia followed by huge black-clad crowds of wailing mourners. Serbian nationalists regard the autonomous province of Kosovo, with an Albanian-Islamic majority population, as lying in the "heartland of our nation." In the meadow of Gazimestan the monument to Lazar expresses vengeful sadness and defeat:

> Whosoever is a Serb and of Serbian birth
> And who does not come to Kosovo Polje to do battle against the Turks
> Let him have neither a male nor a female offspring
> Let him have no crop.

In contemporary nationalist symbolism, "Albanians" in Kosovo and other Islamic minorities elsewhere in former Yugoslavia, especially Bosnia, have substituted for "Turks." In both the Serbian and Croatian national imaginations, the civil war was a replaying of ancient conflicts of west and east, European and Asiatic, "civilization" and "barbarism."

The anniversary commemorations began the revolt against the Yugoslav Federation as nationalist violence triangulated throughout the country. The affect encoded in the Lazar memory informs contemporary discourses of violent conflict. During the fighting in Kosovo early in 1999, the Serbian Democratic Movement (nationalist and close to the Orthodox Church) claimed:

> We Serbs are a proud people who have endured throughout history – and still our homeland suffers the agonies of war. We respond with pride and courage. Never have we needed it more. . . . It is a courageous sacrifice. Before the Battle of Kosovo Prince Lazar told his gallant knights that it was better to die heroically than to live under the enemy yoke. More than ever, we must hold Kosovo dear for all the world to see, for it is a testament to the courage of our people. (*Serbia Information News*, March 1, 1999)

This and similar statements drew their meaning from the particular politics of memory in the Yugoslav Federation in which World War II had been "memorized" through education and public discourse as a people's liberation war – a struggle of class rather than ethnic or national aspiration (Hoepken 1999). The language of socialism had not permitted an open discourse nor subjected Yugoslav history to unrestricted discussion. With the collapse of the Federation the Party lost control of memory and secret histories of trauma and ethnic hatred were opened up. This coincided with a process of "recounting the dead" on all sides of the conflict prior to the civil war. The history of German occupation and conflicts between the Croatian Ustashe and the Chetniks (Serbian partisans) had left largely suppressed historical memories of mass slaughter. The collapse of Federal and communist rule was accompanied by the uncovering of (semi-) hidden massacres followed by new commemorative funerals, which provided a "supreme moment for transforming ritual into political theatre" (Hayden 1994: 172). Each subsequent antagonist in the civil war could mobilize the unexpiated trauma of suppressed memories. The communists were mass murderers (of Ustashas and Chetniks); the Croatian (fascist) state of 1941–5 was a murderer of Serbs; the Muslims were collaborators with Nazi genocide; while the new Croatian state under Tuðjman diminished the extent of Ustashe genocide, thus provoking further trauma-rage. All collective participants imagined themselves victims of unavenged historical wrongs that could be expiated only through the elimination of the enemy.

The ensuing conflict took on the proportions of what René Girard (1977) calls "violent contagion," which was exterminatory and potentially unlimited. This arises, in his view, from an unresolved primal conflict. Mimetic desire to acquire the wholeness of the other (which is experienced as a lack or incompleteness of oneself) leads to feud between incompatible rivals. By taking the other simultaneously as a model and obstacle they form "violent doubles" locked in mutual destruction. Violent doubles are characterized by incommensurable identities – to be X is to fear Y; to be Y is to fear X – locked in a feud in which one's enfranchisement requires another's disenfranchisement. This is resolved, temporarily, by sacrifice, where potentially violent doubles discharge mimetically generated violence on to an arbitrary and innocent victim whom they scapegoat, by attributing to the victim the violence they have just committed. The scapegoat mechanism establishes in-group/out-group differentiations that maintain the communities' structure and cohesion. This sacrificial expulsion is the basis of all social order and ritual through which communities gain control over their violence. Myths bind communities and symbolically discharge rage while disguising the original sacrifice-murder. But a crisis in the social order, a sacrificial crisis, can release the violent desires once renounced.

This is not the place for a detailed examination of this theory, which is dependent on a kind of Durkheimian rewriting of Hegel's master–slave dialectic and makes too ubiquitous a claim to explain specific social conflicts. But it may illuminate the dynamics of bitter and intractable national conflicts in which both sides claim exclusive rights over identical social and territorial space. One excludes the other, yet both share the same space and are destined to be enemies, until the spiral of violent contagion can be broken. In the Yugoslav case, a patchwork of competing national identities entered fields of struggle over incommensurable desires for national homelands. In a triadic pattern, minorities struggled with titular states for a national homeland that was the goal of each. The Krajina Serbs, looking to incorporation in a Serbian homeland, resisted Croatia's nationalizing desire, while Milosevic insisted that Croatia could be independent only without Krajina. In Kosovo the Serbian minority, backed by the Serbian army, resisted independence and the desire for unity with an Albanian homeland, as we have seen. The conflict in Bosnia was particularly exterminatory because it was a field of multiple doubles – Serb/Croat, Islamic/Serb, Islamic/Croat (Brubaker 1995), each struggling for incommensurable spaces.

Our claim is that in order to understand this and similar ethnic conflicts we need to understand the processes of construction and mobilization of collective memory. The Kosovan conflict took place on a landscape of sacred territory, which was an object of mutually exclusive desires for rectification of historical wrongs. Both sides legitimated exterminatory desires with reference to historical memories. Kosovo was alternately the spiritual home of Serb Orthodoxy, marked by holy sites, monasteries, and forced evacuations, both following Prince Lazar's defeat and again led by Patriarch Arsenije III Carnojevic in 1690; or for centuries populated predominantly by Albanians periodically subjected to Serbian genocide. "Ethnic cleansing" is not new to these landscapes. In accounts from both sides, commemorations and rituals demonstrate the loving recitation of harms suffered and revenge inflicted. The massacres and removals of Kosovans by Serbs in 1999 had had many precedents, such as the expulsions of Albanians during the second Serbian–Ottoman war (1877–8).[8]

Melancholia and grief, then, are of particular importance because they constitute the basis for the desire for vengeful justice. Grief and loss may prove to be significant in discourses authorizing violent actions. Unresolved grief does not allow accommodation or reconciliation but perpetuates stereotyped repetitions of thought and behavior. Further, state control and sanctification of national rituals of remembering will both preclude open confrontation with the past and encourage the formation of counter-memories that likewise will not be discursively examined. In this way conflicts become intractable, and an exterminatory violence results from friend/foe enmity in which the very presence of the other sustains yet threatens each identity.

Nonetheless, we should note that for both Durkheim and Girard (in different ways) piacular rites and mimetic scapegoats should operate to *contain* and limit violence. But they do not necessarily do so; on the contrary, they may act as catalysts and authorizations for further violence. In the examples cited above expiatory–sacrificial rituals were the prelude to violence that spilled out into communal destructiveness. Further, while the symbolic discharge of violence may serve to dissipate actual violence, the border between the symbolic and the real is unstable, and under conditions of crisis the former may spill over into the latter.[9] But whether violence is symbolically discharged (thereby being contained) or is real, is of critical importance, and we need to know how this line gets crossed. Rather than contain violence, the kinds of ritual memory discussed here generate an unstable process of national identity formation, which requires continual affirmation. National identity is not fixed or stable but is an unstable hybrid of conflicting passions, as "scraps, patches and rags of daily life must be repeatedly turned into the signs of a national culture" (Bhabha 1995: 297). Maintaining a personal narrative that instantiates and affirms a collective memory continually suppresses the irredeemably plural nature of modern identities. The more the maintenance of a unisonant self is threatened by the presence of competing identities, the more likely that inner conflicts will take the form of paranoid projections.

Postcommunism and Collective Memory

National memories are not only the repository of definable and stable groups. Rather, they are unstable and constructed as a hybrid of conflicting passions that are actively assembled into a narrative of "nationhood." Attempting to maintain a personal narrative that instantiates and affirms a collective memory continually suppresses the irredeemably plural nature of modern identities. The sources of modern "identity" lie in multiple histories, media, and archives that are subject to revision, mobilization, and recombination according to contemporary cultural shifts and politics. In web-based archives, the linearity of text and narrative memory gives way to non-linearity in virtual time, offering multiple levels and entrances, simultaneous presence and virtual "experience." The public nature of archives changes with the proliferation of web-based archives that can be individually appropriated and consumed. Thus Smith's notion of the enduring nature of national identities being to do with their cultural priority and depth may already be outdated. In a culture of "depthlessness" and electronic archives, "memories" and identities can be constructed and appropriated individualistically within plural frames of interpretation. Against this background of instability and reconstruction, nationalism is an allegory of irresolution, an expression of fear of the transient nature of the nation (Kosker 1994).

The postcommunist condition is one of increasing instability, with multiple forms of social identification and rethinking of a past that was often subject to official controls. In particular, the collective memory of trauma, of counting the dead, and the construction of a narrative community with the dead, can invest collective memories with a pathos that under certain circumstances legitimates expiatory violence. The Serbian case shows the potential for violent conflict following from the mobilization of cultural memories where these are the object of melancholic grief rather than memory-work. Various sides in the Yugoslavian civil war mobilized support among diasporic communities, particularly via the Internet.[10] A crucial factor in authorizing violence, then, is the availability of languages of rationalization and legitimation, which draw on the affectively charged pathos of collective loss. These may be inscribed into cultural memories in ritualized ways and therefore not be open to discursive examination. In response to social stress, such as state failure, piacular rituals expiate memories of collective injustice. These have the potential to spiral into a process of "disidentification" between ethnic groups (e.g. Serbs and Albanians), encouraged by campaigns to strengthen identifications within the population. The resulting "dyscivilizing" process gives rise to a society that is compartmentalized into areas where "peaceful" everyday life continues, and those, such as the camps, or the whole area of Kosovo, where extreme violence is perpetrated against the targeted group. This is likely to be most severe where it involves unmediated mimetic conflicts between similar actors competing for an identical object, such as incompatible national homelands. These are extreme cases of routinized processes of commemoration and identity formation. Yet, at the same time, "memory" is becoming less officially and publicly sanctioned and more constructed and consumed in an individualized way. One consequence of this is the detachment of identity and place, as diasporic communities sustain national "belonging" via global systems of communication. In postcommunism there are rhetorical battles for appropriation of representations and commemorations, which relate to wider issues. Important among these is the way in which the heroic forms of commemoration associated with high modernity are increasingly undermined by more ambiguous memorials and rituals of mourning. Postmodern and individualized forms of commemoration are less stable and more contested as the media of commemoration are diversified – alongside public monumental spaces there are privatized and virtual forms of memory and commemoration. A crucial issue for the formation of civil societies able to learn and mediate diversity, though, is its communicative structure. Whether it takes the form of incantations of closed quasi-sacred language, or of communicative communities able to subject identities and histories to reflexive examination will have crucial consequences for the formation of violent oppositions.

9

Concluding Themes

We began this book with the theme of "being taken by surprise" by the fall of communism, and to open this concluding chapter it may be appropriate to review this and the other surprises of the postcommunist transition. If the revolutions of 1989 lacked a major theory, in the sense of an orienting doctrine, they have also not so far inspired fundamental retrospective theories such as Tocqueville provided for the French Revolution. There have been a number of interesting reflections, such as those by Dahrendorf (1990, 1997), Deppe et al. (1991), Beyme (1994), Furet (1995), Lefort (1999), and Kumar (2001), but none of their authors would probably claim to have drawn fundamental theoretical consequences from their analyses.

Indeed, the theme of recuperation and return associated with 1989 by Habermas has proved to be applicable to postcommunist social theory too – some of the major theoretical developments have involved *return* to issues and perspectives that had come to be seen as passé. The theory of civil society, for example, returned to the center of debates about social integration and democratic constitutionalism along with cognate theories of social capital and networks. Another prime example is modernization theory that, although widely rejected in the 1970s, has been defended by advocates such as Rostow and Lipset as having been the only theory with a sufficiently large-scale grasp of social change to predict the end of communism (Tiryakian 1991). At the same time the end of communism has been "claimed" by many theories (e.g. postmodernism, globalization, reflexive modernization, complexity, and neofunctionalism) as illustrating the view of social development they had had all along. Few theoretical developments, though, have attempted to conceptualize both the specificity of postcommunist configurations and how they instantiate yet challenge wider processes of social change.

The revolutions of 1989 were relatively unexpected and took some further unexpected directions. We have already referred to the relatively peaceful nature of the 1989 revolutions and of the post-1989 scene in Europe, with, of course, the tragic exception of Yugoslavia and the partial exception of Russia. The relative absence of violence could have been expected, in the sense that many other late twentieth-century revolutions (such as those in Iran and the Philippines) were rather peaceful, at least in their early stages. But an alternative scenario was just as possible. The communist regimes were, of course, much less brutal than they had been in the past, but they were still authoritarian and fairly ruthless. The Tienanmen Square massacre in the summer of 1989 could easily have been replicated in many of the European states, as the German regime explicitly threatened. The outcome of 1989, as we suggested earlier, lends support to Theda Skocpol's model of revolution, with its stress on regime collapse.

Another surprise, which we have registered from time to time in the course of the book, is that, with the future apparently so open at the end of 1989 and in the early months of 1990, parts of Eastern Europe fell into rather conventional "Western" European patterns. The party political landscape is a striking example. In Germany, in particular, a student of electoral politics might easily overlook the caesura of 1990, which shows up in the figures only in rather marginal shifts in support for the main parties of the old Federal Republic and the appearance of the new ex-communist PDS. Germany is, of course, a special case, but part of the explanation for the rapid adoption of fairly "standard" party forms[1] throughout the former bloc was no doubt the widespread sense that the whole telos of postcommunist transition was indeed to return to "Europe" and to "normality." The prospect of EU accession merely reinforced an existing trend among Central and Eastern European countries.

All this, however, raises broader questions about the determination of social processes.

The issue of what Jon Elster (1978) called "branching points" in history and which have more recently been conceptualized as path-dependence is central to explanations of social change. It was crucial to Weber's attempts to theorize both the potential openness of historical outcomes and developmental logics that made some, such as the growth of bureaucracy, more probable than others.[2] Theories of path-dependence run counter to modernization theories that suggest there is one, or at least an optimal, path to functionally differentiated stable social orders. But path-dependence did not lead directly to the neoliberal strategies of privatization, liberalization, and marketization – these were strategic choices made in the context of the prevailing political and institutional climate. On the other hand, the outcomes of these, where they were pursued (for example in Poland and more briefly in Russia) were the result of configurations of local institutional and cultural conditions melded with global constraints and political strategies. The particular forms of capitalist development in parts of the postcommunist world (such as the growth of insider capitalism, high levels of corruption and illicit dealing) attest to the importance not just of the rather vaguely formulated process of "glocalization" (i.e. the way in which globalization interacts with, and may reinforce, local diversities) but rather to the tolerance of the "global system" to multiple forms of local integration to it. This "combined and uneven" development has been a repeated theme in our discussion.

A related set of questions concerns the weights to be attached to the political, the economic, the social, and the cultural in the analysis of social formations. One can see the collapse of communism as further evidence against Marxist emphases on the primacy of the economic. Although the slow-down and general malaise of the state socialist economies in the 1980s was a crucial element in their loss of legitimacy and their ultimate collapse, one must shift the emphasis, as Habermas had done for "late capitalism" in his *Legitimation Crisis* (1973), away from the initial crisis and toward its metastasis from the economic to the political and cultural domains. In Habermas's model, a capitalist economic crisis of a broadly Marxist sort leads to output crises in the state which attempts to master it, to "rationality crises" in the state apparatus, and to motivational crises at the sociocultural level. It can be argued (Ray 1996: 101) that the politicization of economic processes which was an essential element of Habermas's model of late capitalist crisis is, if anything, reversed in the already politicized economies of state socialism: "communist states attempted to offset the effects of excessive political regulation through increasing reliance on monetary exchange." In the end, however, the malaise was so strong that even if Eastern Europeans had foreseen the dimensions of the transition shock and the general social dislocation, they would no doubt still have "chosen freedom."[3] It was, of course, the same "system" that managed the economy, the polity, and the cultural sphere, and it is this that was rejected and abandoned as a whole.[4]

One could make a strong case for the primacy of the political, since many of the movement activists were motivated more by the pursuit of freedom and democracy than by economic considerations, and it was a specifically political collapse, precipitated by the withdrawal of the Soviet guarantee, that occurred in 1989. As many Western discussions of legitimation in the East rightly stressed, what counted was probably the legitimacy of the regimes in the eyes of their middle-rank officials rather than among the public at large.

The cultural erosion of the regimes may however deserve more attention than it has often received. Pop culture in particular could not easily be regulated or incorporated and it made the regimes seem like something from the past. The cover photo from *Rockszene DDR* (Leitner 1983), featuring an army officer in Soviet-style greatcoat sitting on an underground train next to an extremely punk youth, makes the point neatly. The coming of word processors in the mid-1980s revolutionized *samizdat* in a world where photocopying was scarce and controlled, and the Interfax agency in the USSR, for example, was an effective means of transmitting information.

The 1990s saw the triumph of economically and politically deterministic models at the expense of more socially and culturally oriented ones. As we noted in the Introduction, Ralf Dahrendorf (1990: 85) drew the classic distinction between the "hour of the [constitutional] lawyer" and its successor, "the hour of the politician," though he immediately took back the suggestion of a clear temporal sequence, stressing that "constitution-building and . . . economic policy . . . have to be set in motion at the same time." His chronology also deserves attention.

> The formal process of constitutional reform takes at least six months; a general sense that things are moving up as a result of economic reform is unlikely to spread before six years have passed; the third condition of the road to freedom is to provide the social foundations which transform the constitution and the economy from fair-weather into all-weather institutions . . . and sixty years are barely enough to lay these foundations. . . . Civil society is the key. . . . The hour of the lawyer and the hour of the politician mean little without the hour of the citizen. (Dahrendorf 1990: 92–3)

Even if sixty years is a high estimate, the proportions seem roughly right. We have already questioned some of the more extreme suggestions that one should abandon all reference to society, and we would suggest that the postcommunist experience demonstrates the importance of notions such as society or civil society, and social structure. Social capital and integrative networks can, of course, "stretch" to operate across borders and via virtual communications, but at the same time modern sociality entails a balance of co-presence and absence. Further, social bonds are established through mechanisms of distribution of status and prestige that inculcate a sense of belonging – largely through locally situated facework relations. These presuppose cognitive and emotional connectedness embedded within local institutional, cultural, and economic arrangements. It is these which make it plausible for analysts to speak of a "*sui generis* post-communist political model (Kaldor and Vejvoda 1999[2002]: 2) or to continue to stress the distinctiveness of postcommunist economic and social structures. The language of awakening, trauma, denial, and so forth is probably not ultimately the appropriate way in which to analyze these processes, but it captures an important aspect of them. What is clear, at least, is that the language of chapters and checklists is not up to the task of genuine social and political integration. The example of Yugoslavia indicates how this will require painful encounters with pasts that will need to be overcome and renounced rather than either repressed or reified into melancholic rituals.

EU Enlargement may appear to mark the final chapter of postcommunist transition for Central and Eastern Europe at least, but even here it is going to be a long and open-ended one. The members expected to join in the present decade, and some further potential members in the twenty-teens, will continue, we believe, to afford crucially important material for social scientific analysis. Marx, of course, based his analysis of capitalism on Britain, not just because he happened to end up there but because it was in the forefront of capitalist development. Some analysts of late twentieth- and twenty-first-century capitalism argue that we should focus, similarly, on the cutting edge of capitalist development. While not denying the importance of such research, in East Asia and elsewhere, we believe also that there are crucially important lessons to be learned from this unique process of the development of postcommunist capitalism, taking place in a variety of societies which were all, however, subjected to certain broadly common, at least formally common, patterns of political and social organization. The various trajectories of these societies in the 1990s and the early twenty-first century constitute unique research material for social scientists and raise important questions for the future of world-scale developmental processes.

Over-hasty announcements of convergence reflect the way in which sociology has tended to regard non-Western societies as residual – modernization, postmodernization, and reflexive modernization all regard Western societies as the seat of historical change and the apex of social development. Yet the postcommunist world embodies a paradox of homogeneity and difference. Homogeneity, in that for the first time in history capitalism reaches across virtually the whole planet, yet difference in that its instantiation varies according to local circumstances and adaptations to the exigencies of postcommunism. Although some postcommunist societies have moved closer to Western European systems, Westernization is no longer a valid assumption for the discipline that should not impose notions of "transition" – which affects a form of closure on a diverse process. "Postcommunism" in its spatial sense, referring to the former communist countries, is highly diverse, ranging from accession states to sites of re-Sovietization such as Belarus or Uzbekistan. In its temporal sense, as the condition of postcommunism, it is a complex and contradictory world of heightened uncertainty and competing US and Islamist global projects. A Western-centric sociology is not going to have the conceptual or research skills to grasp this, a diagnosis that leads Wallerstein (2001) to call for a unified historical social science that learns from the world, redistributes research funding away from the center, and involves social scientists working in at least five to seven languages. This is unlikely, perhaps, but the call for a decentered sociology in an age of global postcommunism is surely timely.

To return to a theme which we have addressed at various places in this book, we recognize that, with the collapse in most countries of communism, and its mutation in most of those which have officially preserved it into something significantly different, capitalism is for the moment "the only game in town." During the declining years of the communist systems, as Sakwa (1999) points out, there was a shift of utopian expectations from *time* (the communist society of the future) to *place* (the model offered by the West). At the same time the state socialist critique of Western capitalism became less plausible. As Sklair (2002: 222) says, they "could not pretend western capitalism failed to feed, clothe and house people." But this is not to say that anticapitalism is dead as an ideology; indeed, it has experienced something of a comeback in the early twenty-first century. One cannot conclude from the collapse of communism that global capitalism has solved the problems that gave rise to the socialist critique in the first place. On the contrary, the emergence of frontier "Mafia" capitalism in the East and the social costs of the transition to capitalism render it hard to argue for the moral superiority of capitalism over *all* possible alternatives. Further, the argument for a mixed economy – that certain social goods are either not well provided by the market or that their commercial provision is socially unjust – appears to be poignant as we experience the collapse of railway networks, massive power cuts, and a declining health service. Two lessons here should be learned from the postcommunist transition to capitalism. First, markets are complex institutional structures that require embedding in supportive but constraining cultural norms and, second, social inequality will not be resolved through democratization alone (indeed public resistance to privatization and rising inequalities will be better articulated in democratic systems). These issues and others – notably ecological – are being mobilized by social movements operating at local, global, and virtual levels. However, even though the anticapitalist movements remain fragmented, their global spread suggests that they may have a substantial future as vehicles of what is likely to survive as a counterculture to capitalism.

One future, for parts at least of all the member states of the United Nations, and not just of the European Union, is something similar to what we used to call European modernity, but with heavy qualifications in the area of environmental questions. However, Europe itself has become post-Western in two distinct senses of the extension or re-establishment of "Western" patterns of economic and political, and hence social life to the Eastern half of the continent, and in the globalization and diversification of its own populations and cultural patterns, somewhat lumberingly expressed in discussions of multiculturalism and postcolonialism. Further, the "European model" of social solidarity secured through social welfare rights and insurance, labor protection, democracy, and nationalism is weakening in a context of globalization. At the same time features of West European economies increasingly resemble the illicit exchanges within Soviet systems, for example with a growth of informal economies, "flexible," undocumented labor, and civic disengagement marked, for example, by low electoral participation. Both are perhaps manifestations of (different) crises of governmentality and global restructuring. This is probably already to stray beyond what we can convincingly predict, and it would be pointless to speculate further. The lesson of postcommunist transition is that the interrelations between what Georges Gurvitch (1963) called "[s]ocial determinations and human liberty" are more complex and unpredictable than futurologists can probably afford to admit.

Notes

Introduction: Being Taken by Surprise

1 There is a link here not so much between Comte and Marx as between each of these writers and Saint-Simon. Marx began to study Saint-Simon even before he read Hegel and as a student attended lectures given by Ludwig Gall, a leading Saint-Simonian (Bottomore and Rubel 1970: 25).

2 "In early 1919 Max Weber wrote a letter of doom to his younger colleague and friend Georg Lukács, who had by then become a Communist and whom he regarded as the great promise of German theoretical culture. In this letter Weber warned Lukács that the audacious Russian experiment would bereave socialism of its reputation and authority for a hundred years. Let us conclude with the most optimist sentence of this book: of these hundred, sixty years have already elapsed" (Fehér et al. 1983: 299).

Chapter 1: Theory after the Fall

1 The Mexican "Party of the Institutionalized Revolution" (PRI) remained in power from its revolutionary origins in 1910 right through the century, tolerating but effectively discouraging alternative parties.

2 There was also a substantial degree of patriotism, even in the GDR, expressed, for example, in response to sporting successes and contributions to the space race.

3 When they refer to welfare they mean that there was no Western-style welfare system but rather a "guaranteed society" that tied people in atomized dependence on the state as provider of needs over which people exercised no choice (Fehér et al. 1983: 244–7). It could be noted that similar critiques of Western welfare systems were being developed at around the same time.

4 During the Gorbachev period (when more accuracy was sought) percentage annual rates for the Soviet Union were published with a retrospective inflation adjustment. These were: 7.2 percent (1951–60), 4.4 percent (1961–5), 4.1 percent (1966–70), 3.2 percent (1971–5), 1 percent (1976–80), and 0.6 percent (1981–6).

5   They had, however, a vaguely Arendtian democratic, though not revolutionary, theory, articulated in the language of civil society and "anti-political politics."

6   Giddens made a similar point in his plenary address to the Detraditionalization conference, Lancaster University, July 1993.

7   This has, of course, been the case with critical theories, too, from Marx (who admittedly had a few doubts by the 1870s) through to the Frankfurt School and Habermas. They have all, by and large, assumed that Western capitalism, however dismal, prefigured the destiny of humanity.

Chapter 2: Class: Marx and Weber

1   See ch. 1, n. 1.

2   Theda Skocpol's brilliant book on the French, Russian, and Chinese revolutions (Skocpol 1979) stressed the importance of regime collapse. Her project of "bringing the state back in" (Evans et al. 1985) was conceived in opposition to sociological theories, whether Marxist or non-Marxist, which had treated it as merely dependent on class relations.

3   The subtitle of Moore's classic book, *Social Origins of Dictatorship and Democracy*, is: "lord and peasant in the making of the modern world."

4   Often, of course, nomenklatura privatization has taken an explicitly criminal form, as in the Bulgarian example discussed later (pp. 80–5).

5   Weber is listed in the index to Grabher and Stark's book, but Marx is not.

6   This is not, of course, to deny the very substantial differences between Western societies (for a good discussion, see Bottomore and Brym 1989).

7   King (2001) is an exceptionally useful study of Hungary, the Czech Republic, and Slovakia, with some shrewd evaluations of the diversity of evidence for these theoretical models. He suggests that the aggregate differences between these countries can be best explained by differences in organization and legitimation in the late communist period (see in particular pp. 113–15).

8   The Gini coefficient measures the percentage difference between a hypothetical model of perfect equality (the Lorenz curve) and actual income inequality – so higher Gini coefficients indicate greater income inequality. This is discussed further in chapter 3, pp. 51–4.

9   For an interesting discussion of post-1945 and post-1989 reconstruction in Germany, based on the idea of imitation, see Jacoby (2000).

10 This is, of course, the term popularized in the UK by Blair and Giddens, imitated in Germany under the slogan of the *neue Mitte* and often known in France under the pejorative term of *pensée unique* (see Touraine 1999/2001).

Chapter 3: Society, Solidarity, and Anomie: Durkheim

1   There are, of course, parallels here with later non-Marxists such as Joseph Schumpeter and Daniel Bell.

2   *Solidarité* was to be diffused through the educational system promoting social justice as repayment of a "social debt" by the privileged to the underprivileged.

This assumed mutual interdependence and quasi-contractual obligations between all citizens and implied a program of public education, social insurance, and labor and welfare legislation. Solidarism advocated state intervention, social legislation, and voluntary associations to create a middle way between laissez-faire liberalism and revolutionary socialism. Durkheim shared the desire for social solidarity through reconciliation but believed in more thorough social reconstruction than voluntary associations (Lukes 1973: 350–4).

3 Critics (e.g. Monnerot 1946) often took exception to his claim that social facts are, and should be studied as, things.

4 For the Durkheimians, the welfare state cannot be an adequate solution since it does not assure the necessary moral and social integration, but on the contrary weakens the integrative functions of intermediate structures; by inflating expectations, it promotes anomic tendencies, and by individualizing benefits it encourages "selfish" tendencies in our societies (Flora and Heidenheimer 1981: 363).

5 State provision may actually have exacerbated inequalities; for an early critique see Szelényi (1978). There is, of course, a parallel here with the West, where it was shown that the middle classes tended to derive most benefit from universalistic welfare systems.

6 In Poland Edward Gierek, in power from 1970 to 1980, borrowed wildly to finance investment, to little effect. Hungarian policy was somewhat more successful, but in the early 1990s Hungary was spending 40 percent of its export revenue on debt repayment. In Romania, following a debt crisis at the beginning of the 1980s, Ceaucescu carried through a ruthless repayment policy.

7 Zaslavskaya attacked the rigidity of the planning system, corruption, inflexible work practices, the inhibition of market forces, and identified middle-ranking bureaucrats, planners, and enterprise managers as the most likely opponents of reform, since they would defend their privileges. Signaling an end to any pretense to uphold egalitarian values, she argued that the social mechanism of economic development at present operating in the USSR creates the type of worker who fails to correspond not only to the strategic aims of developed socialist society, but also to the technological requirements of contemporary production.

8 The opening chapters of Bönker et al. (2002) provide a useful retrospective illustration of the divergent perspectives on the shock of transition.

9 Having risen by 26 years between 1926 and 1972 (to age 70), life expectancy in the Soviet Union had fallen by 1985 to 69–73 for women and 64 for men (Holmes 1997: 235).

10 He lists the UK, Ireland, and Italy as a separate category, with mixed public and private provision.

11 King (2000) points out that only the area from Slovenia northeast toward the Baltic countries and Central Europe has escaped stagnation and faltering reform and shown rising growth rates. The pattern of hesitant national revival, fitful liberalization, and authoritarian backlash "now seems the typical path," at least for the former Soviet Union.

12 The Gini coefficient was defined at p. 205, n. 8. There is other evidence that a high Gini coefficient predicts high crime and in particular homicide in a society (Messner and Rosenfeld 1997).

13 A similar pattern is found in China, where following economic reforms since the 1980s income inequalities have widened. The World Bank estimates that 270 million live in poverty, there is a growing urban–rural divide and a Gini coefficient of 0.46 (Welsh 2002).

14 This is marked, for example, in the current title of the Ministère des affaires sociales, du travail et de la solidarité.

15 Eurobarometer 8: <http://europa.eu.int/comm/public_opinion/archives/ceeb_en. htm>. The 2001 and 2002 surveys are more focused on attitudes to the EU and therefore less useful for our purposes.

16 Blair and Schröder (1999) actually co-published a paper linking the two concepts; see also Giddens (2001). In his edited collection, Giddens (2001: 1) writes that "at the time of writing there are self-declared third way parties in power in the UK, New Zealand, Korea, Taiwan, Brazil, Argentina, and Chile, among many other countries." Others, he notes, avoid the term but practice third way politics.

17 Another is, of course, the very significant gender gaps, for example, women attempt suicide more than men, but male suicide rates are much higher – it is reported that the ratio is approximately 4 to 1. In the case discussed below, of what we might tentatively call "transition shock suicide," i.e. increases in suicide rates coinciding with the transition period, it is interesting that in several cases male rates tend to rise more than female, although women were more likely to lose their jobs in the transition.

18 See, for example, the work of Danute Gailiene in Lithuania and Airi Varnik in Estonia.

19 For a critique of these critiques, see Outhwaite (forthcoming) and chapter 6. The representation of states is, of course, also problematic (see Neocleous 2003), but mostly free of such fundamental doubts about their very existence.

20 A sociologist from what he jokingly called Saint Leninsburg, when asked in 1991 about the prospects of its secession, raised the prospect that even certain districts of the city might prefer to separate from others.

Chapter 4: Three Types of Convergence

1 One limitation which became clear somewhat later was the extent to which it relied on what came to be called a Fordist model of accumulation; see below.

2 The term Fordism, invented by the Italian Marxist Antonio Gramsci, was taken up by the "regulation school" in France and Italy, and has since become standard usage. The combination of large-scale production and centralized decision-making (Taylorism involved separating workers not just from the means of production but from independent decisions at the point of production) was common to both East and West, though in the East the frequent need for improvisation may paradoxically have given workers more autonomy.

3   We return to this issue in the final chapter.
4   Leftist opponents of Thatcherism were still often opposed to the EU and disinclined to cite European social or Christian democracy as a viable alternative.
5   Readers familiar with the "39 articles" defining the somewhat vague doctrines of the Church of England might wish there had been 39 chapters, though the governments of Eastern and Central Europe probably felt that 31 was plenty.
6   Similar considerations had arisen with the incorporation of the former GDR in 1990; as David Spence (1991: 362) puts it, it had to be pointed out to the Parliament "that the general public would hardly sympathise with the Community institutions if an issue as historical as German Unification were hindered by a quarrel about committees."
7   For a powerful critique of some aspects of this, see Mayhew (2002). The political screening process seems to have been more sensitive and more benign, producing, *inter alia,* valuable studies such as that by Kaldor and Vejvoda (2000), discussed below.
8   Poznanski (1992: 74) estimates that in Poland assets were sold off at "around 10 percent of the real value" and suggests that the same might be true of Hungary.
9   This can be compared with economistic analyses that suggest, extrapolating from growth trends in the early twentieth century, that without the Revolution and the resulting interruptions to growth Russia might have ended up in much the same position economically as it actually did.
10 We are, of course, referring to the radical American Lincoln Steffens's remark in 1921 after a visit to the USSR that he had "seen the future and it works."
11 For the present, it seems undeniable that the historical past, whether it is viewed in positive or, more often, negative terms, continues to shape these societies. What Kaldor and Vejvoda (1999[2002]: 2) suggest of the political order could be generalized to economic and other social spheres: "it is possible to talk about a *sui generis* political model which is influenced by the legacy of communism and, at the same time, by both the strengths and the weaknesses of contemporary Western democracy."
12 On the effects on "outsiders" see Dyker (2003) and White et al. (2003). Opinions vary on whether EU membership for Russia is unthinkable or merely an open question. A likely scenario is perhaps some sort of rather looser association between the EU and Russia or the Commonwealth of Independent States, along the lines of that with NATO.
13 The World Bank Report on *The First Ten Years* (World Bank 2002) lists many of these areas of inadequate development.
14 Organized crime in postcommunist societies is sometimes described as a *mafya*, although there are no known Italian connections, nor is loyalty based primarily on kinship.
15 We are grateful to Professor Georgi Dimitrov, Sofia University, for his assistance with this section.
16 The Center for the Study of Democracy (2004) reports: "The penetration of the organized crime into the security sectors of the countries in transition is one of the darkest aspects of the post-communist transformations of states. During the

past 15 years the growing impact and influence of organized criminal groups was felt not only in the countries in transition but also in the European Union. This process was facilitated by the increasingly free movement of people, goods and finances around Europe."

17 The alternation in government between the BSP and the broad anticommunist coalition, the Union of Democratic Forces (UDF) ended in June 2001 when a coalition led by the former King Simeon Koburg-Gotha, the National Movement Simeon II, won a landslide victory with 42.7 percent of the vote. The inability of either of the other parties to tackle rising crime showed in polls as the main reason for support for the new party (*East European Constitutional Review*, 10, 2/3 (2001): 9).

18 This included the attempted removal of tenure for judges appointed after 1989 in the proposed Law on Judicial Power; reduction of justices' salaries and abolition of pension rights; reduced budget allocation to the judicial branch; denial of the judiciary's access to the media; eviction of the Constitutional Court from their offices, in August 1995. This was described as a "massive effort to undermine the independence of courts and prosecutors" (Ganev 1995).

19 This is an area in which official statistics are not reliable, because the administrative machinery is not working well and there is a low rate of conviction for organized criminals. So it is difficult to assess the extent of organized crime with any precision. There was a widespread fear of crime that may have exceeded its actuality.

20 These have included the Central Bureau for Fighting Against Organized Crime, which coordinates official responses to the problem of crime and corruption; the Measures Against Money Laundering Act (1997); the Insurance Act (1997), which introduced insurance licensing, attempted to prohibit the formation of joint security and insurance companies.

21 See <http://www.online.bg/coalition2000/>.

Chapter 5: Socialism, Modernity and Beyond

1 This was especially so with convergence theories. The concept of totalitarianism did, it is true, differentiate between the two systems but in a largely descriptive fashion, and could not explain why Soviet systems changed (e.g. Ray 1996: 50–60).

2 Some classical statements of modernization theory are: Almond and Powell (1966), Deutsch (1961), Huntington (1968), Lerner (1958), Lipset (1960), Parsons (1964), Rostow (1979).

3 By the 1970s the CIA accepted Soviet data suggesting that the Soviet economy was growing and had already reached 60 percent of the American output (Lipset and Bence 1994).

4 Magnitogorsk became a symbol of Soviet industrial growth. Constructed by "pioneers" in the southern Ural Mountains deep in the heart of the Russian Steppe, the city was created during the first Five Year Plan in 1929 around a steel plant that dominates the eastern bank of the Ural river. It was designed to

follow a linear plan in which a central city and housing strip would be aligned parallel to a strip of factory production providing a short home-to-work commute for 100,000 workers. The two would be separated by a green belt that would keep the noise and pollution of the factory from the housing. For unanticipated technical reasons the linear model was not entirely followed, but the city was proclaimed a model for socialist planning and design.

5   For Rostow's views on postcommunist modernization after the end of communism see Rostow (1991), where he argues for an essentially Keynesian program of liberalization with direct foreign investment and a New Deal.

6   Created in 1948 by the UN, the Economic Commission for Latin America and the Caribbean developed an analysis of center–periphery relations in the world system that favored central industrial countries. See Larrain (1994: 102ff) for a discussion of its impact.

7   Named after the Soviet economist, Nikolai Kondratieff, who proposed the theory in 1926. Each cycle lasts 50–60 years and goes through development and boom to recession. The first cycle was based on steam power, the second on railways, the third on electricity and the motor car, and the fourth on electronics and synthetic materials. Kondratieff argued that one of the forces which initiates long waves is the large number of important discoveries and inventions that occur during a depression and are usually applied on a large scale at the beginning of the next upswing. Chase-Dunn claims that the accumulation process expands within a certain political framework to a point where the framework is no longer adequate to the scale of world commodity production and distribution. Then world wars and violent reorganization of production follow as accumulation adjusts on a new political foundation (Chase-Dunn 1989: 132–3). This occurs when K-wave price swings are at their peak but the investment cycle is about to downswing.

8   Built between 1931 and 1933 largely by *zeks*, slave labor from the Gulag, the White Sea–Baltic Canal was grandiose and useless, and by 1966 had almost ceased to be used (Hosking 1992: 198).

9   Out of a total population of less than 16 million the Stasi had over 85,000 full-time members of staff and many more people engaged in other activities, especially as "unofficial employees" (Fricke 1992). But the result was the generation of mass archives that were not read.

10 From *Nasze Wiadomosci* (no. 42, February 28, 1989), one of many illegal student magazines launched in Poland during military rule.

11 This claim, it should be noted, is not new. The philosopher and poet Georg Philipp Friedrich von Hardenberg (Novalis) (1772–1801) claimed that art had ended and that all that was left was irony and parody.

12 Family life was extolled, divorce more difficult, abortion prohibited in 1944, homosexuality criminalized, and women resubordinated in the workplace and at home. History teaching returned to "important events, personages and dates," Ivan the Terrible and Peter the Great were once again national heroes (Hosking 1992: 215–16). Rather than promote a utopian, modernist reconstruction of society, Stalinist culture was conservative, a development that reflected the victory of the young, careerist, status-conscious petty-bourgeoisie (*meschanstvo*) over the revolutionary intelligentsia (Dunham 1976).

13 Indeed, Weber's fragmentary analysis of communism suggested that it was a precapitalist ethos based on the comradeship of rebellious soldiers, the utopian mentality of intellectuals, and the revolutionary aspirations of the peasantry (Turner 1994).

Chapter 6: Globalization and Convergence

1 On the eastern side there was an illuminated control area (the "death area") in which refugees were shot without warning. At least 100 people were killed at the Berlin Wall; the last of them was Chris Gueffroy on February 6, 1989.
2 The economy did recover more rapidly than in most post-communist countries in the later 1990s, with GDP growth of 35 percent in 1992–7, consumption exceeding pre-1990 levels by 1995 and a reorientation of trade towards the EU, which rose from 30 percent ($7 billion) in 1989 to 67 percent ($50.3 billion) in 1998 (Polish Government Center for Strategic Studies). However, the social cost was borne by particular groups – women experienced higher unemployment than men, and it was highest in the North, where it remained above 20 percent. Agriculture absorbed much of the "shock" as farm yields fell by 50 percent during 1990–4, while many unemployed from the cities returned to family farms in the country (Say 2000).
3 This list is not exhaustive, but most of these principles will be found in most neoliberal programs. For example, Balcerowicz (1993) and Radygin (1995).
4 This was more complicated in postcommunist countries where neoliberals were often modernizers who were liberal on social issues – such as the Yabloko (Apple) Party in Russia.
5 Quah describes the weightless economy as one where "the economic significance of knowledge achieves greatest contemporary resonance" and it has four main features: (1) information and communications technology (ICT) and the Internet; (2) intellectual assets: not only patents and copyrights but also, more broadly, namebrands, trademarks, advertising, financial and consulting services, and education; (3) electronic libraries and databases: including new media, video entertainment, and broadcasting; (4) biotechnology: carbon-based libraries and databases, pharmaceuticals (Quah 2002). A similar idea is suggested in Ritzer's concept of "nothing" – a social form that is "generally centrally conceived, controlled, and comparatively devoid of distinctive substantive content" (2003: 3). He documents the global process of movement from "something" (local and substantive forms) to nothing – but it is not clear that he offers more than new terms for this familiar process.
6 It is not entirely clear, though, whether they regard globalization as real (but a projection of Americo-centrism) or an illusion projected on to the world
7 The polarization of the debate into "radicals" and "skeptics" might be useful for teaching purposes, to guide students through a maze of conflicting positions, but it is not particularly illuminating in academic discussion.
8 This included the Soviet Union, the communist states of Eastern Europe (except Yugoslavia and Albania) and Vietnam, Cuba, and Mongolia. The Soviet Union was by far the most powerful member of Comecon and the Warsaw Pact,

although its exercise of political dominance was sometimes at the expense of economic interest – providing oil and gas at less than international prices (Holmes 1997: 33–5).

9 Examples of this model might be the Chelyabinsk tractor factory built by Ford in 1930s, which had a higher caterpillar output than the US (Murray 1992), or the East German *Kombinate* in the 1960s (Voskamp and Wittke 1991).

10 In particular, critics of the decline of the nation state argument regard this as an obstacle to developing an egalitarian and welfare-based socialist strategy (notably Hirst and Thompson 1996). Further, the hollowing out and the emergence of the regulatory state is not necessarily equivalent to the implosion of nation states that retain crucial and arguably increasing powers over the management of space and mobility.

11 By the early 1980s foreign lenders were insisting on austerity programs, as part of adjustment packages, which involved cuts in inventory investment, imports, and consumption. This left the Soviet Union with the burden of underwriting costs in the People's Democracies as its hard currency subsidies rose to $6.2 billion in 1981, the value of rouble credits to $3 billion by the end of the 1970s, and Soviet trade subsidies to $79.5 billion. Austerity created additional problems for state socialism since it was difficult to expand exports while reducing investment, and cuts in social consumption were already provoking protests. Further austerity programs, such as the Hungarian stabilization of 1977–8, increased dependence on informal private sources of welfare and hence increased differentiation between official and second societies (Ray 1996: ch. 5).

12 See Gorbachev (1997: 517–50) for an account of Soviet thinking about the Cold War, the arms race, and SDI.

13 This rather awkward term captures the important point that the local and global are tightly linked but does not offer much in the way of theorization of its articulations, which the current chapter attempts to do.

14 Per capita direct foreign investment in 1994 in Bulgaria was $12 million, Czech Republic $83 million, Estonia $158 million, Hungary $111 million, Poland $14 million, and Russia $7 million (EBRD 1995).

15 Even so, the banking collapse in August 1998 demonstrated that Russia had moved from a command economy and was now vulnerable to global markets (Gustafson 1999). Further, Russia has become a significant global actor in the energy sector (Sakwa 2004).

16 Also known as "neocons," this group, including Donald Rumsfeld, William Kristol, Elliott Abrams, Paul Wolfowitz, John Bolton, and Richard Perle, organized in the 1990s the "Project for the American Century" that lobbied for regime change in Iraq.

17 Marx famously noted in the *Eighteenth Brumaire* how actors in the present "conjure up the spirits of the past to their service and borrow from their names . . . in order to present the new scene of world history in this time-honoured disguise." The present is resonant with images of the past, for example British Prime Minister Tony Blair invoking images of the Blitz and World War II when mobilizing support for an attack on Iraq.

18 We are aware of the ambiguities around the term "terrorist" and the difficulties of distinguishing terrorism, insurgence, guerrilla war, and indeed any other act of war. Terrorism we take to mean the deployment of violence as a spectacle aimed primarily at civilian populations, in pursuit of political, religious, or other ends. The literature on terrorism is vast and this brief section does not attempt to address it, which would require another book. Readers may want to pursue Worcester et al. (2002), Lutz and Lutz (2004), and Hewitt (2002) for comprehensive accounts of current work.

19 We use the term "imaginary" in the sense of powerful and pervasive constructions of the world that do not correspond to "rational" or "real" elements but become the symbolic ground on which actions take place and therefore have real effects.

Chapter 7: Civil Society East and West

1 This relates to a wider issue of the way in which the Jews have been constructed as the epitome of cosmopolitan modernity and enemies of authentic community and solidarity (e.g. Adorno and Horkheimer 1989).

2 Western social democratic parties in the early twentieth century were largely democratic in practice even if still revolutionary in rhetoric. Leading Marxists in Western Europe – such as Karl Kautsky and Eduard Bernstein – were vehement critics of Bolshevism after 1917. The Russian Mensheviks similarly favored supporting the "bourgeois democratic revolution" of February 1917.

3 "Social capital" refers to features of social organization such as networks, norms, and social trust that facilitate coordination and cooperation for mutual benefit, that people can draw upon to solve common problems. Networks of civic engagement, such as neighborhood associations, sports clubs, and cooperatives, are an essential form of social capital, and the denser these networks, the more likely that members of a community will cooperate for mutual benefit. This is so, even in the face of persistent problems of collective action (tragedy of the commons, prisoner's dilemma, etc.), because of networks of civic engagement. However, there is disagreement about the locus of social capital. Some (e.g. Fukuyama 1995; Inglehart 1997) see social capital as a property of cultures (everyone has a similar predisposition to cooperate in all situations), while others treat it as a property of individuals (some people in a society are more cooperative or trusting than others; e.g. Putnam 1993). Coleman (1990) again regards social capital as situational – some situations encourage cooperation while others do not. For example, buying an airline ticket involves a modern impersonal network whereas childcare can involve informal exchanges with neighbors. We will not consider these differences here – the concept is being used as one of the possible meanings of "civil society."

4 Kumar does subsequently say that "I am less convinced than I was earlier that we should simply discard the concept of civil society," and proposes instead guidelines to give the concept coherence (Kumar 2001: 167ff).

5 Literally, "self-publication," this referred to underground publication of papers and journals critical of the system.

6 Since a great deal of these exchanges were non-monetary, it is difficult to estimate the size of the informal sector, even if reliable data were available. A report to the Central Committee of the CPSU in 1987 estimated that 1.5 billion roubles a year were tied up in the second economy (White et al. 1993: 118) (i.e. 0.2 percent of GNP), but this was a gross underestimation. Grossman (1977) estimated *legal* private activity in the Soviet Union as accounting for 31 percent of value added in agriculture; 32 percent in housing; 5 percent in services; amounting to 10 percent of GDP overall, and suggested that the illegal and semi-legal sectors would have been larger.

7 On the other hand, Holmes (1997: 301) points out that with the exception of the former DDR and some prominent communist leaders, lustration and prosecution of former communists has been limited and pursued in a "very civil" way.

8 In Hungarian national elections the percentage participation (for two-stage elections) was, in 1990: 65 and 45; 1994: 68 and 55; in 1998: 56 and 57. The latter result could be evidence of widespread disaffection with the political system. In Bulgaria, with a traditionally high level of political participation in mass organizations, participation in the 1990 election was 91 percent and in 1991, 87 percent (Nikolov 1993: 142) but by 2001 it was 66.7 percent. In the 1994 elections to the Russian Duma participation was 50 percent, and in 2004 was 56 percent.

9 It is true that enterprise managers underreport output to avoid taxes, which depresses the rate further. But the extent of the collapse is visible, in underused or derelict plant. Underreporting is not sufficient to account for the extent of the "transition recession."

10 None of the contributors to this volume note that when close to governmental power, in Afghanistan, Al-Qaeda destroyed what was left of civil society and participated in one of the most repressive regimes in history.

11 For example, holding prisoners at Guantanamo Bay, beyond the jurisdiction of US and international law, pursuing war against Iraq without UN agreement, failing to ratify the Kyoto climate treaty.

12 The potential for these is indicated, for example, in MADRE international women's human rights organization, the International Association of Refugee Law Judges, the International Criminal Defense Lawyers Association, and 50 Years is Enough – a network that aims at increasing awareness among the US public of global inequalities 50 years after the Bretton Woods Agreement (Sassen 2002a).

Chapter 8: Modernity, Memory, and Postcommunism

1 There is some dispute whether "genocide" is the right term to apply to "ethnic cleansing" in Kosovo. But Martin Shaw points out that "genocide does not always involve the slaughter of the majority, let alone the entirety, of the 'enemy' group. This is because perpetrators can often achieve the destruction of a group through relatively limited killings, accompanied by other measures. For example, in March 1999 the Serbian regime of Slobodan Milosevic aimed to destroy the Albanian community within Kosovo, primarily by expelling large

numbers of its members from the province. In this context, the killing of around 10,000 people, and the forcible eviction and deportation of many others, was more than sufficient to terrorize over a million people out of Kosovo. Many who were not personally forced to leave nevertheless fled on hearing of the murder and terror that was being practised elsewhere in the province" (Shaw 2003).

2 This can be illustrated in many ways, including the Irving vs. Penguin Books Ltd and Deborah Lipstadt libel case in the UK in 2000 and the contentions over commemoration or "exploitation" of the Holocaust and its significance (e.g. Finkelstein 2000).

3 For example: Yad Vashem <http://www.yadvashem.org.il/>; Survivors of the Shoa <http://www.vhf.org/>; <http://www.bethshalom.com/>; Spielberg's Holocaust site <http://www.vhf.org/>.

4 This is a Georgian film, deploying multiple frames and fantasy sequences. The mayor of a small Georgian town dies, and the day after his funeral, his body is exhumed and dumped on his son's front lawn. Baffled but not wanting to make a fuss, the son has the body reburied, only for the corpse to keep returning. The woman who accuses the dead mayor of Stalin-like purges of the town does not want the man to rest since repentance cannot be delivered without confronting the past.

5 Martin Amis comments that "right up to 1989 the Auschwitz Museum itself was a monument to Holocaust denial" (Amis 2002: 222).

6 Similarly, the Romany Holocaust, previously "forgotten" in European history, is subject to remembrance and the search to document witness from survivors. See Kapralski (1997, 2001), Kenrick (1995), Sonneman (2002), and Acton (2002).

7 The inexpressibility of concentration camp memories is frequently reported. Many survivors express their frustration at attempting to articulate memories but finding no ready way to fully make their experience answer a generally accepted account (Langer 1991). Lacking narrative coherence, the Holocaust is often described as unrepresentable in memory, unavailable to the stories of life embedded in traditional practices, accountable and sanctioned by community (Turner 1996).

8 The instruction given to Serbian soldiers was: "The fewer Arnavuts [Albanians] and Turks remain with us, the greater will be your contribution to the country." Putting these instructions into practice had familiar results. According to one witness, "In the winter, very cold and frosty, of 1877–1878, I saw people running away, weakly dressed and barefoot, that had abandoned their warm and wealthy rooms. . . . On the way from Grdelica to Vranje, all the way to Kumanova, on both sides of the road corpses of children and old people could be seen that had died of the cold" (Institute of History 1998: 6).

9 A further example of this is the way that in medieval Europe Easter rituals often spilled over into anti-Semitic violence. Although the Easter passion is a representation of a sacrifice, the pathos invoked incited actual killing in "revenge." See for example Wistrich (1992).

10 For opposing "sides" see Srpska Mreza <http://www.srpska-mreza.com/> and <http://www.kosova.com/>.

Chapter 9: Concluding Themes

1 The content, of course, was not always reflected in official titles (liberal, social democratic, or whatever).

2 Elster has made a fundamental contribution to theorizing postcommunist transition, in a major collective work on constitutional and institutional reform (Elster et al. 1998). Theories or models of path-dependence, stressing the effects of the past on current possibilities, have been developed mainly within economics but can readily be seen to have relevance to the social sciences in general and post-communist transition in particular. For an overview, see Rona-Tas (1998) at <http://hi.rutgers.edu/szelenyi60/intro.html>.

3 One should note however another surprise in this context, that the old communist parties were not wiped out electorally like the fascist parties after 1945. They had, of course, to relabel themselves, and to perform a certain amount of lustration and purging, but they were often the surprised beneficiaries of hostility to the first postcommunist administrations.

4 Compare the Nazi critique of the Weimar Republic as the *Systemzeit* and the radical critiques of "the [capitalist] system" in the West in the 1960s and 1970s. It is interesting to recall that Tocqueville acutely picked up a similar critique of "the system" in Britain at the time of the Crimean War. In a letter to Nassau senior he wrote: "Your people seem . . . to be tired of their public men, and to be losing faith in their institutions. What else do these complaints of what is called 'the system' mean?" (quoted in Olive Anderson, *A Liberal State at War*, New York: St Martins, 1967, p. 80). The rapid acceptance in the GDR of the idea of reunification is a striking index of this rejection of the old regime.

5 In fairness, we must point out that their study was commissioned by the EU itself in 1995, and conducted in conjunction with the Forward Studies Unit of the European Commission and the Research Department of the Council of Europe. This study was also significant in that its country chapters were mostly written by local experts.

Bibliography

Acton, T. (ed.) (2002), *Scholarship and the Gypsy Struggle: Commitment in Romani Studies*, Hatfield: University of Hertfordshire Press.

Adorno, T. W. (1994), *Adorno: The Stars Down to Earth and Other Essays on the Irrational in Culture*, ed. with an introduction by S. Crook, London: Routledge.

Adorno, T. W. and Horkheimer, M. (1989), Elements of anti-Semitism: the limits of enlightenment. In *Dialectic of Enlightenment*, London: Verso, pp. 168–208.

Aganbegyan, A. (1988), *The Challenge: The Economics of Perestroika*, London: Hutchinson.

Ahrne, G. (1996), Civil society and civil organizations, *Organization*, 3, 1: 109–210.

Albert, M. (1991), *Capitalisme contre capitalisme*, Paris: Seuil. (Tr. as *Capitalism against capitalism*, London: Whurr.)

Alexander, J. (1995), *Fin de Siècle Social Theory: Relativism, Reduction, and the Problem of Reason*, London: Verso.

Alford, C. F. (1998), Freud and violence. In A. Elliott (ed.), *Freud 2000*, Cambridge: Polity Press, pp. 61–87.

Almond, G. A. (1963), *The Civic Culture: Political Attitudes and Democracy in Five Nations*, Princeton, NJ: Princeton University Press.

Almond, G. and Powell, B. (1966), *Comparative Politics: A Developmental Approach*, Boston: Little, Brown.

Almond, G. and Verba, S. (1963), *The Civic Culture: Political Attitudes and Democracy in Five Nations*, Princeton, NJ: Princeton University Press.

Almond, G. A. and Verba, S. (eds.) (1980), *The Civic Culture Revisited*, Boston: Little, Brown.

Amis, M. (2002), *Coba the Dread*, London: Jonathan Cape.

Andersen, M. S. (2002), Ecological modernization or subversion? The effect of Europeanization on Eastern Europe, *American Behavioral Scientist*, 45: 1394–1416.

Anderson, B. (1993), *Imagined Communities: Reflections on the Origin and Spread of Nationalism*, London: Verso.

Andor, A. and Summers, M. (2000), *Market Failure: A Guide to the East European "Economic Miracle,"* London: Pluto Press.

Anheier, H., Glasius, M., and Kaldor, M. (2001), *Global Civil Society*, Oxford: Oxford University Press.

Appadurai, A. (1996), *Modernity at Large, Cultural Dimensions of Globalization,* London: University of Minnesota Press.

Arato, A. (1981), Civil society against the state: Poland 1980–81, *Telos,* 47 (Spring): 23–47.

Arato, A. (1982), Critical sociology and authoritarian state socialism. In J. B. Thompson and D. Held (eds), *Habermas: Critical Debates,* London: Macmillan.

Arato, A. (1991), Social theory, civil society and the transformation of authoritarian socialism. In F. Fehér and A. Arato (eds.), *The Crisis in Eastern Europe,* New Brunswick, NJ: Transaction Books, pp. 1–26.

Aricanli, T. and Thomas, M. (1994), Side-stepping capitalism: on the Ottoman road to elsewhere, *Journal of Historical Sociology,* 7, 1: 25–48.

Arnason, J. P. (1993), *The Future that Failed: Origins and Destinies of the Soviet Model,* London: Routledge.

Aron, R. (1962), *Dix-huit leçons sur la société industrielle,* Paris: Gallimard. (Tr. as *Eighteen Lectures on Industrial Society,* London: Weidenfeld.)

Aron, R. (1965), *Démocratie et totalitarianisme,* Paris: Gallimard. (Tr. as *Democracy and Totalitarianism,* London: Weidenfeld.)

Bachrach, P. and Baratz, M. S. (1970), *Power and Poverty: Theory and Practice,* Oxford: Oxford University Press.

Back, L. (2002a), Aryans reading Adorno: cyber-culture and twenty-first century racism, *Ethnic and Racial Studies* 25, 4: 628–51.

Back, L. (2002b), New technologies of racism. In D. T. Goldberg and J. Solomos (eds.), *A Companion to Racial and Ethnic Studies,* Oxford: Blackwell, pp. 365–77.

Bahro, R. (1978), *The Alternative in Eastern Europe,* London: NLB.

Bakhtin, M. (1981), Forms of time and the chronotype in the novel. In M. Holquist (ed.), *The Dialogic Imagination,* Austin: University of Texas Press.

Bakos, G. (1994), Hungarian transition after 3 years, *Europe–Asia Studies,* 46, 7: 1189–1214.

Balcerowicz, L. (1993), *Common Fallacies in the Debate on the Economic Transition in Central and Eastern Europe,* Working Paper 11, London: EBRD.

Baldwin, P. (1990), *The Politics of Social Solidarity,* Cambridge: Cambridge University Press.

Balla, B. (1972), *Kaderverwaltung: Versuch zur Idealtypisierung der Bürokratie sowjetisch-volksdemokratischen Typs,* Stuttgart: Enke.

Baron, N. (1997), Perestroika, politicians and Pandora's box: the collective memory of Stalinism during Soviet reform, *European Review of History,* 97, 4: 73–91.

Baudrillard, J. (1993), *The Transparency of Evil: Essays on Extreme Phenomena,* London: Verso.

Bauman, Z. (1987), *Legislators and Interpreters,* Cambridge: Polity Press.

Bauman, Z. (1992), *Intimations of Postmodernity,* London: Routledge.

Bauman, Z. (1994), After the patronage state: a model in search of class interests. In Bryant and Mokrzycki, *The New Great Transformation?,* pp. 14–35.

Bauman, Z. (1998), *Globalization: The Human Consequences,* Cambridge: Polity Press.

Bauman, Z. (1999), *Modernity and the Holocaust,* Cambridge: Polity Press.

Bauman, Z. (2001), *Liquid Modernity,* Oxford: Polity Press.

Beck, U. (1992), *Risk Society: Towards a New Modernity,* London: Sage.

Beck, U. (1994), The reinvention of politics. In U. Beck, A. Giddens, and S. Lash, *Reflexive Modernization: Politics, Tradition and Aesthetics in the Modern Social Order,* Oxford: Polity Press, pp. 1–55.

Beck, U. (1995), *Ecological Politics in the Age of Risk,* Atlantic Highlands, NJ: Humanities Press.

Beck, U. (1997), *The Reinvention of Politics,* Cambridge: Polity Press.

Beck, U. and Beck-Gernsheim, E. (1995), *The Normal Chaos of Love,* Cambridge: Polity Press.

Beck, U. and Beck-Gernsheim, E. (2001), *Individualization: Institutionalized Individualism and its Social and Political Consequences,* London: Sage.

Beck, U., Bonss, W., and Lau, C, (2003), The theory of reflexive modernization: problematic, hypotheses and research programme, *Theory, Culture and Society,* 20, 2: 1–33.

Bell, D. (1980), The social framework of the information society. In T. Forester (ed.), *The Microelectronics Revolution,* Oxford: Basil Blackwell.

Bell, D. (1987), The world and the US in 2013, *Daedalus,* 116, 3: 1–32.

Benacek, V. (1997), Fiscal convergence of the lands of the European Union and the border states, *Politicka Ekonomie,* 45, 4: 514–21.

Bendix, R. and Roth, G. (1971), *Scholarship and Partisanship: Essays on Max Weber,* Berkeley: University of California Press.

Benjamin, W. (1979), The story teller. In *Illuminations,* London: Fontana.

Berger, S. and Dore, D. (1996), *States Against Markets,* London: Routledge.

Bergesen, A. J. (2003), Is terrorism globalizing? *Protosociology,* 18–19: 32–55.

Berman, M. (1985), *All that is Solid Melts into Air,* London: Verso.

Bernhard, M. (1996), Civil society after the first transition, *Communist and Post-Communist Studies,* 29, 3: 309–33.

Best, S. (2003), *A Beginner's Guide to Social Theory,* London: Sage.

Beyme, K. von (1994), *Systemwechsel in Osteuropa,* Frankfurt am Main: Suhrkamp.

Bhabha, H. (1995), DissemiNation: time, narrative and the margins of the modern nation. In H. Bhabha (ed.), *Nation and Narration,* London: Routledge, pp. 219–322.

Billig, M. (1997), *Banal Nationalism,* London: Sage.

Blair, T. and Schröder, G. (1999), Europe: The Third Way (June 8). Available at <www.labour.org.uk>.

Blaney, D. L. and Inayatullah, N. (2002), Neo-modernization? IR and the inner life of modernization theory. *European Journal of International Relations,* 8: 103–37.

Blatt, J. (1991), *East Central Europe from Reform to Transition,* London: Pinter.

Boccioni, U. et al. (1909), *Manifesto of the Futurist Painters* [Signed: Umberto Boccioni, Carlo D. Carrà, Luigi Russolo, Giacomo Balla, Gino Severini]. Milan.

Bogorov, V. (2002), In the Temple of Sacred Motherland: Representations of National Identity in the Soviet and Russian WWII Memorials. Available at <http://www.dartmouth.edu/~crn/groups/geographies_group_papers/Finalpapers / Bogorov02.pdf>.

Böhm-Bawerk, E. von (1896[1949]), *Karl Marx and the Close of his System,* London: Unwin. (Republished New York: Kelley, 1949.)

Bönker, F., Müller, K., and Pickel, A. (eds.) (2002), *Postcommunist Transformation and the Social Sciences: Cross-disciplinary Approaches,* Lanham, MD: Rowman and Littlefield.

Booth, K. and Dunne, T. (eds.) (2002), *Worlds in Collision: Terror and the Future of Global Order,* Basingstoke: Palgrave Macmillan.

Bottomore, T. and Brym, R. (eds.) (1989), *The Capitalist Class: An International Study,* New York: Harvester Wheatsheaf.

Bottomore, T. and Rubel, M. (eds.) (1970), *Karl Marx: Selected Writings in Sociology and Social Philosophy,* Harmondsworth: Penguin.

Bourdieu, P. (1983), Ökonomisches Kapital, kulturelles Kapital, soziales Kapital (tr. R. Kreckel). In R. Kreckel (ed.), *Soziale Ungleichheiten. Sonderheft 2 der Zeitschrift "Soziale Welt,"* Göttingen: Vlg. Otto Schwartz, pp. 183–19. (Tr. as The (three) forms of capital. In A. H. Halsey, P. Brown, and A. Stuart Wells (eds.), *Education, Culture, Economy, and Society,* Oxford: Oxford University Press, 1997, pp. 46–58.)

Bourdieu, P. (1984), *Distinction,* London: Routledge.

Bourdieu, P. and Wacquant, L. (1999), On the cunning of imperialist reason, *Theory Culture and Society,* 16, 1: 41–58.

Boyer, R. (1996), The convergence hypothesis revisited: globalization but still the century of nations? In Berger and Dore (eds.), *States Against Markets,* pp. 29–59.

Brown, P. and Lauder, H. (2001), *Capitalism and Social Progress: The Future of Society in a Global Economy,* Basingstoke: Palgrave Macmillan.

Brubaker, R. (1995), National minorities, nationalizing states and external national homelands in the New Europe, *Daedalus* (Spring): 107–32.

Bruner, E. (1996), *Russian and Other Former Soviet Armed Forces,* Washington, DC: Foreign Affairs and National Defense Division.

Bryant, C. G. A. (1995), Civic nation, civil society, civil religion. In Hall (ed.), *Civil Society,* pp. 146–57.

Bryant, C. G. A. and Mokrzycki, E. (1994), *The New Great Transformation? Change and Continuity in East-Central Europe,* London: Routledge.

Bucher, G. (2000), Struggling to survive: Soviet women in the postwar years, *Journal of Women's History,* 12, 1: 137–59.

Budapest Analytica (2003), at <http://www.budapestanalyses.hu/docs/En/Ba_Archive/analysus_14_en.html>.

Budge, I., et al. (1997), *The Politics of the New Europe: Atlantic to Urals,* London: Longman.

Bugajski, J. and Pollack, M. (1989), *East European Fault Lines,* Boulder, CO: Westview Press.

Bunce, V. (1983), The political economy of the Brezhnev era: the rise and fall of corporatism, *British Journal of Political Science,* 13: 129–58.

Bunce, V. (1999), *Subversive Institutions: The Design and the Destruction of Socialism and the State,* Cambridge: Cambridge University Press.

Burawoy, M. (ed.) (2002), *American Journal of Sociology,* special issue.

Burawoy, M. and Wright, E. O. (2002), Sociological Marxism. In J. Turner (ed.), *The Handbook of Sociological Theory,* New York: Plenum Books, pp. 459–86.

Byers, M. (2002), Terror and the future of international law. In Booth and Dunne (eds.), *Worlds in Collision*, pp. 118–27.

Castells, M. (1998), *End of the Millennium*, Oxford: Blackwell.

Caute, D. (1988), *Fellow Travellers: Intellectual Friends of Communism*, London: Yale University Press.

Centre for the Study of Democracy (2004), *Partners in Crime: The Risks of Symbiosis between the Security Services and Organized Crime in South East Europe*, Sofia. Available at <http://www.csd/bg/artShow.php?id=2033>.

Chalcraft, D. (1994), Bringing the text back in: on ways of reading the two editions of the Protestant Ethic. In Ray and Reed, *Organizing Modernity*, pp. 16–45.

Chase-Dunn, C. (1983), The kernel of the capitalist world economy: three approaches. In W. Thompson, *Contending Approaches to World Systems Analysis*, London: Sage, pp. 55–78.

Chase-Dunn, C. (1989), *Global Formation: Structures of the World Economy*, Oxford: Basil Blackwell.

Chase-Dunn C. (2002), Globalization from below: toward a collectively rational and democratic global commonwealth, *Annals of the American Academy of Political and Social Science*, 581: 48–61.

Chirot, D. (1991), What happened in Eastern Europe in 1989? In D. Chirot (ed.), *The Crisis of Leninism and the Decline of the Left*, Seattle: University of Washington Press.

Clegg, S. (1989), *Frameworks of Power*, London: Sage.

Clegg, S. (1994), Max Weber and contemporary sociology of organizations. In Ray and Reed, *Organizing Modernity*, pp. 46–80.

Coalition 2000 (2001), *Corruption Assessment Report 2001*, Sofia. Available at <http://www.online.bg/coalition2000/eng/CAR_content.html>.

Cohen, J. and Arato, A. (1992), *Civil Society and Political Theory*, Cambridge, MA: MIT Press.

Coleman, D. (1996), *Europe's Population in the 1990s*, Oxford: Oxford University Press.

Coleman, J. (1990), *Foundations of Social Theory*, Cambridge, MA: Harvard University Press.

Collins, R. (1986), *Weberian Sociological Theory*, Cambridge: Cambridge University Press.

Comte, A. (1976), *The Foundation of Sociology*, ed. K. Thompson, London: Nelson.

Condorcet, M. J. A. (1976), Sketch for the historical picture of the progress of the human mind. In K. M. Baker (ed.), *Selected Writings*, Indianapolis: Bobbs-Merrill. (First published 1794.)

Connerton, P. (1989), *How Societies Remember*, Cambridge: Cambridge University Press.

Cook, L. (1992), Brezhnev's social contract and Gorbachev's reforms, *Soviet Studies*, 44, 1: 37–56.

Corin, C. (1992), *Superwomen and the Double Burden: Women's Experience of Change in Central and Eastern Europe and the Former Soviet Union*, London: Scarlet Press.

Cottey, A., Edmunds, T., and Forster, A. (1999), *Democratic Control of the Armed Forces in Central and Eastern Europe: A Framework for Understanding*

Civil Military Relations, Brighton: ESRC "One Europe or Several?" Working Paper.

Cox, T. and Mason, B. (1999), *Social and Economic Transformation in East Central Europe: Institutions, Property Relations and Social Interests*, Cheltenham: Edward Elgar.

Cressy, D. (1994), National memory in Early Modern England. In Gillis, *Commemorations*, pp. 61–73.

Crook, S., Pakulski, J., and Waters, M. (1994), *Postmodernization: Change in Advanced Societies*, London: Sage.

Crouch, C. and Streeck, W. (1997), *Political Economy of Modern Capitalism: Mapping Convergence and Diversity*, London: Sage.

Crow, G. (2002), *Social Solidarities: Theories, Identities and Social Change*, Buckingham: Open University Press.

Currie, C. C. and Ray, L. J. (1986), On the class location of contract farmers in Kenya, *Economy and Society*, 15, 4: 445–75.

Dahrendorf, R. (1959), *Class and Class Conflict in Industrial Society*, London: Routledge.

Dahrendorf, R. (1990), *Reflections on the Revolution in Europe: In a Letter Intended to Have Been Sent to a Gentleman in Warsaw*, London: Chatto and Windus.

Dahrendorf, R. (1997), *After 1989: Morals, Revolution and Civil Society*, Basingstoke: Macmillan.

Dallago, B. (1990), *The Irregular Economy*, Aldershot: Dartmouth.

Danecki, J. (1993), Social costs of system transformation in Poland. In S. Ringen and C. Wallace, *Societies in Transition: East-Central Europe Today*, Prague Papers on Social Responses to Transformation, vol. 1. Prague: Central European University, pp. 47–60.

Dawisha, K. and Parrott, B. (eds.) (1997), *Democratization and Authoritarianism in Post-communist Societies*, Cambridge: Cambridge University Press.

De Atkine, N. (1999), Why Arabs lose wars, *Middle East Quarterly*, 6, 4: 17–27.

Delhey, J. (2001), *Osteuropa zwischen Marx und Markt: Soziale Ungleichheit und soziales Bewusstsein nach dem Kommunismus*, Hamburg: Krämer.

Deppe, R., Dubiel, H., and Rödel, U. (eds.) (1991), *Demokratischer Umbruch in Osteuropa*, Frankfurt am Main: Suhrkamp.

De Swaan, A. (2001), *Human Societies: An Introduction*, Cambridge: Polity Press.

Deutsch, K. (1961), Social mobilization and political development, *American Political Science Review*, 55: 493–514.

DiMaggio, P. and Powell, W. (1983), The iron cage revisited, *American Sociological Review*, 48, 1: 147–60.

Djilas, M. (1957), *The New Class: An Analysis of the Communist System*, London: Unwin Books.

Djilas, M. (1966), *The New Class: An Analysis of the Communist System*, London: Thames and Hudson.

Docherty C. (2002), *Berlin 1983*. Available at <http://www.restless-soul.co.uk/berlin1.htm>.

Donnan, H. and Wilson, T. M. (1999), *Borders*, Oxford: Berg.

Donzelot, J. (1984), *L'invention du social: essai sur le déclin des passions politiques*, Paris: Seuil.

Dore, R. (1973), *British Factory: Japanese Factory. The Origins of National Diversity in Industrial Relations,* London: Allen and Unwin.

Drakokhurst, Y. (1997), Republic of Belarus: crushing civil society, *Belarusian Chronicle,* 9, 8. Available at <http://chronicle.home.by/resources/doc/ccs/9708a.htm>.

Dubet, F. and Martuccelli, D. (1998), *Dans quelle société vivons-nous?* Paris: Seuil.

Dunham, V. (1976), *In Stalin's Time,* Cambridge: Cambridge University Press.

Dunning, E. and Mennell, S. (1998), Elias on Germany, Nazism and the Holocaust: on the balance between "civilizing" and "decivilizing" trends in the social development of Western Europe, *British Journal of Sociology,* 49, 3: 339–57.

Dunning, E. G. and Hopper, E. I. (1966), Industrialization and the problem of convergence: a critical note, *Sociological Review,* 14, 2: 163–86.

Durkheim, E. (1969), Individualism and the intellectuals, *Political Studies,* 17: 14–30.

Durkheim, E. (1976), *Elementary Forms of the Religious Life,* London: Allen and Unwin.

Durkheim, E. (1984), *The Division of Labour in Society,* tr. W. Douglas Halls, London: Macmillan.

Dwyer, K. (1991), *Arab Voices,* London: Routledge.

Dyker, D. (2003), The impact of eastwards enlargement of the European Union on non-applicant and delayed-accession countries. In *Eastern Europe and the Commonwealth of Independent States,* London: Europa, ch. 6.

Easterly, W. and Fischer, S. (1994), The Soviet economic decline: historical and republican data. Cambridge, MA: National Bureau of Economic Research Working Paper 4735.

Eatwell, J., Ellman, M., Karlsson, M., Nuti, D. M., and Shapiro, J. (1997b), *Not Just Another Accession: The Political Economy of EU Enlargement to the East,* London: Institute for Public Policy Research.

Eatwell, R. (ed.) (1997a), *European Political Cultures: Conflict or Convergence?* London: Routledge.

EBRD (1995), *Transition Report,* London: European Bank for Reconstruction and Development.

EBRD (1999), *Transition Report,* London: European Bank for Reconstruction and Development.

EBRD (2000), *Transition Report,* London: European Bank for Reconstruction and Development.

Eder, K. (1976), *Die Entstehung staatlich organisierter Gesellschaften: ein Beitrag zu einer Theorie sozialer Evolution,* Frankfurt am Main: Suhrkamp.

Eder, K. (1985), *Geschichte als Lernprozess? Zur Pathogenese politischer Modernität in Deutschland,* Frankfurt am Main: Suhrkamp.

Einhorn, B. (1993), *Cinderella Goes to Market: Citizenship, Gender and Women's Movements in East Central Europe,* London: Verso. (2nd edn. 2002.)

Einhorn, B., Kaldor, M., and Kavan, Z. (1996), *Citizenship and Democratic Control in Contemporary Europe,* Cheltenham: Edward Elgar.

Eisenstadt, S. N. (ed.) (1987), *Patterns of Modernity,* London: Pinter.

Eisenstadt, S. N. (1992), The breakdown of communist regimes and the vicissitudes of modernity, *Daedalus,* 121, 2 (Spring): 21–41.

Eisenstadt, S. N. (1996), The Jacobin component of fundamentalist movements, *Contention*, 5, 3: 155–70.

Eisenstadt, S. (2000), The reconstruction of religious arenas in the framework of "multiple modernities," *Millennium*, 29, 3: 591–611.

Eisenstadt, S. (2001), The civilizational dimension of modernity: modernity as a distinct civilization, *International Sociology*, 16, 3: 320–40.

Elias, N. (1994), *The Civilizing Process*, Oxford: Blackwell.

Elias, N. (1996), *The Germans*, Oxford: Polity Press.

Elliott, A. (2003), *Critical Visions: New Directions in Social Theory*, New York: Rowman and Littlefield.

Ellman, M. (1984), *Collectivisation, Convergence and Capitalism: Political Economy in a Divided World*, London: Academic Press.

Elster, J. (1978), *Logic and Society: Contradictions and Possible Worlds*, Chichester: Wiley.

Elster, J., Offe, C., and Preuss, U. (1998), *Institutional Design in Post-Communist Societies: Rebuilding the Ship at Sea*, Cambridge: Cambridge University Press.

Ely, J. (1992), The politics of "civil society," *Telos*, 93: 173–91.

Esping-Andersen, G. (1989), The three political economies of the welfare state, *Canadian Review of Sociology and Anthropology*, 26, 2.

Evans, P., Rueschemeyer, D., and Skocpol, T. (1985), *Bringing the State Back In*, Cambridge: Cambridge University Press.

Eyal, G., Szelényi, I., and Townsley, E. (1998), *Making Capitalism without Capitalists: Class Formation and Elite Struggles in Post-communist Central Europe*, London: Verso.

Eyal, G., Szelényi, I., and Townsley, E. (2003), On irony: an invitation to neoclassical sociology, *Thesis Eleven*, 73: 5–41.

Fainsod, M. (1963), Bureaucracy and modernization: the Russian and Soviet case. In J. LaPalombara (ed.), *Bureaucracy and Political Development*, Princeton, NJ: Princeton University Press, pp. 233–67.

Falk, R. (1999), *Predatory Globalization: A Critique*, Cambridge: Polity Press.

Featherstone, M. (2000), Archiving cultures, *British Journal of Sociology*, 51, 1: 161–84.

Fehér, F. (1982), Paternalism as a mode of legitimation in Soviet-type societies. In T. H. Rigby and F. Fehér (eds.), *Political Legitimation in Communist Regimes*, London: Macmillan, pp. 64–81.

Fehér, F. and Heller, A. (1986), *Eastern Left – Western Left*, Oxford: Polity Press.

Fehér, F., Heller, A., and Márkus, G. (1983), *Dictatorship over Needs*, Oxford: Blackwell.

Feminist Review (1991), Special Issue on Shifting Territories – Feminisms and Europe, 39.

Ferguson, A. (1966), *An Essay on the History of Civil Society*, Edinburgh: Edinburgh University Press. (First published 1767.)

Filippov, A. (1992), Eliten im postimperialen Reichsraum, *Berliner Debatte INITIAL*, 6: 45–9.

Filtzer, D. (1992), *Soviet Workers and De-Stalinization*, Cambridge: Cambridge University Press.

Finkelstein, N. (2000), *The Holocaust Industry*, London: Verso.

Fischer, M. E. (ed.) (1996), *Establishing Democracies*, Boulder, CO: Westview Press.

Flaherty, P. (1992), Cycles and crises in statist economies, *Review of Radical Political Economics*, 24: 111–53.

Fligstein, N. (2001), *Architecture of Markets*, Princeton, NJ: Princeton University Press.

Fligstein, N. and Sweet, S. S. (2002), Constructing markets and politics: an institutionalist account of European integration, *American Journal of Sociology*, 107, 5: 1206–43.

Flora, P. and Heidenheimer, A. J. (eds.) (1981), *The Development of Welfare States in Europe and America*, New Brunswick, NJ: Transaction.

Foley, M. and Edwards, B. (1996), The paradox of civil society, *Journal of Democracy*, 7, 3: 38–52.

Forest, B. and Johnson, J. (2002), Unraveling the threads of history: Soviet-era monuments and post-Soviet national identity in Moscow, *Annals of the Association of American Geographers*, 92, 3: 524–47.

Foucault, M. (1975), *Surveiller et punir: Naissance de la prison*, Paris: Gallimard. (Tr. as *Discipline and Punish: The Birth of the Prison*, London: Allen Lane, 1977.)

Foucault, M. (1980), *Power/Knowledge*, Brighton: Harvester.

Fraser, N. (1989), *Unruly Practices: Power, Discourse and Gender in Contemporary Social Theory*, Cambridge: Polity Press.

Freitag, M. (2002), *L'oubli de la société. Pour une théorie critique de la postmodernité*, Rennes: Presses Universitaires de Rennes.

Freud, S. (1984), Mourning and melancholia [1915]. In *Pelican Freud Library*, vol. 11, Harmondsworth: Penguin Books.

Fricke K. W. (1992), The state security apparatus of the Former GDR and its legacy, *Aussenpolitik*, 43, 2: 153–63.

Friedman, T. (2000), *The Lexus and the Olive Tree*, New York: Anchor Books.

Frijda, N. (1997), Commemoration. In J. Pennebaker, D. Pacz, and B. Rimé, *Collective Memory of Political Events*, Mahwah, NJ: Lawrence Erlbaum, pp. 103–27.

Frost, M. (1998), Migrants, civil society and sovereign states: investigating an ethical hierarchy, *Political Studies*, 46, 5: 871–85.

Fukuyama, F. (1992), *The End of History and the Last Man*, London: Hamish Hamilton.

Fukuyama, F. (1995), *Trust*, London: Hamish Hamilton.

Fulcher, J. (2000), Globalization, the nation-state and global society, *Sociological Review*, 48, 4: 522–43.

Furet, F. (1995), *Le passé d'une illusion: essai sur l'idée communiste au XXe siècle*, Paris: Calmann-Lévy. (Tr. D. Furet as *The Passing of an Illusion: The Idea of Communism in the Twentieth Century*, Chicago: University of Chicago Press, 1999.)

Ganev, V. (1995), Prisoners' rights, public services and institutional collapse in Bulgaria, *East European Constitutional Review*, 4, 1: 76–83.

Ganev, V. (2001), The Dorian Gray effect: winners as state breakers in postcommunism, *Communist and Post-Communist Studies*, 34, 1: 1–25.

Garrett, G. (2000), The causes of globalization, *Comparative Political Studies*, 33, 6–7: 941–91.

Gellner, E. (1994), *Conditions of Liberty: Civil Society and its Rivals*, Harmondsworth: Penguin.

Gellner, E. (1995), The importance of being modular. In Hall (ed.), *Civil Society*, pp. 32–55.

Geremek, B. (1992), Civil society and the present age. In National Humanities Center, *The Idea of a Civil Society*. Available at <http://www.nhc.rtp.nc.us/publications/civilsoc/geremek.htm>.

Gergen, K. (1994), Mind, text and society. In U. Neisser and R. Fivush (eds.), *The Remembering Self*, Cambridge: Cambridge University Press.

Gibson, L. (1998), *Social Networks and Civil Society in Processes of Democratization*, Studies in Public Policy no. 301, Glasgow: Centre for the Study of Public Policy, University of Strathclyde.

Giddens, A. (1973), *The Class Structure of the Advanced Societies*, London: Hutchinson.

Giddens, A. (1985), *The Nation-state and Violence*, Cambridge: Polity Press.

Giddens, A. (1990), *Consequences of Modernity*, Cambridge: Polity Press.

Giddens, A. (1994), Living in a post-traditional society. In U. Beck, A. Giddens, and S. Lash, *Reflexive Modernization: Politics, Tradition and Aesthetics in the Modern Social Order*, Oxford: Polity Press, pp. 56–109.

Giddens, A. (1998), *The Third Way: The Renewal of Social Democracy*, Cambridge: Polity Press.

Giddens, A. (1999a), The Director's Lectures: Politics after Socialism, Lecture 5. Available at <http://www.lse.ac.uk/Giddens/pdf/20-jan-99.pdf>.

Giddens, A. (1999b), The Director's Lectures: Politics after Socialism, Lecture 6. Available at <http://www.lse.ac.uk/Giddens/pdf/27-jan-99.pdf>.

Giddens, A. (ed.) (2001), *The Global Third Way Debate*, Cambridge: Polity Press.

Gillis, J. R. (1994), *Commemorations: The Politics of National Identity*, Princeton, NJ: Princeton University Press.

Gimpelson, V., Treisman, D., and Monusova, G. (2000), Public employment and redistributive politics: evidence from Russia's regions. Discussion Paper No. 61, Bonn: Institute for the Study of Labor.

Girard, R. (1977), *Violence and the Sacred*, Baltimore: Johns Hopkins University Press.

Glasius, M. and Kaldor, M. (2002), The state of global civil society. In Glasius et al., *Global Civil Society 2002*, pp. 3–33.

Glasius, M., Kaldor, M., and Anheier, H. (eds.) (2002), *Global Civil Society 2002*, Oxford: Oxford University Press.

Glasman, M. (1994), The Great Deformation: Polanyi, Poland and the terrors of planned spontaneity, *New Left Review*, 204: 59–86.

Glenny, M. (1999), *The Balkans*, London: Granta Books.

Goetz, K. H. (2001), Making sense of post-communist central administration: modernization, Europeanization or Latinization? *Journal of European Public Policy*, 8: 1032–51.

Goff, P. M. (2000), Invisible borders: economic liberalism and national identity, *International Studies Quarterly*, 44, 4: 533–62.

Goldman, M. (1991), *What Went Wrong with Perestroika*, London: W. W. Norton.

Gooding, J. (1990), Gorbachev and democracy, *Soviet Studies*, 422: 195–231.

Gorbachev, M. (1997), *Memoirs,* London: Bantam Books.

Gorbachev, M. (1986), Politichesky doklad tsentralnogo komiteta KPSS XXVII syezdu kommunisticheskoy partii Sovetskogo soyuza [Political Report of the CPSU Central Committee to the 27th Congress of the CPSU], *Pravda,* 25 February: 2–10.

Gouldner, A. (1971), *The Coming Crisis of Western Sociology,* London: Heinemann.

Grabher, G. and Stark, D. (1997), *Restructuring Networks in Post-socialism: Legacies, Linkages, and Localities,* Oxford: Oxford University Press.

Granick, D. (1979), *The Red Executive: A Study of the Organization Man in Russian Industry,* London: Macmillan.

Granovetter, M. (1973), The strength of weak ties, *American Journal of Sociology,* 78, 6: 1360–80.

Greenfeld, L. (1992), *Nationalism: Five Roads to Modernity,* Cambridge, MA: Harvard University Press.

Grix, J. (2001), Social capital as a concept in the social sciences: the state of the debate, *Democratization,* 8, 3: 189–210.

Grødeland, Å., Koshechkina, T., and Miller, W. (1998), Foolish to give and yet more foolish not to take: in depth interviews with post-communist citizens on their everyday use of bribes and contacts, *Europe–Asia Studies,* 50, 4: 651–77.

Grossman, G. (1977), The second economy of the USSR, *Problems in Communism,* 26: 25–40.

Guldimann, T. (1984), *Moral und Herrschaft in der Sowjetunion,* Frankfurt: Suhrkamp.

Gurvitch, G. (1963), *Déterminismes sociaux et liberté humaine: vers l'étude sociologique des cheminements de la liberté,* 2nd, rev. edn., Paris: Presses Universitaires de France. (Orig. published Paris: Presses Universitaires de France, 1955.)

Gustafson, T. (1999), *Capitalism Russian-style,* Cambridge: Cambridge University Press.

Habermas, J. (1973), *Legitimationsprobleme im Spätkapitalismus,* Frankfurt am Main: Suhrkamp. (Tr. as *Legitimation Crisis,* London: Heinemann, 1976.)

Habermas, J. (1985), *Die neue Unübersichtlichkeit,* Frankfurt: Suhrkamp. (Tr. as *The New Conservatism,* Cambridge: Polity Press.)

Habermas, J. (1986), *Eine Art Schadensabwicklung,* Frankfurt: Suhrkamp.

Habermas, J. (1989a), *The Theory of Communicative Action, Lifeworld and System: A Critique of Functionalist Reason,* vol. 2, Cambridge: Polity Press.

Habermas, J. (1989b), *The Structural Transformation of the Public Sphere,* Cambridge: Polity Press.

Habermas, J. (1990), *Die nachholende Revolution,* Frankfurt am Main: Suhrkamp.

Habermas, J. (1992), Citizenship and national identity: some reflections on the future of Europe, *Praxis International,* 12, 1: 1–19.

Habermas, J. (1994), *The Past as Future,* Cambridge: Polity Press.

Habermas, J. (2001), *The Postnational Constellation,* Cambridge: Polity Press.

Hacking, I. (1994), Memoro-politics and the soul, *History of the Human Sciences,* 7, 2: 29–53.

Halbwachs, M. (1992), *On Collective Memory,* ed. L. Coser, Chicago: Chicago University Press.

Hall, J. (ed.) (1995), *Civil Society: Theory, History, Comparison,* Oxford: Polity Press.

Hallam, E. and Hockey, J. (2001), *Death, Memory and Material Culture,* Oxford: Berg.

Hankiss, E. (1991), The "Second Society": is there an alternative social model emerging in contemporary Hungary? In F. Fehér and A. Arato, *The Crisis in Eastern Europe,* New Brunswick, NJ: Transaction Books.

Hann, C. M. (1990), Second economy and civil society. In C. M. Hann (ed.), *Market Economy and Civil Society in Hungary,* London: Frank Cass, pp. 21–44.

Hann, C. M. (1995), Philosophers' models on the Carpathian Lowands. In Hall (ed.), *Civil Society,* pp. 158–82.

Hardt, M. and Negri, A. (2000), *Empire,* Cambridge, MA: Harvard University Press.

Hartmann, H. (1981), *The Unhappy Marriage of Marxism and Feminism,* London: Pluto.

Harvey, D. (1994), *The Condition of Post-Modernity,* Oxford: Blackwell.

Harvey, D. (1996), *Justice, Nature and the Geography of Difference,* Oxford: Basil Blackwell.

Hauslohner (1989), Gorbachev's social contract. In F. Fehér and A. Arato, *Gorbachev: The Debate,* Cambridge: Polity Press, pp. 83–123.

Hausner, J. and Nielsen, K. (1992), The post-socialist transformation process. Paper to the Post Socialism: Problems and Prospects Conference, Charlotte Mason College, Cumbria, UK, July.

Hausner, J., Jessop, B., and Nielsen, K. (eds.) (1995), *Strategic Choice and Path Dependency in Post-Socialism: Institutional Dynamics in the Transformation Process,* Aldershot: Edward Elgar.

Havel, V. (1988), Anti-political politics. In Keane (ed.), *Civil Society,* pp. 381–98.

Havel, V. (1994), The need for transcendence in the postmodern world, Independence Hall, Philadelphia, July 4. Available at <http://www.worldtrans.org/whole/havelspeech.html>.

Hayden, P. M. (1994), Recounting the dead. In Watson (ed.), *Memory, History and Opposition,* pp. 167–84.

Hechter, M. (1995), Introduction: reflections on historical prophecy in the social sciences, *American Journal of Sociology,* 100, 6 (May): 1520–7.

Hedlund, S. and Sundström, N. (1996), The Russian economy after systemic change, *Europe–Asia Studies,* 48, 6: 887–914.

Heffernan, M. (1995), For ever England: the Western Front and the politics of remembrance in Britain, *Ecumene,* 2, 3: 293–323.

Hegel, G. (1967), *Philosophy of Right,* Oxford: Oxford University Press. (First published 1821.)

Held, D. (1995), *The Problem of Autonomy and the Global Order,* Cambridge: Polity Press.

Held, D. (2002), Violence, law and justice in a global age. OpenDemocracy.net.

Held, D. and McGrew, A. (eds.) (2000), *The Global Transformations Reader: An Introduction to the Globalization Debate,* Cambridge: Polity Press.

Held, D., McGrew, A., Goldblatt, D., and Perraton, J. (2000), *Global Transformations,* Cambridge: Polity Press.

Heller, A. (1988), On formal democracy. In J. Keane, *Civil Society and the State: New European Perspectives,* London: Verso, pp. 129–46.

Hellman, J. (1998), Winners take all: the politics of partial reform in post-communist transitions, *World Politics,* 50: 203–34.

Hertz, N. (2001), *Silent Takeover,* London: William Heinemann.

Hewitt, C. (2002), *Understanding Terrorism in America,* London: Routledge.

Higley, J. and Lengyel, G. (2000), *Elites after State Socialism: Theories and Analysis,* Lanham, MD: Rowman and Littlefield.

Hirst, P. and Thompson, G. (1996), *Globalization in Question, the International Economy and the Possibilities of Governance,* Cambridge: Polity Press.

Hirszowicz, M. (1980), *The Bureaucratic Leviathan: A Study in the Sociology of Communism,* London: Martin Robertson.

Hjerm, M. (2003), National sentiments in Eastern and Western Europe, *Nationalities Papers,* 31, 4: 413–29.

Hobbes, T. (1994), *Leviathan,* London: Everyman. (First published 1660.)

Hobsbawm, E. J. (1995), *Age of Extremes: The Short Twentieth Century 1914–1991,* London: Abacus.

Hodges, D. C. (1981), *The Bureaucratization of Socialism,* Amherst: University of Massachusetts Press.

Hoepken, W. (1999), War, memory and education in a fragmented society: the case of Yugoslavia, *East European Politics and Society,* 13, 1: 190–227.

Hoffman, D. (2002), *The Oligarchs: Wealth and Power in the New Russia,* New York: Public Affairs.

Holmes, L. T. (1993), *The End of Communist Power,* Cambridge: Polity Press.

Holmes, L. T. (1997), *Post-communism: An Introduction,* Cambridge: Polity Press.

Holmes, S. (2001), Introduction to "From Postcommunism to Post-September 11," *East European Constitutional Review* (Winter): 78–81.

Hölscher, B. and Dittrich, R. (1999), Russia goes West? *Journal of Sociology and Social Anthropology,* 2: 1. (In Russian; German original kindly provided by the authors.)

Hörschelmann, K. (2002), History after the end: post-socialist difference in a (post)-modern world, *Transactions of the Institute of British Geographers,* 27: 52–66.

Hosking, G. (1992), *A History of the Soviet Union, 1917–1991,* London: Fontana.

Hough, J. (1969), *Soviet Prefects: The Local Party Organs in Industrial Decision-making,* Cambridge: Cambridge University Press.

Hough, J. (1978), The Cultural Revolution and Western understandings of the Soviet system. In S. Fitzpatrick, *The Cultural Revolution in Russia,* London: Indiana University Press, pp. 241–53.

Howard, M. M. (2000), *Free not to Participate: The Weakness of Civil Society in Post-Communist Europe,* Studies in Public Policy No. 325, Glasgow: Centre for the Study of Public Policy, University of Strathclyde.

Hradil, S. (2001), *Soziale Ungleichheit in Deutschland,* 8. Aufl., Opladen: Leske and Budrich.

Hradil, S. and Schiener, J. (2002), *Soziale Ungleichheit in Deutschland,* Stuttgart: UTB.

Hudson, R. (1999), *Who Becomes a Terrorist and Why: The 1999 Government Report on Profiling Terrorists,* Guildford: Lyons Press.

Hume, D. (1955), *Inquiry Concerning Human Understanding*, London: Bobbs-Merrill. (Orig. published 1758.)

Hunt, L. (1990), The sacred and the French Revolution. In J. Alexander (ed.), *Durkheimian Sociology*, Cambridge: Cambridge University Press.

Huntington, S. (1968), *Political Order in Changing Societies*, New Haven, CT: Yale University Press.

Huntington, S. (1999), *Clash of Civilizations and the Remaking of World Order*, London: Touchstone.

Ignatieff, M. (1995), On civil society, *Foreign Affairs*, 74, 2: 128–36.

Inglehart, R. (1990), *Culture Shift in Advanced Industrial Society*, Princeton, NJ: Princeton University Press.

Inglehart, R. (1997), *Modernization and Postmodernization: Cultural, Economic and Political Change in 43 Societies*, Princeton, NJ: Princeton University Press.

Inkeles, A. (1991), Transitions to democracy, *Society*, 28, 4: 67–7.

Institute of History (1998), *Expulsions of Albanians and Colonisation of Kosova*, Prishtina: Kosova Information Center.

Jacoby, R. (1975), *Social Amnesia*, Boston, MA: Beacon Press.

Jacoby, W. (2000), *Imitation and Politics: Redesigning Modern Germany*, Ithaca, NY: Cornell University Press.

Jacoby, W. (2002), Talking the talk and walking the walk: the cultural and institutional effects of Western models. In F. Bönker, K. Müller, and A. Pickel (eds.), *Postcommunist Transformation and the Social Sciences: Cross-disciplinary Approaches*, Lanham, MD: Rowman and Littlefield.

Janos, A. C. (1991), Social science, communism and the dynamics of political change, *World Politics*, 44: 81–112.

Jessop, B. (1992), *From the Keynesian Welfare to the Schumpeterian Workfare State*, Lancaster: Lancaster Regionalism Group: Working Paper no. 45.

Jessop, B. (1999), Globalization and the national state [draft]. Department of Sociology, Lancaster University. Available at: <http://www.comp.lancs.ac.uk/sociology/papers/jessop-globalization-and-the-national-state.pdf>.

Jessop, B. (2000), The crisis of the national spatio-temporal fix and the ecological dominance of globalizing capitalism, *International Journal of Urban and Regional Studies*, 24: 273–310.

Jessop, B. (2002), *The Future of the Capitalist State*, Cambridge: Polity Press.

Johnson, C. (2000), *Blowback: The Costs and Consequences of American Empire*, New York: Henry Holt.

Johnson, C. (2003), *The Sorrows of Empire: How the Americans Lost Their Century*, New York: Metropolitan Books.

Jowitt, K. (1978), *The Leninist Response to National Dependence*, Berkeley, CA: Institute of International Relations.

Jowitt, K. (1983), Soviet neotraditionalism: the political corruption of a Leninist regime, *Soviet Studies*, 35, 3: 275–97.

Kaldor, M. (1993), Yugoslavia and the new nationalism, *New Left Review*, 197: 96–112.

Kaldor, M. (1998), *New and Old Wars*, Cambridge: Polity Press.

Kaldor, M. and Vejvoda, I. (eds.) (1999), *Democratization in Central and Eastern Europe*, London: Pinter. (Republished London: Continuum, 2002.)

Kaldor, M. and Vejvoda, I. (eds.) (2000), *Democratization in Central and Eastern Europe*, London: Continuum.

Kaplan, R. (1993), *Balkan Ghosts*, London: Macmillan.

Kaplan, R. (1994), The coming anarchy, *Atlantic Quarterly*, 273 (February): 44–76.

Kapralski, S. (1997), Identity building and the Holocaust: Roma political nationalism, *Nationalities Papers*, 25, 2: 269–83.

Kapralski, S. (2001), Battlefields of memory: landscape and identity in Polish–Jewish relations, *History and Memory*, 13, 2: 35–58.

Karagiannis, N. (2004), *A Critique of the EU's Development Policy: The Politics of Development Discourse Revisited*, London: Pluto.

Kazimierz, Z. (1993), *Constructing Capitalism: The Reemergence of Civil Society and Liberal Economy in the Post-communist World*, Boulder, CO: Westview Press.

Keane, J. (ed.) (1988), *Civil Society and the State: New European Perspectives*, London: Verso.

Keck, M. E. and Sikkink, K. (1998), *Activists Beyond Borders*, Ithaca, NY: Cornell University Press.

Kemp, S. and Holmwood, J. (2003), Realism, regularity and social explanation, *Journal for the Theory of Social Behaviour*, 33, 2: 165–87.

Kenney, P. (1999), What is the history of 1989? New scholarship from east-central Europe, *East European Politics and Societies*, 13, 2: 419–31.

Kenrick, D. (1995), *Gypsies under the Swastika*, Hatfield: University of Hertfordshire Press.

Killias, M. and Aebi, M. F. (2000), Crime trends in Europe from 1990 to 1996: how Europe illustrates the limits of the American experience, *European Journal of Criminal Policy and Research*, 8, 1: 43–63.

King, C. (2000), Post-postcommunism: transition, comparison, and the end of "eastern Europe," *World Politics*, 53, 1: 143–72.

King, L. P. (2001), *The Basic Features of Postcommunist Capitalism in Eastern Europe: Firms in Hungary, the Czech Republic, and Slovakia*, Westport and London: Praeger.

Klein, E. (2001), *The Battle for Auschwitz: Catholic–Jewish Relations under Strain*, London: Vallentine Mitchell.

Koch, T. and Thomas, M. (1997), The social and cultural embeddedness of entrepreneurs in Eastern Germany. In Grabher and Stark (eds.), *Restructuring Networks in Post-Socialism*, pp. 243–60.

Kolodko, G. (2002), *Globalization and Catching-up in Transition Economies*, Rochester, NY: University of Rochester Press.

Konrád, G. (1984), *Antipolitics*, London: Harcourt Brace Jovanovich.

Konrád, G. and Szelényi, I. (1979), *The Intellectuals on the Road to Class Power*, Brighton: Harvester.

Kornai, J. and Eggleston, K. (2001), *Welfare, Choice and Solidarity in Transition: Reforming the Health Sector in Eastern Europe*, Cambridge: Cambridge University Press.

Koselleck, R. K. (1985), *Futures Past: On the Semantics of Historical Time*, Cambridge, MA: MIT Press.

Kosker, R. J. (1994), Building pasts: historic preservation and identity in twentieth century Germany. In Gillis, *Commemorations*, pp. 215–38.

Kostov, G. R. (1993), Changing the political system in Bulgaria. In J. Anson, E. Todorova, G. Kressel, and N. Genov (eds.), *Ethnicity and Politics in Bulgaria and Israel*, Aldershot: Avebury, pp. 224–7.

Krastev, J. M. (1998), Drug abuse in Eastern Europe. In J. Millar and S. Wolchik (eds.), *The Social Legacy of Communism*, Cambridge: Cambridge University Press, pp. 149–77.

Kravchenko, V. A. (1947), *I Choose Freedom: The Personal and Political Life of a Soviet Official*, Garden City, NY: Garden City Publishing.

Kugelmass, J. (1993), The rites of the tribe: the meaning of Poland for American Jewish tourists. In *YIVO Annual 21*, Evanston, IL: Northwestern University Press and the YIVO Institute for Jewish Research.

Kumar, K. (1978), *Prophecy and Progress: The Sociology of Industrial and Post-industrial Society*, London: Allen Lane.

Kumar, K. (1993), Civil society: an inquiry into the usefulness of an historical term, *British Journal of Sociology*, 44, 3: 375–95.

Kumar, K. (1995), *From Post-industrial to Post-modern Society*, Oxford: Blackwell.

Kumar, K. (2001), *1989 Revolutionary Ideas and Ideals*, London: University of Minnesota Press.

Kurtz, M. J. and Barnes, A. (2002), The political foundations of post-communist regimes: marketization, agrarian legacies, or international influences, *Comparative Political Studies*, 35: 524–53.

Lane, D. (1985), *Soviet Economy and Society*, London: Martin Robertson.

Langer, L. (1991), *Holocaust Testimonies: The Ruins of Memory*, New Haven, CT: Yale University Press.

Laqueur, T. W. (1994), Memory and naming in the Great War. In Gillis, *Commemorations*, pp. 150–76.

Larrain, J. (1994), *Theories of Development*, Cambridge: Polity Press.

Lash, S. (1999), *Another Modernity*, Cambridge: Polity Press.

Lash, S. and Urry, J. (1994), *Economies of Signs and Space*, London: Sage.

Latour, B. (1991), *We Have Never Been Modern*, Hemel Hempstead: Harvester Wheatsheaf.

Lazarenko, V. and Sobolev, V. (2001), Employment structure and management in transitional post-command economies. Proceedings of the IIRA 6th European Industrial Relations Congress, Oslo.

Ledeneva, A. V. (1998), *Russia's Economy of Favours: Blat, Networking and Informal Exchange*, Cambridge: Cambridge University Press.

Lefort, C. (1981), *L'invention démocratique: les limites de la domination totalitaire*, Paris: Fayard.

Lefort, C. (1999), *La complication. Retour sur le communisme*, Paris: Fayard.

Leitner, O. (1983), *Rockszene DDR: Aspekte einer Massenkultur im Sozialismus*, Reinbek bei Hamburg: Rowohlt.

Lemert, C. (1997), *Social Things*, New York: Rowman and Littlefield.

Lerner, D. (1958), *The Passing of Traditional Society*, New York: Free Press.

Levinson, C. (1978), *Vodka Cola*, London: Gordon and Cremonesi.

Lipset, M. (1960), *Political Man: The Social Basis of Politics*, Garden City, NY: Doubleday.

Lipset, S. M. (1994), The social prerequisites of democracy revisited, *American Sociological Review*, 59, 1: 1–22.

Lipset, S. M. and Bence, G. (1994), Anticipations of the failure of Communism, *Theory and Society*, 23: 169–210.

Lloyd, C. (2000), Globalization: beyond the ultra-modernist narrative to a critical realist perspective on geopolitics in the cyber age, *International Journal of Urban and Regional Research*, 24, 2: 258–73.

Lloyd, D. (1998), *Battlefield Tourism: Pilgrimage and Commemoration of the Great War in Britain, Australia and Canada, 1919–1939*, Oxford: Berg.

Locke, J. (1980), *Second Treatise on Civil Government*, ed. C. B. Macpherson, Indianapolis, IN: Hackett. (First published 1681–3.)

Lockwood, D. (1992), *Solidarity and Schism*, Oxford: Clarendon Press.

Lockwood, D. (2000), *The Destruction of the Soviet Union*, London: Macmillan.

Lomax, B. (1997), The strange death of civil society in Hungary, *Journal of Communist Studies and Transition Studies*, 13, 1: 41–63.

Lotspeich, R. (1995), Crime in the transition economies, *Europe–Asia Studies*, 47: 555–89.

Lowenthal, D. (1979), Age and artefact: dilemmas of appreciation. In D. W. Meinig, *The Interpretation of Ordinary Landscapes*, Oxford: Oxford University Press.

Ludz, P. C. (1972), *The Changing Party Elite in East Germany*, Cambridge, MA: MIT Press. (Orig. published as *Parteielite im Wandel*, Köln: Westdeutscher Verlag, 1968.)

Luhmann, N. (1982), *The Differentiation of Society*, New York: Columbia University Press.

Lukes, S. (1973), *Emile Durkheim: His Life and Work*, Harmondsworth: Penguin.

Lury, C. (1998), *Prosthetic Culture*, London: Sage.

Lutz, J. M. and Lutz, B. J. (2004), *Global Terrorism*, London: Routledge.

Lyotard, J.-F. (1979), *La Condition postmoderne: rapport sur le savoir*, Paris: Minuit. (Tr. as *The Postmodern Condition: A Report on Knowledge*, Minneapolis: University of Minnesota Press, 1984.)

Maaz, H.-J. (1990), *Der Gefühlsstau. Ein Psychogramm der DDR*, Berlin: Argon.

McCann L. (ed.) (2004), *Russian Transformations*, London: Curzon.

McFaul, M. (1993), *Post-Communist Politics*, Washington, DC: Center for Strategic and International Studies.

Macnaughton, P. and Urry, J. (1998), *Contested Natures*, London: Sage.

Maffesoli, M. (1996), *The Time of Tribes: The Decline of Individualism in Mass Society*, London: Sage.

Mal'kov, V. L. (1993), *Organizatsiia truda i trudovaia etika: drevnost', srednie veka, sovremennost'*, ed. V. L. Mal'kov and L. T. Mil'skaia, Moscow: Russian Academy of Sciences, Institute of Social history.

Marcuse, H. (1934), Der Kampf gegen den Liberalismus in der totalitären Staatsauffassung, *Zeitschrift für Sozialforschung*, 3, 2. (Tr. in *Negations*, London: Allen Lane, The Penguin Press, 1968.)

Marcuse, H. (1936), Autorität und Familie in der deutschen Soziologie bis 1933, In *Studien über Autorität und Familie*, Schriften des Instituts für Sozialforschung, 5, Paris: Alcan.

Marcuse, H. (1958), *Soviet Marxism: A Critical Analysis,* New York: Columbia University Press.

Marcuse, H. (1964), *One Dimensional Man,* London: Routledge.

Marmor, T. and Okma, K. G. H. (1998), Cautionary lessons from the West: what (not) to learn from other countries' experiences in the financing and delivery of health care. In P. Flora et al. (eds.), *The State of Social Welfare 1997*, Aldershot: Ashgate, pp. 327–50.

Marquand, D. (1979), *Parliament for Europe,* London: Cape.

Marshall, T. H. (1992), Citizenship and social class. In T. H. Marshall and T. B. Bottomore, *Citizenship and Social Class*, London: Pluto Press, pp. 3–54.

Marx, K. (1844), *On the Jewish Question,* and *The Capacity for Present-day Jews and Christians to Become Free.* In *Deutsch-Französische Jahrbücher.* Reprinted at <http://www.marxists.org/archive/marx/works/1844/jewish-question/index.htm>.

Marx, K. (1977), *The Poverty of Philosophy,* Peking: Foreign Languages Press. (First published 1847.)

Marx, K. and Engels, F. (1969), *Manifesto of the Communist Party,* Moscow: Progress Publishers. (Orig. published 1848.)

Mayhew, A. (2002), The negotiating position of the European Union on agriculture, the structural funds and the EU budget, Brighton: Sussex European Institute Working Paper No. 52.

Mennell, S. (1995), Civilisation and decivilisation, civil society and violence, *Irish Journal of Sociology*, 5: 1–21.

Mény, Y. (2003), De la démocratie en Europe, *Journal of Common Market Studies*, 41, 1: 1–13.

Merton, R. (1938), Social structure and anomie, *American Sociological Review*, 3: 672–82.

Messner, S. F. and Rosenfeld, R. (1997), Political restraint of the market and levels of criminal homicide: a cross-national application of institutional-anomie theory, *Social Forces*, 75, 4: 1393–1416.

Mestrovic, S. G. (1994), *The Balkanization of the West: The Confluence of Post-modernism and Postcommunism,* London: Routledge.

Meuschel, S. (1992), *Legitimation und Parteiherrschaft: zum Paradox von Stabilität und Revolution in der DDR, 1945–1989,* Frankfurt: Suhrkamp.

Michnik, A. (1999), The rebirth of civil society. Public lecture, Centre for the Study of Global Governance.

Michnik, A. (2001), Confessions of a converted dissident. Public lecture presented at the LSE, October 20, 1999, as part of the Ideas of 1989 Public Lecture Series.

Miller, T. (1993), *The Well-tempered Self: Citizenship, Culture, and the Post-modern Subject,* London: Johns Hopkins University Press.

Misztal, B. (1996), *Trust in Modern Societies: The Search for the Bases of Social Order,* Cambridge: Polity Press.

Misztal, B. (2000), *Informality,* London: Routledge.

Misztal, B. (2003), *Theories of Social Remembering,* Maidenhead: Open University Press.

Monnerot, J. (1946), *Les faits sociaux ne sont pas des choses,* Paris: Gallimard.

Montesquieu, C. de S. (1949), *The Spirit of the Laws,* London: Collier-Macmillan. (First published 1748.)

Moore, B. (1966), *Social Origins of Dictatorship and Democracy,* Harmondsworth: Penguin.

Muller, K. (1992), Modernizing Eastern Europe: theoretical problems and political dilemmas, *Archives Européennes de Sociologie,* 33, 1: 109–50.

Münch, R. (1990), Differentiation, rationalization, interpretation: the emergence of modern society. In J. Alexander and P. Colomy (eds.), *Differentiation Theory and Social Change,* New York: Columbia University Press, pp. 441–64.

Murer, J. (2002), The clash within: intrapsychically created enemies and their roles in ethnonationalist conflict. In Worcester et al., *Violence and Politics,* pp. 209–25.

Murray, R. (1992), Flexible specialization and development strategy: the relevance for Eastern Europe. In H. Ernste and V. Meier, *Regional Development and Contemporary Industrial Response,* London: Belhaven, pp. 197–218.

Nagle, J. D. and Mahr, A. (1999), *Democracy and Democratization: Post-communist Europe in Comparative Perspective,* London: Sage.

Naishul, V. (1993), Liberalism, customary rights and economic reforms, *Communist Economies and Economic Transformation,* 5, 1: 29–44.

Neocleous, M. (2003), *Imagining the State,* Maidenhead: Open University Press.

Nikolov, S. E. (1993), Depoliticization of an over-politicized society. In J. Anson, E. Todorova, G. Kressel, and N. Genov, *Ethnicity and Politics in Bulgaria and Israel,* Aldershot: Avebury, pp. 138–48.

Nove, A. (1991), *The Economics of Feasible Socialism,* London: HarperCollins.

O'Dowd, L. (1998), Negotiating state borders: a new sociology for a new Europe. Inaugural Lecture, Queen's University Belfast.

Offe, C. (1991), Capitalism by democratic design? Democratic theory facing the triple transition in East Central Europe, *Social Research,* 58: 865–92.

Offe, C. (1996), *Varieties of Transition: The East European and East German Experience,* Cambridge: Polity Press. (Orig. published as *Der Tunnel am Ende des Lichts: Erkundungen der politischen Transformation im neuen Osten,* Frankfurt: Campus, 1994.)

Offe, C. (2000), The democratic welfare state: a European regime under the strain of European integration, *Reihe Politikwissenschaft,* 68, Vienna: Institute for Advanced Studies.

Offe, C. and Preuss, U. (1991), Democratic institutions and moral resources. In D. Held (ed.), *Political Theory Today,* Cambridge: Polity Press, pp. 143–72.

Ohmae, K. (1993), The rise of the region state, *Foreign Affairs,* 72, 2: 78–87.

Ohmae, K. (1994), *The Borderless World: Power and Strategy in the Interlinked Economy,* London: HarperCollins.

Okin, S. M. (1991), Gender, the public and the private. In D. Held (ed.), *Political Theory Today,* Cambridge: Polity Press, pp. 67–90.

Okun, A. (1981), *Prices and Qualities,* Washington, DC: Brookings Institution Press.

Olick, J. K. and Robbins, J. (1998), Social memory studies, *Annual Review of Sociology,* 24, 1: 105–41.

Oliviero, M. B. and Simmons, A. (2002), Who's minding the store? Global civil society and corporate responsibility. In Glasius et al., *Global Civil Society 2002,* pp. 77–107.

Ossowski, S. (1963), *Class Structure in the Social Consciousness*, London: Routledge.

Ost, D. (1990), *Solidarity and the Politics of Antipolitics: Opposition and Reform in Poland since 1968*, Philadelphia: Temple University Press.

Ost, D. (1995), Labor, class and democracy: shaping political antagonisms in post-communist society. In B. Crawford (ed.), *Markets, States, Democracy: The Political Economy of Post-Communist Transformation*, Boulder, CO: Westview Press.

Ott, T. (2001), From concentration to deconcentration: migration patterns in the post-socialist city, *Cities*, 18: 403–12.

Outhwaite, W. (1986), Newspeak Est–Ouest, *Sociolinguistics*, 16, 2 (December): 45–50. (English version (abridged), in *Aspects*, 1986.)

Outhwaite, W. (1992), Critical theory and modernization. In A. Sogomonov and E. Danilova (eds.), *Social Critique of the Theory of Modernization*, Moscow: Institute of Sociology, Russian Academy of Sciences.

Outhwaite, W. (1996), Steering the public sphere: communication policy in state socialism and after. In Einhorn et al. (eds.), *Citizenship and Democratic Control*, pp. 159–72.

Outhwaite, W. (forthcoming), *The Future of Society*, Oxford: Blackwell.

Ozouf, M. (1988), *Festivals of the French Revolution*, Cambridge, MA: Harvard University Press.

Paez, D., Basabe, N., and Gonzalez, J. L. (1997), Social processes and collective memory. In J. Pennebaker, D. Pacz, and B. Rimé, *Collective Memory of Political Events*, Mahwah, NJ: Lawrence Erlbaum.

Pakulski, J. (1986), Legitimacy and mass compliance: reflections on Max Weber and Soviet type societies, *British Journal of Political Science*, 16, 1: 35–56.

Pakulski, J. and Waters, M. (1995), *The Death of Class*, London: Sage.

Papastergiadis, N. (2000), *The Turbulence of Migration*, Oxford: Polity Press.

Parkin, F. (1971), *Class Inequality and Political Order: Social Stratification in Capitalist and Communist Societies*, London: Macgibbon.

Parsons, T. (1964), Evolutionary universals in society, *American Sociological Review*, 29: 339–57.

Parsons. T. (1970), *The Social System*, Glencoe, IL: Free Press.

Patai, R. (1976), *The Arab Mind*, New York: Charles Scribner's Sons.

Pateman, C. (1988), *The Sexual Contract*, Cambridge: Polity Press.

Patomáki, H. and Pursianen, C. (1999), Western models and the Russian idea: beyond "inside/outside" in discourses on civil society, *Millennium*, 28, 1: 53–77.

Pelczynski, Z. A. (1988), Solidarity and the rebirth of civil society in Poland 1976–81. In Keane, *Civil Society and the State*, pp. 361–80.

Petras, J. and Veltmeyer, H. (2001), *Globalization Unmasked: Imperialism in the 21st Century*, London: Zed Books.

Pierson, C. (1996), *The Modern State*, London: Routledge.

Poggi, G. (2001), State and society, *International Encyclopedia of the Social and Behavioral Sciences*, Amsterdam: Elsevier, pp. 14961–4.

Polanyi, K. (1944), *The Great Transformation*, Boston, MA: Beacon Press.

Polonsky, M. and Taylor, R. (1986), *USSR: From an Idea by Karl Marx*, London: Faber.

Poppi, C. (1997), Wider horizons with larger details: subjectivity, ethnicity and globalization. In A. Scott (ed.), *Limits of Globalization*, London: Routledge, pp. 284–305.

Potůček, M. (2000), *Not Only the Market: The Role of the Market, Government and Civic Sector in the Development of Post-communist Central Europe*, Warsaw: Central European Press.

Poznanski, K. Z. (1992), *Constructing Capitalism: The Reemergence of Civil Society and Liberal Economy in the Post-communist World*, Boulder, CO: Westview Press.

Prager, J. (1998), *Presenting the Past*, Cambridge, MA: Harvard University Press.

Pridham, G., Herring, E., and Sanford, G. (1994), *Building Democracy? The International Dimension of Democratisation in Eastern Europe*, London: Leicester University Press.

Pryce-Jones, D. (1995), *The War that Never Was: The Fall of the Soviet Empire, 1985–1991*, London: Weidenfeld and Nicolson.

Putnam, R. D. (1993), *Making Democracy Work: Civic Traditions in Modern Italy*, Princeton, NJ: Princeton University Press.

Putnam, R. D. (2000), *Bowling Alone*, London: Simon and Schuster.

Pye, L. (1990), Political science and the crisis of authoritarianism, *American Political Science Review*, 84, 1: 3–19.

Quah, D. (2002), The weightless economy. Available at <http://econ.lse.ac.uk/staff/dquah/tweir10.html>.

Quah, D. T. (1996), *The Invisible Hand and the Weightless Economy*, Occasional papers, no. 12, London: London School of Economics and Political Science, Centre for Economic Performance.

Radygin, A. (1995), *Privatisation in Russia: Hard Choice, First Results, New Targets*, London: Centre for Research into Communist Economies New Series.

Ramet, S. P. (1991), *Social Currents in Eastern Europe: The Sources and Making of the Great Transformation*, London: Duke University Press.

Ray, L. J. (1993), *Rethinking Critical Theory: Emancipation in an Age of Global Social Movements*, London: Sage.

Ray, L. J. (1995), The rectifying revolutions? Organizational futures in the new Eastern Europe, *Organization*, 2, 3/4: 441–65.

Ray, L. J. (1996), *Social Theory and the Crisis of State Socialism*, Cheltenham: Edward Elgar.

Ray, L. J. (1997), Post-communism: post-modernity or modernity revisited? *British Journal of Sociology*, 48, 4: 543–60.

Ray, L. J. (1999a), Social differentiation, transgression, and the politics of irony. In L. Ray and A. Sayer (eds.), *Culture and Economy after the Cultural Turn*, London: Sage, pp. 189–210.

Ray, L. J. (1999b), "Fundamentalism," modernity and the new Jacobins, *Economy and Society*, 28, 2: 198–221.

Ray, L. J. (1999c), *Theorizing Classical Sociology*, Buckingham: Open University Press.

Ray, L. J. (1999d), Memory, trauma and genocidal nationalism, *Sociological Research Online*, 4, 2. Available at <http://www.socresonline.org.uk/socresonline/4/2/ray.html>.

Ray, L. J. (2000), Memory, violence and identity. In J. Eldridge, J. Macinnes, S. Scott, C. Warhurst, and A. Witz (eds.), *For Sociology*, Durham: The Sociology Press, pp. 145–59.

Ray, L. J. (2002), Crossing borders? Sociology, globalization and immobility, *Sociological Research Online*, 7, 3. Available at <http://www.socresonline.org.uk/7/3/ray.html>.

Ray, L. J. and Reed, M. (eds.) (1994), *Organizing Modernity: New Weberian Perspectives on Work, Organization and Society*, London: Routledge.

Ritzer, G. (2003), *The Globalization of Nothing*, London: Sage.

Rivera-Batiz, F. (1999), Undocumented workers in the labor market, *Journal of Population Economics*, 1: 91-116.

Rizzi, B. (1939), *La bureaucratisation du monde*, Paris: Les Presses Modernes. (Tr. as *The Bureaucratization of the World*, ed. A. Westoby, London: Tavistock, 1985.)

Robertson, R. (1992), *Globalization, Social Theory and Global Culture*, London: Sage.

Rödel, U., Frankenberg, G., and Dubiel, H. (1989), *Die demokratische Frage*, Frankfurt: Suhrkamp.

Rose, R. (1995), Russia as an hour-glass society: a constitution without citizens, *East European Constitutional Review*, 4, 3: 34–42.

Rosenau, P. M. (1992), *Post-modernism and the Social Sciences*, Princeton, NJ: Princeton University Press.

Rosser, J. B., Jr., Rosser, M. V., and Ahmed, E. (2000), Income inequality and the informal economy in transition economies, *Journal of Comparative Economics*, 28: 156–71.

Rostow, W. (1979), *The Stages of Economic Growth: A Non-Communist Manifesto*, Cambridge: Cambridge University Press. (First published 1960.)

Rostow, W. (1991), Eastern Europe and the Soviet Union: a technological time warp. In Chirot (ed.), *The Crisis of Leninism and the Decline of the Left*, pp. 61–73.

Rousseau, J.-J. (1968), *The Social Contract*, Harmondsworth: Penguin. (First published 1762.)

Rueschemeyer, D. (1986), *Power and the Division of Labour*, Cambridge: Polity Press.

Rupnick, J. (1999), The post-communist divide, *Journal of Democracy*, 10, 1: 57–62.

Sacks, J. (1993), *Poland's Jump to the Market Economy*, Cambridge, MA: MIT Press.

Said, E. (2001), The clash of ignorances, *The Nation* (October 22).

Sakwa, R. (1999), *Postcommunism*, Buckingham: Open University Press.

Sakwa, R. (2004), Russia and globalisation. In L. McCann (ed.), *Russian Transformations*, London: Curzon.

Sartorius, N. (1996), Recent changes in suicide rates in selected Eastern European and other European countries. In J. L. Pearson and Y. Conwell (eds.), *Suicide and Aging*, New York: Springer.

Sassen, S. (1998), *Globalization and its Discontents*, New York: New Press.

Sassen, S. (2000), Regulating immigration in a global age, *Annals of the American Academy of Political and Social Science*, 570: 65–77.

Sassen, S. (2002a), Global cities and diasporic networks: microsites in global civil society. In Glasius et al., *Global Civil Society 2002*, pp. 217–38.

Sassen, S. (2002b), Governance hotspots: challenges we must confront in the post-September 11 world. In Booth and Dunne (eds.), *Worlds in Collision*, pp. 313–24.

Say, B. (2000), The Polish economic transition: outcome and lessons, *Communist and Post-Communist Studies*, 33, 1: 49–70.

Sayer, A. (1995), *Radical Political Economy*, Oxford: Blackwell.

Scharpf, F. (2002), The European social model: coping with the challenges of diversity, *Journal of Common Market Studies*, 40, 4: 645–70.

Scholte, J. A. (1996), Beyond the buzzword: towards a critical theory of globalization. In E. Kofmann and G. Youngs (eds.), *Globalization: Theory and Practice*, London: Pinter, pp. 43–57.

Schwartz, J. A. (1982), The social control of commemoration: a study in collective memory, *Social Forces*, 61, 2.

Schwinn, T. (2001), *Differenzierung ohne Gesellschaft*, Weilerswist: Velbrück.

Seldon, R. (1991), The rhetoric of enterprise. In R. Keat and N. Abercrombie (eds.), *Enterprise Culture*, London: Routledge, pp. 58–71.

Seligman, A. (1993), The fragile ethical vision of civil society. In Turner (ed.), *Citizenship and Social Theory*, pp. 139–62.

Seligman, A. (1995), Animadversions upon civil society and civic virtue in the last decade of the twentieth century. In Hall (ed.), *Civil Society*, pp. 200–23.

Serbian Academy of Arts and Sciences (1986), *Memorandum*. Available at <http://zagreb.hic.hr/books/greatserbia/sanu/htm>.

Shane, S. (1995), *Dismantling Utopia: How Information Ended the Soviet Union*. Chicago: Elephant Paperbacks.

Shannon, U. (2002), Private armies and the decline of the state. In Worcester et al., *Violence and Politics*, pp. 32–47.

Shaw, M. (2000), *Theory of the Global State: Globality as Unfinished Revolution*, Cambridge: Cambridge University Press.

Shaw, M. (2003), *War and Genocide: Organized Killing in Modern Society*, Oxford: Polity Press.

Shlapentokh, V. (2003), Hobbes and Locke at odds in Putin's Russia, *Europe-Asia Studies*, 55, 7: 981–1007.

Sica, A. and Turner, S. (forthcoming), *The Disobedient Generation: 68ers and the Transformation of Social Theory*, Chicago: University of Chicago Press.

Sidorenko, E. (1999), Neo-liberalism after communism: constructing a sociological account of the political space of post-1989 Poland. PhD thesis, London University.

Sik, E. (1988), Reciprocal exchange of labour in Hungary. In R. E. Pahl (ed.), *On Work: Historical, Comparative and Theoretical Approaches*, Oxford: Blackwell, pp. 527–47.

Simmel, G. (1990), *The Philosophy of Money*, ed. and tr. D. Frisby and T. Bottomore, London: Routledge.

Sivan, E. (1989), The Islamic resurgence: civil society strikes back, *Journal of Contemporary History*, 25, 2/3: 353–62.

Skapska, G. (1994), Beyond constructionism and rationality of discovery: economic transformation and institution-building processes. In G. Alexander and G. Skapska (eds.), *A Fourth Way? Privatization, Property and the Emergence of New Market Economies*, London: Routledge, pp. 150–62.

Sklair, L. (1991), *Sociology of the Global System*, London: Harvester.

Sklair, L. (2002), *Globalization: Capitalism and its Alternatives*, Oxford: Oxford University Press.

Skocpol, T. (1979), *States and Social Revolutions: A Comparative Analysis of France, Russia and China*, Cambridge: Cambridge University Press.

Skultans, V. (1998), *Testament of Lives: Narrative and Memory in post-Soviet Latvia*, London: Routledge.

Slepyan, K. D. (1993), The limits of mobilization: party, state, and the 1927 Civil Defence Campaign, *Europe-Asia Studies*, 45, 5: 851–68.

Smart, B. (1992), *Modern Conditions, Postmodern Controversies*, London: Routledge.

Smart, B. (2003), *Economy, Culture, and Society: A Sociological Critique of Neoliberalism*, Buckingham: Open University Press.

Smith, A. (1993), *Russia and the World Economy: Problems of Integration*, London: Routledge.

Smith, A. (1996), LSE Centennial Lecture: The resurgence of nationalism? Myth and memory in the renewal of nations, *British Journal of Sociology*, 47, 4: 575–98.

Smith, A. (1997), Towards a global culture? In M. Featherstone (ed.), *Global Culture, Nationalism, Globalization and Modernity*, London: Sage, pp. 171–91.

Smith, J. (1998), Global civil society? Transnational social movement organizations and social capital, *American Behavioral Scientist*, 42, 1: 93–107.

Smith, K. E. (1996), *Remembering Stalin's Victims: Popular Memory and the End of the USSR*, Ithaca, NY: Cornell University Press.

Smith, S. (1994), Writing the history of the Russian Revolution after the fall of communism, *Europe–Asia Studies*, 46, 4: 563–78.

Sójka, J. (1994), Transition to democracy: the challenge of the unexpected. In A. Jawłowska and M. Kempny, *Cultural Dilemmas of Post-Communist Societies*, Warsaw: IfiS Publishers, pp. 21–32.

Sonneman, T. (2002), *Shared Sorrows: A Gypsy Family Remembers the Holocaust*, Hatfield: University of Hertfordshire Press.

Spence, D. (1991), *Enlargement without Accession*, London: Royal Institute of International Affairs.

Spiegel (2004), Tabuzone Ost, 15 (April 5).

Staniszkis, J. (1985), *Poland's Self-Limiting Revolution*, Princeton, NJ: Princeton University Press.

Staniszkis, J. (1992), *The Ontology of Socialism*, Oxford: Clarendon Press.

Staniszkis, J. (1999), *Post-Communism: The Emerging Enigma*, Warsaw: ISP/PAN.

Stark, D. (1996), Recombinant property in East European capitalism, *American Journal of Sociology*, 101, 4: 993–1027.

Stark, D. and Bruszt, L. (1998), *Postsocialist Pathways: Transforming Politics and Property in East Central Europe*, Cambridge: Cambridge University Press.

Starr, S. F. (1978), Visionary town planning during the Cultural Revolution. In Fitzpatrick, *Cultural Revolution*, pp. 207–40.

Szalai, J. (1989), The dominance of the economic approach in reform proposals in Hungary and some of the implications of the crisis of the 80s. In V. Gathy (ed.), *State and Civil Society: Relationships in Flux*, Budapest: Institute of Sociology.

Szamuely, T. (1988), *The Russian Tradition*, London: Secker and Warburg.

Szelényi, I. (1978), Social inequalities in state socialist redistributive economies: dilemmas for social policy in contemporary socialist societies of eastern Europe, *International Journal of Comparative Sociology*, 19, 1–2.

Szelényi, I. and Konrád, G. (1991), Intellectuals and domination in post-communist societies. In J. Coleman and P. Bourdieu (eds.), *Social Theory for a Changing Society*, Boulder, CO: Westview Press, pp. 337–61.

Sztompka, P. (1993), *The Sociology of Social Change*, Oxford: Blackwell.

Tamás, G. M. (1994), A disquisition on civil-society, *Social Research*, 61, 2: 205–22.

Taylor, C. (1989), *Sources of the Self: The Making of Modern Identity*, Cambridge: Cambridge University Press.

Therborn, G. (1995), *European Modernity and Beyond: the Trajectory of European Societies, 1945–2000*, London: Sage.

Thomas, G. D. (1998), Civil society: historical uses versus global context, *International Politics*, 35: 49–64.

Thompson, E. (1967), *The Making of the English Working Class*, Harmondsworth: Penguin.

Tilly, C. (1995), To explain political processes, *American Journal of Sociology*, 100, 6 (May): 1594–1610.

Tiryakian, E. (1991), Modernization: exhumetur in pace (rethinking macrosociology in the 1990s), *International Sociology*, 6, 2: 165–80.

Tiryakian, E. (2001), The civilization of modernity and the modernity of civilizations, *International Sociology*, 16, 3: 277–92.

Tocqueville, A. de (1946), *Democracy in America*, London: Oxford University Press. (First published 1835.)

Tocqueville, A. de (1969), *Democracy in America*, London: Oxford University Press.

Tomson, W. (1999), The price of everything and the value of nothing? Unraveling the workings of Russia's "virtual economy," *Economy and Society*, 28, 2: 256–80.

Touraine, A. (1983), *Solidarity: the Analysis of a Social Movement: Poland, 1980–1981*, tr. D. Denby, Cambridge: Cambridge University Press.

Touraine, A. (1997), *Pourrons-nous vivre ensemble?* Paris: Fayard. (Tr. as *Can We Live Together? Equality and Difference*, Cambridge: Polity Press, 2000.)

Touraine, A. (1999), *Comment sortir du libéralisme?* Paris: Fayard. (Tr. as *Beyond Neoliberalism*, Cambridge: Polity Press, 2001).

Touraine, A. et al. (1982), *Solidarité*, Paris: Fayard. (Tr. D. Denby, as *Solidarity*, Cambridge: Cambridge University Press, 1983.)

Transparency International (2002). Available at <www.gwdg.de>,

Turner, B. (ed.) (1993), *Citizenship and Social Theory*, London: Sage.

Turner, B. S. (1994), Max Weber on individualism, bureaucracy and despotism: on political authoritarianism and contemporary politics. In Ray and Reed (eds.), *Organizing Modernity*, pp. 122–40.

Turner, C. (1996), Holocaust memories and history, *History of the Human Sciences*, 9, 4.

Urry, J. (1998), Globalisation and citizenship [draft]. Published by the Department of Sociology, Lancaster University. Available at <http://www.comp.lancs.ac.uk/sociology/papers/urry-globalisation-and-citizenship.pdf>.

Urry, J. (1999), Automobility, car culture and weightless travel: a discussion paper. Lancaster Department of Sociology On-line papers. Available at <http://www.comp.lancs.ac.uk/sociology/papers/urry-automobility.pdf>.

Urry, J. (2000a), Mobile sociology, *British Journal of Sociology*, 51, 1: 185–203.

Urry, J. (2000b), *Sociology beyond Societies: Mobilities for the Twenty-first Century*, London: Routledge.

Urry J. (2002), *Global Complexity*, Cambridge: Polity Press.

Vajda, M. (1988), East-Central European perspectives. In Keane, *Civil Society*, pp. 333–60.

Van der Pijl, K. (1998), *Transnational Classes and International Relations*, London: Routledge.

Van der Pijl, K. (2001–2), Globalization or class society in transition, *Science and Society*, 65, 4 (Winter): 492–500.

Van Zon, H. (1993), Problems of transitology: towards a new research agenda and new research practice. Paper to the conference on Transforming Post-Socialist Societies, Cracow Academy of Economics, October 1993.

Varese, F. (1994), Is Sicily the future of Russia? Private protection and the rise of the Russian mafia, *Archives Européennes de Sociologie*, 35, 2: 224–58.

Vassilev, R. (1999), Modernization theory revisited: the case of Bulgaria, *East European Politics and Societies*, 13, 3: 567–99.

Veltz, P. (1996), *Mondialisation: villes et territoires: l'économie archipel*, Paris: Economica.

Virilio, P. and Lotringer, S. (1983), *Pure War*, New York: Semiotexte.

Vitosha Research Group and Centre for Economic Development (2001), *Global Competitiveness Survey*, Sofia. Available at <http://www.vitosha-research.com/agency.htm>.

Voskamp, U. and Wittke, V. (1991), Industrial restructuring in the Former GDR, *Politics and Society*, 19, 3: 341–71.

Voslensky, M. (1984), *Nomenklatura: Anatomy of the Soviet Ruling Class*, London: Bodley Head.

Wagner, P. (1994), *A Sociology of Modernity: Liberty and Discipline*, London: Routledge.

Wagner, P. (2001), *A History and Theory of the Social Sciences: Not All that is Solid Melts into Air*, London: Sage.

Wagner, P. (2003), Die westliche Demokratie und die Möglichkeit des Totalitarismus. Über die Motive der Gründung und der Zerstörung in *The origins of totalitarianism*. In A. Grunenberg (ed.), *Totalitäre Herrschaft und republikanische Demokratie: Fünfzig Jahre* The Origins of Totalitarianism *von Hannah Arendt*, Bern: Peter Lang.

Walby, S. (1994), Is citizenship gendered? *Sociology*, 28, 2: 379–95.

Walby, S. (2003), The myth of the nation-state: theorizing society and polities in a global era, *Sociology*, 37, 3: 529–46.

Walicki, A. (1991), From Stalinism to post-communist pluralism: the case of Poland, *New Left Review*, 185: 92–121.

Walker, R. (1994), Social movements/world politics, *Millennium*, 23, 3: 669–700.

Wallerstein, I. (1979), Modernization: requiescat in pace. In I. Wallerstein, *The Capitalist World Economy*, Cambridge: Cambridge University Press.

Wallerstein, I. (2001), *Unthinking Social Science: the Limits of Nineteenth-century Paradigms*, 2nd edn. with new preface, Philadelphia: Temple University Press. (Orig. published Cambridge: Polity Press, 1991.)

Waltz, K. N. (1999), Globalization and governance. James Madison Lecture. Available at <www.apsanet.org./PS/dec99/waltz.cfm>.

Waters, M. (1995), *Globalization*, London: Routledge.

Waters, M. (1997), Inequality after class. In D. Owen (ed.), *Sociology after Postmodernism*, Beverly Hills: Sage.

Watson, C. W. (2000), *Multiculturalism*, Buckingham: Open University Press.

Watson, R. (ed.) (1994a), *Memory, History and Opposition under State Socialism*, Santa Fe: Schools of American Research Press.

Webb, B. and Webb, S. (1936), *Soviet Communism: A New Civilization*, London: Longman.

Weber, M. (2002), *The Protestant Ethic and the Spirit of Capitalism*, tr. S. Kalberg, Los Angeles: Roxbury. (Orig. published 1905.).

Weber, M. (1978), *Economy and Society*, tr. and ed. G. Roth and C. Wittich, New York: Bedminster Press.

Weber, M. (1984), *General Economic History*, New Brunswick, NJ: Transaction Books.

Weiler, J. (2002), A constitution for Europe? Some hard choices, *Journal of Common Market Studies*, 40, 4: 563–80.

Weiss, L. (1998), *The Myth of the Powerless State: Governing the Economy in a Global Era*, Cambridge: Polity Press.

Wellmer, A. (1993), *Endspiele*, Frankfurt: Suhrkamp. (Tr. as *Endgames*, Cambridge, MA: MIT Press, 1998.)

Welsh, B. (2002), Globalization, weak states, and the death toll in East Asia. In Worcester et al., *Violence and World Politics*, pp. 67–89.

West, R. (1982), *Black Lamb and Grey Falcon*, London: Macmillan.

Whetten, L. L. (1989), *Interaction of Political and Economic Reforms within the Eastern Bloc*, London: Crane Russak.

White, H. (2001), *Markets from Networks*, Princeton, NJ: Princeton University Press.

White, S., Gill, G., and Slider, D. (1993), *The Politics of Transition: Shaping a Post-Soviet Future*, Cambridge: Cambridge University Press.

White, S., Batt, J., and Lewis, P. G. (eds.) (2003), *Developments in Central and East European Politics*, vol. 3, Basingstoke: Palgrave Macmillan.

Winter, J. (1999), Forms of kinship and remembrance in the aftermath of the Great War. In J. Winter and E. Sivan (eds.), *War and Remembrance in the Twentieth Century*, Cambridge: Cambridge University Press.

Wistrich, R. (1992), *Antisemitism: The Longest Hatred*, New York: Pantheon Books.

Wolton, D. (1993), *La dernière utopie: naissance de l'Europe démocratique*, Paris: Flammarion.

Worcester, K., Bermanzohn, S. A., and Unger, M. (eds.) (2002), *Violence and Politics: Globalization's Paradox*, London: Routledge.

World Bank (2002), *Transition: The First Ten Years: Analysis and Lessons for Eastern Europe and the Former Soviet Union*, Washington, DC: World Bank.

Yakovlev, A. (1993), *The Fate of Marxism in Russia*, tr. C. A. Fitzpatrick, London: Yale University Press.

Yeung, H. W. C. (1998), Capital, state and space: contesting the borderless world, *Transactions of the Institute of British Geographers*, 23, 3: 291–309.

Zack, M. and McKenney, J. (1995), Social context and interaction in ongoing computer-supported management groups, *Organization Science*, 6, 4: 394–422.

Zaslavskaya, T. (1984), The Novosibirsk Report, *Survey*, 28, 1: 88–108.

Zaslavskaya, T. (1989), *The Second Socialist Revolution: an Alternative Soviet strategy*, London: Tauris.

Zeldin, T. (1973), *France 1848–1945*, vol. 1: *Ambition, Love and Politics*, Oxford: Clarendon Press.

Zloch-Christy, I. (1987), *Debt Problems of Eastern Europe*, Cambridge: Cambridge University Press.

Index